HUMAN
RELATIONS
IN THE
INDUSTRIAL
SOUTHEAST

HUMAN
RELATIONS
IN THE
INDUSTRIAL
SOUTHEAST

A STUDY OF THE TEXTILE INDUSTRY

BY GLENN GILMAN

CHAPEL HILL
The University of North Carolina Press

COPYRIGHT, 1956, BY
GLENN GILMAN

Manufactured in the United States of America

Foreword

i

THE STUDY UPON which this work is based and the preparation of
the work itself were originally undertaken with rather a limited
objective in mind—to furnish the future supervisors, administrators,
and executives of the southeastern cotton textile industry with an
orientation toward industrial relations that would enable them to
maintain those relationships to the long-run advantage of the industry, the region, and the nation. This primary purpose has not
been abandoned. As the work progressed however, it became
apparent that this limited objective could not be attained by a limited
approach.

The present nature of industrial relations in the southeastern
cotton textile industry cannot be understood even by their prac-
titioners except in terms of the story that lies behind them. The past
that created them has been rolled up, like the core of a snowball,
to serve as the foundation of their present shape. There is more
involved than a mere recounting and analysis of past and present
worker-management relationships—and far more than a mere cataloging of personnel practices in the industry. The story is even more
than that of the industry. It is the story of the Piedmont region
itself, and of its regeneration after the desolation of war and reconstruction had brought not only its economy but its society to the
edge of disaster. The emerging pattern of industrial relations was
an integral part of that regeneration, and it cannot be understood
except as a part of the context with which it was in interaction—
which created it, but which it in turn helped to create.

The mills were built by the region itself, for its salvation, out of
the desperate hope and unwavering faith in an ultimate future that

were all that was left in those bleak days. They opened a new avenue into the future for a society that had come to a dead end, that had seen traditional lines of activity prove ineffective in dealing with problems of the gravest nature.

The building of the mills was essentially a social movement rather than an economic development. They were "built from the combined capital of many of little means" for the social and economic rehabilitation of the region rather than primarily for the private profit of individual entrepreneurs. In the usual case, the factories use the folk, and in the process they create a mass society if one is not already in existence. In the present instance, the folk have used the factories; they have woven modern industrial processes into the warp and woof of a dynamic folk culture. It does not really matter who possesses legal title to the textile mills that dot the southeast from Lynchburg to Laurel. They have become an institution; and as an institution they belong to the society that brought them into being.

But in turning to industry for a solution to the problems that arose out of war and reconstruction, the Piedmont fell heir to another problem—the basic problem of industrial relations (which we shall define in the first chapter) that is inherent in the industrial process and that must be solved if any industrially based society is to survive in the long run. It is the nature of this second solution that engages our attention in this study. It appears at first sight to be a unique solution for a unique set of circumstances and thus of no more than passing interest to anyone except those whom it immediately involves; but closer inspection reveals it to have been worked out in terms so basically fundamental to the whole problem of man in the industrial milieu as to merit the attention of a wider audience. There is the possibility that in certain respects at least this Piedmont solution to the problem of industrial relations is a prototype, a guide for the future that can be expeditiously used by other industries in other regions.

The Piedmont solution is at any rate one that deserves the attention of social scientists; for it is a case study, classic in its proportions, of the interaction between culture and civilization—and an illustration of the fact that the technics of civilization are not necessarily destructive to the basic structuring of a folk culture.

ii

The shape of the study is oriented by two fundamental assumptions, the first of which is that the life patterns of any people (including the patterns of their industrial relationships) cannot be understood except as a function of the interaction of three components:

1. Basic human nature and human needs
2. Natural resources available for the satisfaction of human needs
3. Cultural resources available for implementing these needs

(Students of sociology will recognize this as nothing new. It is a restatement of Patrick Geddes' "work, place, people" concept, which is in turn a modification of Le Play's approach in *The European Worker* as laid down more than a hundred years ago.)

Attempting to understand industrial relations in any specific industry in a specific locality unless these three dimensions of their nature are taken into account can lead only to superficial generalizations. Yet conclusions are often based on an investigation of only one dimension—the human factor—without grounding them in the realities of particular industries in particular locations. Such generalizations fall into one of two classes. Either they are undeniably true of every worker-management relationship everywhere, but necessarily so broad in order to achieve this wide applicability as to possess no predictive value in any particular case; or they may on the other hand be restricted generalizations valid for the situation studied, but possessing no real applicability to any other.

In following the "work, place, people" concept, we do essentially what the mathematician would do. We define our problem first, which arises out of an inevitable conflict between basic elements of human nature ("people") and certain basic attributes of the industrial process ("work"); and then we determine the nature of the boundary conditions ("place") that set up certain limitations under which the problem must be worked out. The process is not quite as simple as the above would indicate, for we have to take certain other factors into account. (1) Basic human nature will have been modified by previous work and previous habitat—"culture" must be considered, in other words; (2) other modifications will be introduced by present work and habitat, which cannot be ignored; (3) the natural features of the habitat will themselves inevitably be changed by the people; and (4) the work will be influenced by changes in human nature and habitat. We must recognize, in other words, that we are dealing with an on-going process that has its roots in the past and its orientation toward the future and that a continuous process of interaction between the three components changes the nature of each through time. But even so, we have a much better chance of gaining some real insight into real industrial relations between real people in real situations by facing up to these complications and attempting to work in terms of them, than by denying that they exist.

iii

The pattern of the study may seem strange to those who are familiar with a more conventional treatment. Those who expect it immediately to offer technics for the solution of industrial relations problems will be disappointed. Those who think that it at least ought to get down immediately to a discussion of industrial relations as such will feel that it is moving too slowly. Yet despite his knowledge that these objections will be offered, the writer can neither feel that industrial relations can be lifted for study out of the context in which they occur nor that specific and detailed solutions can be offered in advance for real industrial relations problems. We can merely make certain generalizations about human nature and the industrial process, and then attempt to understand (and perhaps in the light of this understanding later to predict) the manifestations of the interaction between the two in real industrial situations.

In our introductory chapter we outline those invariant aspects of human nature and the industrial process that, coming into conflict, generate the basic problem of industrial relations. In Part II of the study we examine the context in which the problem has been worked out in the Piedmont region—the nature of the region and its people, and of the underlying social structure which enables them to live and work together; and we see how the Piedmont textile industry has itself emerged as a means of survival for the regional society.

Only then, after we have become aware of the nature of the factors which must necessarily limit, shape, and give direction to the emerging pattern of industrial relations, do we turn to a consideration of actual worker-management relationships themselves. Against the background we have sketched in Part II we see them generated, not as expedients or as a set of arbitrary technics, but as the inevitable solution (given the circumstances that prevailed) to the basic problem of industrial relations defined in the opening chapter. We will be able to understand them not only as they have occurred in the past but as they will develop in the future. We will have become familiar with their generating principles and thus be able to perceive the elemental simplicity that underlies their day to day manifestations.

iv

Some pages back we mentioned that the shape of the study has been oriented by two fundamental assumptions. We have discussed the first and its implications at some length; but we have not yet mentioned the second. It has been simply and beautifully put by Alfred North Whitehead in his *Adventures of Ideas*: "Life can only be understood as an aim at that perfection which the conditions of its environment allow."

We assume, in other words, that man will invariably attempt to do his best in the situation in which he finds himself, that he will attempt to do "the right thing" as the conditions of his existence have led him to define "the right thing." Consequently the reader who seeks to find in the study either vindication or condemnation of a particular course of conduct will be disappointed. If he seeks a basis for sympathetic understanding of it, he may be more successful.

Acknowledgment

FOR THE FRAME of reference that has made his personal orientation meaningful in the present study, the writer must thank such men of the University of Chicago faculty during his residence there as Herbert Blumer, Tomatsu Shibutani, and the late Louis Wirth who, carrying on the work of Cooley, Dewey, Mead, Park and Thomas, made him explicitly aware of what is entailed in living like a human being; Lloyd Warner and Robert Redfield, who showed him that men's differences only emphasize their essential kinship; and Fred Harbison and Robert Burns, who gave him additional insight into what it means to work for a living in the modern industrial world. Though he has never come under their personal influence, the writer must also give particular credit to Howard Odum, Harriet Herring, and Rupert Vance of the University of North Carolina for the understanding their studies have given him of the special circumstances that surround living and working in a human fashion in southeastern United States. And there is finally Broadus Mitchell, to whose definitive study of *The Rise of the Cotton Mills in the South* all students of the industry owe much —and from which all students of the rise and crystallization of human institutions could learn much.

The writer wishes to express his appreciation to those countless people of the Piedmont textile industry itself, from presidents of multi-unit companies to colored roustabouts in the yard, without whose co-operation the study could never have been made. The writer set the stage for them, but they wrote the last five chapters. It is their story —necessarily generalized and compressed, but still their story. It was told to the writer with candor and frankness; with the honesty characteristic of most people when the past is examined with an eye toward its usefulness for the future, and they are permitted to pull their mistakes out into the light and examine them critically without having to defend the fact that they were made in the first place. Particular credit must be given those twenty-four companies that, in addition to permitting the routine of their productive activities to be upset by personal visits from the writer, supplied him with exhaustive statistical analyses of the nature of their workforces, supervisory forces, and management groups, and of such dimensions of their personnel practices as could be quantitatively assayed.

The writer wishes also to thank Hubert Dennison, Director of the School of Industrial Management at Georgia Tech., for his personal interest in the project while it was under way; and The University of North Carolina Press for its helpful advice in the reducing of the first draft of the manuscript to manageable proportions. The writer is also indebted to Thomas A. Quigley, Director of Industrial Education of the State of Georgia, for his constructively critical reading of the manuscript and his suggestions for its improvement during the final revision. While those mentioned above have contributed to whatever virtues the study may have, they must in no way be held accountable for its faults; those, whatever they may be, can be credited to no one but the writer.

There are two additional people who cannot be overlooked, the writer's wife and daughter, whose patience, forbearance, and understanding have been taxed to the limit since the project has been under way and who have stood the test. To his wife, the writer is particularly grateful for her sympathetic reading of the manuscript as it has come from his typewriter, which has made a joint venture of the result.

GLENN GILMAN.

Atlanta, Georgia
May 15, 1955

Contents

Foreword v

Acknowledgment xi

PART ONE
PROLOGUE

I.   The Problem of Industrial Relations   3

PART TWO
THE CONTEXT OF THE RELATIONSHIP

II.   The Piedmont Region and Its People 27

III.   Origin and Development of the Piedmont Cotton Textile
Industry 64

IV. The Piedmont in the National Market 91

PART THREE
THE PATTERN OF THE RELATIONSHIP

V.   The Developing Pattern of Industrial Relations 127

VI.   Time for Decision 170

VII. The Decision Is Made 206

VIII. The Present Pattern 249

IX.   The Solution of the Textile Piedmont 288

Index 319

Illustrations

Following page 317

One of the Earliest Textile Mill Plants *Circa* 1887

Modern Textile Plants

Loom-Weaving Operation

High Speed Warper

Warper Tender at Warper Creel

The Lunch Hour Break

Mill Cafeteria for Employees

Employees Leaving Mill at Shift Change

The Mill Community

Mill Housing Around the Plant

Mill Houses

Textile Mill Employee Homes

School Buildings

Employee and Community Recreational Facilities

Employee Vocational School Class

Community Center for Employees

A Mill Baseball Diamond

Textile Clinic for Employees and Their Families

Hospital in Mill Community

Modern Textile Engineering School

PART ONE

PROLOGUE

CHAPTER I

The Problem of Industrial Relations

THE CENTRAL TOPIC of our study is "industrial relations." We use the term in its broadest sense as meaning the whole matrix of human relationships that is brought into being by the existence and operation of an industrial enterprise. Our immediate attention throughout the study will be directed toward one particular set of those relationships comprising the worker-management axis; but as the study progresses it will become apparent that these latter can neither be meaningfully studied nor understood if we endow them with autonomous existence, standing apart from and substantially independent of their enveloping context. In no field is the whole complexity of man's interdependence better demonstrated than in modern-day industry. This we must accept as a fact, despite the difficulties it may interject into an attempt to study any one facet of the industrial world.

We simplify our difficulties somewhat by confining ourselves to a case study. We concern ourselves only with one industry, cotton textiles in one particular area, the southeastern Appalachian Piedmont region.[1] We claim no validity beyond the industry and the region for any generalizations that may develop out of it. Yet obviously if the study is to have any value even in this restricted sense it must be projected against a much broader background. Neither we nor others can understand it except as we see it in perspective against a frame of reference that is sufficiently fundamental to serve the same purpose for many industries in many regions.

In this first chapter, then, we attempt to sketch such a background. We are afforded a clue by noting the definition that social scientists

[1]. The "cotton textile industry" as the term is used in this study actually embraces all textile manufacture employing cotton system spindles. It includes many mills that spin and weave synthetics as well as some that have adapted the cotton system to the manufacture of woolens.

apply to industrial relations as a field for study and research. They call it a "problem-centered discipline." Rather than being defined by the existence of a particular body of knowledge, point of view, or set of technics, it is outlined by the existence of a particular set of related problems for the solution of which various points of view, technics, and bodies of knowledge may be enlisted. Implicit in this definition are two important assumptions: (1) that human relationships in industry constitute a problem; and (2) that there must be some basic, over-riding problematical situation that is common to all industry everywhere, the presence of which furnishes the thread of similarity that justifies our regarding as "related" what would otherwise be nothing more than an arbitrarily assembled jumble of individual problems having diverse origins despite their common "industrial" context.

Common sense as well as logic suggest that it is with this "problematical situation" that we ought concern ourselves in seeking the common ground. If it can be identified and defined, the differences we observe among particular industrial relationships may perhaps no longer perplex us but may actually point up their common origin. We may be able to see their diversity as arising from the necessity for seeking satisfactory solutions to the same problem but under differing conditions and with differing resources. What we must do initially is ask ourselves this question, "Why *should* human existence in an industrial *milieu* create a basic problem?" and then attempt to answer it in terms that are fundamental to humanity and to industrial processes.

So to provide a ground against which we can view this study of industrial relations in the southeastern cotton textile industry, we begin by talking in terms that are applicable to all workers and all industries everywhere. For the moment, we concern ourselves with similarities rather than with differences: with the obvious fact that the Piedmont textile worker is a human being who must depend upon industrial employment for a livelihood and that his enterprise employs the basic industrial process of division of labor, depending upon human beings to man its machines. We consider first those attributes of the Piedmont textile worker that are significant of him as a human being. Then we investigate those aspects of the Piedmont textile industry that are typical of it because of its employment of the basic industrial process.

Finally we place our worker, sketched only in universally representative terms, in a Piedmont textile industry that has been reduced to its universally representative dimensions; and we define those elements of industrial relations that emerge out of the interaction simply because they display basic human responses to the basic industrial *milieu*. Our analysis should outline the dimensions of the fundamental problem that must be solved by any society in which modern industrial processes are employed to an important degree or, perhaps, reveal the absence of any such problem and thus the impracticability of our hypothesis!

THE NATURE OF HUMAN NATURE[2]

We live by predicting the future. This simple fact, so obvious that we are quite likely to overlook it, nevertheless holds the clue to the most perplexing problems of human behavior, including those that are industrially grounded. We human beings are hardly unique in this respect. Prediction of the shape of impending events is the basic living technic of all sensate organisms. The senses develop only that the organism may become aware of the nature of its environment be-

2. The compressed character of the discussion of human nature that follows is such as to make detailed documentation unwieldy. The general foundation of theory orienting it, however, has its roots in the work of several men. Particular credit must be given to Charles Horton Cooley's *Human Nature and the Social Order* (New York: Charles Scribner's Sons, 1922); to John Dewey's *Experience and Nature* (Chicago: Open Court Publishing Company, 1926); to George Herbert Mead's *Mind, Self and Society* (Chicago: University of Chicago Press, 1934); and to Kurt Riezler's *Man: Mutable and Immutable* (Chicago: Henry Regnery Company, 1950). The writer is indebted also to the socio-psychological concepts implicitly or explicitly defined in many of the papers of Edward Sapir, Robert E. Park, and W. I. Thomas and those explicitly stated in the courses of Herbert Blumer and Tomatsu Shibutani.

The above sources are perhaps not sufficiently grounded in experimental data to suit many present-day students of human nature. The writer has found, however, that their major hypotheses have not only been validated by, but lend additional significance to, the findings of modern psychiatrists and psycho-analysts, particularly as presented by Harry Stack Sullivan in his *Conceptions of Modern Psychiatry* (Washington, D. C.: The William Alanson White Foundation, 1940) and by Karen Horney in her *New Ways in Psycho-Analysis* (London: Kegan Paul, Trench, Truhner and Company, Ltd., 1939).

For a more elaborately developed and better documented discussion of the general point of view by which the writer is oriented, the reader is referred to Richard Dewey's and W. J. Humber's *Development of Human Behavior* (New York: The Macmillan Company, 1951).

The final test of the validity of the picture of human nature presented in this first chapter must rest with the reader himself. If he cannot verify it in terms of his own life experience, he is entitled to doubt its accuracy; for if the events of his own life disprove any of its generalizations, it does not possess that universality which is the first requisite for any portrayal of the dimensions of human conduct.

fore it comes into decisive contact with it so that it may take in advance
such steps as seem necessary or desirable to insure its survival. From
this point of view, the whole pattern of the evolutionary process can
be seen as the constant searching of the life force for a more effective
predictive relationship between the lifebearing organism and its world.

Our uniqueness as human beings lies in the way by which we make
our predictions. We have traded instinctive certainty as to the nature
of our world for potential adaptability to it, to such a degree that we
possess practically no inherited preparation for dealing with it, aside
from a few primitive reflexes such as flinching, blinking, and grasping.
We must base our predictions as to the future entirely upon what we
ourselves are able to learn about the meaning of the world we sense.
Here we run into a problem. We have had to develop a delicate and
highly discriminatory sensing apparatus to deal with the world in
terms of our own experience, and we now discover a world so complex
and confusing that we can never learn enough about it to enable us
to survive and carry on the species! We would have to die from a
rattlesnake bite, for example, to become acquainted with its lethal
properties. To add further to our difficulties, our human mode of
existence has itself become so complicated that many of the crucial
problems we encounter, even after we have become adults, are beyond
our individual capacity to solve even though we may be aware of how
the solution should be accomplished.

Animal learning is through direct experience, protected by instinctive awareness of the possibility of danger. Animal co-operation is
either biological or instinctive. Virtually without instincts, these animal patterns of learning and co-operating are denied to us. The animal that was about to become man had to find a new way to learn
and a new way to co-operate, not only to become man, but even to survive in the bewildering world that must have faced him.

The Quality of Sympathy[3]

From somewhere, the homonoid acquired an attribute that made
him human. *The breakthrough point of human behavior came when*

3. The importance in human affairs of this quality of sympathy was first noted in
a formal way in modern times by that group of social philosophers called the
"Scottish Moralists," notably by David Hume in his *Treatise on Human Nature* and
by Adam Smith in his *Theory of Moral Sentiments.* Mead and Cooley assume its
existence as a basic premise in their explanations of human conduct: see Cooley's
Chapter IV, *op. cit.,* on "Sympathy or Understanding as an Aspect of Society"; and

potential man developed the quality of sympathetic identification—
sympathy in the sense of ability to take the role of the other, to feel
that to a degree what is happening to the other is also happening to
oneself. (The quality is also quite frequently called *sympathetic
introspection* or *empathy*.) Those of us who are Christians impute
possession of this attribute in its highest degree to Christ, of whom we
say that He suffered for all mankind; and He himself said, "Even as
ye have done it unto the least of these, so have ye done it unto Me."
All the great religions of the world regard the attribute as that most
assiduously to be cultivated by man, and with good reason, for upon
it is based all of man's behavior that distinguishes him from the beasts.

Our superior brain structure, an animal attribute, makes it potentially possible for us to conceptualize, to hold on to ideas and deal
with them as if they were actual physical objects or physical relationships. Our superior vocal equipment, an animal attribute, makes it
potentially possible for us to identify these ideas with audible symbols
that not only enable us to pass them on to others, but to fix them in
our own minds. But neither the power to conceptualize nor the power
to speak, singly or in combination, makes us human. The spark of
sympathy is necessary before we can realize as men the potentialities
we possess as animals.

Turning experiences into concepts and passing them vocally on to
others will not develop as a teaching process, a means of sharing experience, unless those others can feel that to some degree the experience that is being related is happening to them. Learning even
from observation depends upon this ability to take the role of the other.
*We make the experiences of others our own by putting ourselves in
their place, feeling the impact of their experience as if it were happening to us, sharing vicariously their successes and their failures, their
pleasures and their pains, their sorrows and their joys.* In our endless
childhood games of "Let's pretend" we are perfecting our use of the
attribute that makes us human; our ability to imagine that we are
someone else, to look at the world through the eyes of others.

Upon this same quality of sympathy rests our ability to engage in

---

Mead's discussion of "The Nature of Sympathy," pp. 298-303, *op. cit.* Sullivan, using
the somewhat more restricted but closely related term empathy (used synonymously by
some writers), offers it as the only explanation for "the acculturation or cultural con-
ditioning" of the child (*op. cit.*, pp. 8-9).

co-operative activity without instinctive preparation for it, to "figure out" a co-operative pattern of action on the spur of the moment whether it be in the weave room or on the football field. We are able to enlist the aid of others basically because they are able to visualize our need for it, by looking at the situation which faces us from *our,* as well as from their own, points of view. Once the co-operative project is under way, it can proceed only because the lines of action of each of us who is engaged in it are fitted together in such a way as to reinforce one another; and this can initially be achieved only by each of us taking the roles of all the others, anticipating their actions in this way, and then laying out our own course of action accordingly. We perfect our ability to do this through the formally or informally organized play and games of childhood and adolescence. As pitcher for the sandlot softball team, for example, we must have in mind what our teammates, the man at bat, and the opposing players on base are likely to do in the event of a sacrifice bunt or a long hit out to right field; and we achieve this knowledge basically by saying to ourselves, "What would I do if I were in his place?"

As human beings, the whole quality of our predictive behavior is colored by our sympathetic relationship with our fellows. Since we cannot live except in the context of a society in order that (1) we may share its accumulated experiences, its "culture" and (2) obtain the help of its other members in solving those of our life problems that are beyond our individual capacities, *our most important predictions are social predictions.* Social predictions are those estimates of the future that must take into account, not only the "objective" aspects of a situation, but also the probable attitudes, intentions, and contemplated actions of others who are or who may be involved. Perhaps most important of all are the probable responses and judgements that others are likely to make as a result of one's own contemplated actions if they are carried out. Sympathetic awareness of others is the primary basis of the human pattern of predictive behavior. "The brotherhood of man" is no theological platitude; it is a socio-psychological necessity for the human way of life.

Self-Realization[4]

Sympathetically based prediction of the probable actions of others is not enough to account for human behavior, however. If we stop

4. The following discussion of the development and importance of self-awareness is

here we are overlooking the most important component of our prediction equations for the future, our concept of our *self*. We are a part
of every situation we project into the future; and unless we are aware
of our own natures, our knowledge of what others may do is not of
much help. We can, as a matter of fact, look into the future with
confidence when we possess little more to go on than what we consider
to be a reliable estimate of our *self;* we can think of ourselves as persons
who can meet every situation, no matter what its nature, and deal with
it successfully! It is characteristic of man that when the future seems
dim in other respects, he seeks to increase his "self-confidence" as a
compensating factor.

This concept of our self which we possess is, so far as we know, a
uniquely human attribute. We do not think of animals as "self
conscious." It is not an attribute that we are born possessing; we have
all noted that babies lack self-consciousness. Our estimate of our self
is built up in interaction with others, through exercise of the attribute
of sympathetic identification. We put ourselves in the place of others
and look at the world from their points of view, and *our self* is one of
the things we see from the new vantage point, something that was hidden before. Our judgements of our self are built up out of the judgements that we believe others make concerning us. We feel that others
respect us, for example, so we are self-respecting; or perhaps the actions
of others as we interpret them indicate that we are held in contempt,
and we may become self-contemptuous.

We acquire the ability to take the role of "other people in general"
(Mead's "generalized other," or Freud's "super-ego"), and on this
basis we make self-judgements. We recall our own past history, for
example, and decide that we can rely upon our self, have confidence in
our self, or that we cannot rely upon or have confidence in our self.
We praise our self, pity our self, hate our self; we permit our self to do
this, forbid our self to do that, suggest to our self something else, but
always we do it by virtue of our ability to take the points of view of
others and thus look back upon our self as if we were someone else.
If for some reason we are lacking in the ability to take the roles of
others, we find it difficult to form a reliable self-concept. If we live

based largely on the work of Mead (*op. cit.,* pp. 135-226). See also Cooley (*op. cit.,*
pp. 183-84 and 246-49), Riezler (*op. cit.,* p. 84 *et passim*), and Sullivan (*op. cit.,* pp.
8-13).

in an environment where we attribute widely varying and conflicting points of view to others, we find ourselves perplexed as to our own nature.

Just as our self-image is formed in interaction with others, so must it be refreshed and renewed by interaction with others. Its skeletal framework is formed during childhood; the hated, the unwanted, the unloved, or the isolated child may form so warped an image of his own nature as to be severely crippled in social interaction in later life; but the skeleton is clothed with flesh in the on-going social process, through day-by-day contacts with others. We are continually seeking to discover what others think of us, in order that we may keep our image of our self up to date. We hope particularly for, and seek out, the kind of judgements that will substantiate an image of self-confidence and self-respect; but we prefer even an unflattering self-concept, if we feel that we can depend upon it, to a vague and wavering image. There is only one thing worse than being judged, and that is *not* being judged. When we are completely ignored by others as a *person*, as a human individuality, our concept of our self may shrivel to the point that self destruction seems actually to be rather a minor step.[5] We seek response from others, not only as a check on the acceptability of our course of action, but even more fundamentally to reassure ourselves of the validity and the very existence of our self.

This uniquely human attribute of the self, though it is a derivative from it, stands equal in importance to the uniquely human attribute of sympathy as a basis for the human way of life. Even under the very best conditions there must inevitably be so much of the future that cannot be predicted on any other basis that we can look forward to it without anxiety only by virtue of an abiding faith in our self. Self-confidence, self-reliance, self-respect—without these it is impossible to "live like a human being." Just as the great religions admonish us to be in sympathy with our fellows, so do they charge us so to conduct our lives that we can think well of ourselves. The two basic ideas upon which the Christian ethical code is founded are brotherly love and the dignity of the individual human spirit. Christ combined the two in a single bit of advice to us: "Love thy neighbor as thyself."

5. See Emile Durkheim's *Le Suicide* (Paris: F. Alcan, 1897; new ed., 1930); particularily for his discussion of that class of suicides resulting from the social condition he calls *anomie*. See also Sullivan, *op. cit.*, pp. 11-12.

He did not contemplate the submergence of the individual in the brotherhood of man. He saw the two in dynamic interaction, maintaining the marvellously balanced system of tensions that is the total pattern of the human way of life. In any real situation, the operation of the Christian ethic serves to achieve at one and the same time the maximum degree of self-realization and of fellowship. Quite apart from its religious significance, it has lasted down through the centuries because it is founded on a valid imagery of the nature of human nature.

The Human Way

Human nature is essentially a particular way of remaining in predictive contact with the future. This human pattern of prediction is founded upon two uniquely human attributes, the quality of sympathy and the possession of self-consciousness. We are able to profit by the experiences of others and work co-operatively with them by our ability to take their roles. Role-taking inevitably results in self-awareness, and we take our own natures into account in all our speculations as to the shape of the future; we see our self as a part of the environment that will shape our future course of action. This human way of life, however, requires the maintenance of rather special enabling conditions if it is to be successfully pursued.

Security.—Man's need for security springs out of his necessity for membership in that human brotherhood, society, that is based on the attribute of sympathy. We do not use the word *security* in the cheap and superficial sense it has come to assume far too often, but rather in the basic sense of that which affords us a secure foundation from which to orient our sight into the future. We cannot live without the accumulated experiences, the culture, of some enduring social group to supplement our own nor without the assistance of its membership in meeting many of our most crucial problems. Yet social membership is not ours by right even though we may be "born" into a society. In the latter case we have acquired nothing more than a kind of candidacy for membership. We can experience no real sense of belonging to any society, whether it be that of the family, the state, the industrial enterprise, or any other formally or informally organized group in which we regard membership as necessary to the working out of our life problems unless we can feel that three important conditions are being fulfilled.

We can enjoy the sense of security arising out of social membership only when we feel that we possess (1) function, (2) recognition,
and (3) status within those groups that we define as essential to our
welfare.[6] The group, we feel, will not admit us to membership or
countenance our continued membership unless we perform a *function*
that it judges to be in some way worthwhile from its own point of
view. Obviously, performance of the function must be *recognized* if
social membership is to be awarded and re-affirmed. Finally, if the
membership is to be meaningful to us in predictive terms, a *status* must
be assigned to us based on the value of the recognized function that
will let us know "where we stand"; that will permit us to project the
consequences of our membership into the future with a satisfactory
degree of reliability.

We learn our lesson early as to the need for function, recognition,
and status within a group. Even as small children we do that which
we hope will please, we go to great lengths to insure recognition, and
we are jealous of our status and fearful of being displaced. (Part of
this behavior also arises out of our need to build up and re-affirm a
satisfactory self-image, of course. There are few human activities
that have but a single socio-psychological motive.) As adults we are
even more persistent in our efforts to secure and retain legitimate
membership in various organized groups that will either help us to
carry forward necessary activities or that will re-inforce our self-confidence. We are consciously as well as intuitively aware that without
such membership we cannot make even first approximations as to the
shape of the future. Membership in a work group, in the present
study the workforce of an industrial enterprise, is one of the most important of these memberships in the modern world.

6. This is more usually discussed in terms of "role" and "status." See for example,
Ralph Linton's "Concepts of Role and Status" in T. M. Newcomb and E. L. Hartley,
editors, *Readings in Social Psychology* (New York: Henry Holt and Company, 1947).
On this basis, "role" refers to the actual behavior of an individual as observed and
classified by himself and others; "status" is assigned on the basis of expected behavior
which is supposed to, but does not of necessity, coincide with what one actually does.
The role-status concept is not adequate for our purposes, however. Role is equivalent
to recognized function, but part of the worker's anxiety springs from his conviction
in many cases that his function is *not* properly recognized. He may have grave
doubts that management's concept of his role agrees with his own. Peter Drucker
discusses the problem of the industrial worker in terms of function-status in his *The
Future of Industrial Man* (New York: John Day Company, 1942) along lines that
parallel our own; but while the importance of recognition is implicit in his discussion,
he does not spell it out.

Understanding.[7]—Man's need for understanding arises out of his realization of himself as an individual and his necessity therefore to relate himself to the context in which he finds himself. Function, recognition, and status, though of prime importance, are still not sufficient. Our continued acceptance by any society is dependent upon our ability to "get along" with its membership, to fit our own activities in with those of its other members in such a way that we will re-inforce them in co-operative situations and, at the least, not interfere with them in others. We must be able to make many short-run predictions within the social context if we are to be able to make those long-run predictions based on social membership that spell out security for us.

There are three components to our prediction equations within the social environment. We must possess three dependable sets of ideas with which to work: adequate concepts of the nature of (1) our world, (2) our fellows, and (3) our self. With these, we have understanding.[8]

Our conceptual imagery of our world is the frame of reference by which we measure and judge the meanings of the things, relationships, and actions we observe. A good share of it is the heritage of our culture. If it is to be of value to us in a social situation, it must be shared by the others with whom we are in significant contact. We must be in basic agreement with them as to what is good or bad, desirable or undesirable, right or wrong, honest or dishonest. We do not respond directly to situations, but rather to our interpretations of their meanings; and so if we are to be able to make even a first approximation as to the probable responses of others to a shared situation, their definitions of it must correspond to ours in their essential aspects. If they do not, we can neither predict what they are likely to do nor

7. For a masterful discussion of the role of "understanding" in human society, see Riezler, *op. cit.,* Chapter III. Max Weber's concept of *verstehen* as the basis of social action, "such action as, according to its subjective meaning to the actor or actors, involves the attitudes and actions of others and is oriented to them in its course," is significant. Weber uses *verstehen* in much the same sense that we have used the term "sympathy"; he applies it to the grasping of subjective motivation. For understanding when it is based on external, overt action, he uses the term *begreifen.* See his *Gesammelta Aufszatze zur Wissenschaftslehre* (Tubingen: Mohr, 1924), p. 2 and pp. 67 ff. See also Talcott Parson's Chapter XVI in his *The Structure of Social Action* (New York: McGraw-Hill Book Company, 1937) for a further discussion of Weber's methodology.

8. For a more extended discussion of conceptual behavior in human conduct, see Mead's supplementary essay on "The Function of Imagery in Human Conduct," *op. cit.,* pp. 337 ff. See also Riezler and Weber as cited above.

how they are likely to respond to what we consider the "right" thing to do. We will neither understand nor be understood.

There is the possibility, of course, that a particular point of view, by labelling certain phenomena as of no importance, may effectively blind us to aspects of our environment that are actually of great importance. It may label other aspects incorrectly. This is nevertheless the price that we and our society must pay for being able to come to any conclusions at all. In a changing world, we must finally decide that some things are one way and some things are another or we will never act at all. We cannot rid the world of bias. We can only hope that the particular bias of ourselves and our society will be successful in identifying and correctly explaining the important events of a kaleidoscopic world.[9]

Yet even in the most perfect society a mere sharing of a common set of definitions of the meaning of things, relations, and actions is not sufficient; for points of view will inevitably vary from individual to individual because of differences in particular functions, statuses, characters, and temperaments. We must be able to predict, not only what the "typical" member of our society is likely to do, but also how the real individuals with whom we are in contact are likely to deviate from the generalized action pattern of this mythical personality. We may make certain specialized generalizations about classes of people, old people, young people, employers, employees, but too great reliance upon these means that we act toward a stereotype rather than the real individual in many cases where the stereotype is not actually representative.

If we are to fit our own action patterns in with those of others with whom we are engaged in a common activity, we need intimate knowledge of them as individuals. If we are to take their roles adequately, look at the world through their eyes and predict their probable responses, we need to know how their points of view differ from our own and from the "average." The latter does no more than put us on target, so to speak; it gives us a clue as to the probable range of response, but not of its particular nature. Only when we can rely upon our concepts of what others are like can we act with ease and

9. This is the central assumption of the sociology of knowledge which has been best developed by Karl Mannheim in his *Ideology and Utopia,* translated by Louis Wirth and Edward Shils (New York: Harcourt, Brace and Company, 1949). Wirth's Introduction to this work is particularly worthy of attention.

assurance in a situation involving those others. We must be aware of the private little variations they are likely to introduce into their estimation of the meaning of things, or we will have to proceed hesitantly, feeling our way, hoping anxiously that others will subscribe in every essential respect to a frame of reference identical with our own.

There is finally the matter of man's concept of himself. He sees himself as a part of every situation that he projects into the future; and unless he has reliable knowledge of his own nature, an important element of the pattern of the future is hidden or misrepresented. His image of himself must be more than reliable; for the sake of his peace of mind it must possess a particular kind of reliability. Only on the basis of self-confidence and self-reliance can he fill in the inevitably missing parts of the picture of tomorrow and face its approach with equanimity and serenity. Not only must we be in sympathy with our fellows, but we must be able to respect ourselves as individuals if we are to maintain that dynamic relationship between the person and the group that is the basis of human behavior.

Novelty.—In addition to security and understanding, there is one other basic condition necessary to the maintainence of a human way of life. It springs from our necessity to think well of ourselves, to have confidence in our ability to deal with the unknown. We can do this only if we have in the past met and mastered a sufficient variety of unexpected events to substantiate our faith that we can continue to do so in the future. In man, the life process has created an organism endowed with the ability to keep one step ahead of a changing world. We seek out and face up to novelty if for no other reason than to reassure ourselves that we are human beings. The life experience of the race, as embodied in its culture, has demonstrated to man that if he is to survive he cannot wait for the world to come to him; he must seek out its novelty. If we were to attribute to him one remaining instinct of importance, it would be that of a tremendous and overpowering curiosity. At any rate, it is only through new experience, met and mastered, that we develop our faith in our ability to deal with the aleatory element; and when we do not meet with new experience in the ordinary course of events, we are inclined to seek it out.

The Industrial Worker and the Human Way.—Whether his job is in textiles or basic steel, in southeastern United States or in northern China, the industrial worker like all the rest of us must enjoy the conditions necessary for the maintenance of a human way of life if he is to feel that he is living like a human being. Like all of us, his need for security, understanding, and novelty is so basic to his very existence that if he is denied them under a particular set of circumstances he will seek to alter those circumstances if he cannot escape them. Because of its central importance to all his other activities, he must realize these essential conditions in the industrial *milieu* above all. If there is a basic problem of industrial relations, it must arise out of some inherent challenge offered by the fundamental nature of the industrial process to their realization.

The Basic Industrial Process

Modern industry is based on the technological possibilities afforded by division of labor.[10] This technic (an idea in itself much older than modern industry) permitted man, when sufficient demand had been built up for consumer goods, to plan machines to perform the relatively simple tasks that emerged. Further perfection of machine operations called for even more minute division of tasks, until the modern industrial process developed with its complexity of numerous apparently individual and unrelated operations that become integrated and meaningful only in the final end product.

The perfection and elaboration of these specialized machines had three further and very important effects. (1) The skills required to operate them were highly specialized and in most cases reduced as well. (2) The investment necessary to turn out even one article, through utilization of a series of such machines, grew far beyond the capacity of the individual workingman ever to accumulate. (3) The whole process of manufacture itself became so complicated that a more or less elaborate superstructure of supervisory, administrative, and executive personnel was necessary to co-ordinate its otherwise unrelated activities, and very often only the top echelon of command in any one plant had any real idea of the nature of the total operation.

We can say that the modern industrial process, in its universal and basic form, wherever it may be found in whatever industry, is marked by:

10. For an excellent account of the emergence of the present industrial system and of its impact upon society, see Lewis Mumford's *Technics and Civilization* (New York: Harcourt, Brace and Company, 1934).

1. A complex division of labor
2. High capital investments
3. Specialized and for the most part reduced worker skills
4. A differentiated managerial structure

These are the distinguishing features of mass production industry, as opposed to the earlier handicraft industry, that have so increased the material wealth of the world as to permit even the factory worker himself to enjoy material comforts today that were not possessed by the very rich of a century ago. They have had the further effect of supplying him with sufficient leisure so that he has a practical opportunity to enjoy them. This is rather an important factor since he has become in many cases his own best customer.

THE PROBLEM OF INDUSTRIAL RELATIONS

Yet the very characteristics of the process by which man has eased the rigours of his existence in one direction have created a problem in another.[11] It is no criticism of modern industry to say that this is so. We have become and remain human through the development and exercise of our ability to meet and master situations that appear inherently to threaten the human way of life. Yet each new challenge is also a threat. No guarantee of survival has been handed to the human race. We dare not be complacent about any fundamental problem that faces us; we have to solve it to stay human.

The nature of the obstacles that arise in this case will become apparent as we survey the practical difficulties that lie in the way of realizing the conditions necessary for maintenance of the human pattern of predictive behavior when we limit the problem by placing it in an industrial context. (It should be kept in mind that in the dis-

11. For a well-documented case history of the emergence of this problem as the shoe industry changed from a handicraft to a mechanized basis, see Lloyd Warner's and J. C. Low's *The Social System of the Modern Factory*, Vol. IV, *The Yankee City Series* (New Haven: Yale University Press, 1947), especially Chapter II. See also their "The Factory and the Community" in *Industry and Society*, W. F. Whyte, editor (New York: McGraw-Hill Book Company, 1946).

The problem in its essential aspects has also been well discussed by Elton Mayo in his *Human Problems of an Industrial Civilization* (New York: The Macmillan Company, 1933) and his *The Social Problems of an Industrial Civilization* (Cambridge: Harvard University Press, 1945). Peter Drucker's first two chapters of the work cited are well worth reading for further insight into the nature of the basic problem of industrial relations, as are the first three chapters of Frank Tannenbaum's *A Philosophy of Labor* (New York: Alfred A. Knopf, 1951). The genesis of the problem is well presented in the latter reference.

cussion immediately following we concern ourselves only with the raw and unameliorated impact of the basic industrial process upon basic human nature. We deliberately avoid, at this point, consideration of any cushioning factors that might cloud the stark and logical necessity of what emerges out of the interaction.)

Division of Labor and the Industrial Worker

We have pointed out the necessity that man, for the sake of his own peace of mind, feels that he is performing a useful function. The division of labor as it has developed in modern mass production industry strikes at the very heart of this assurance. In many cases the task performed has developed out of so intricate a subdivision of function that it appears to the worker to have no real and intrinsic meaning. He may be quite convinced that his job is due to nothing more than a product designer's whim or a production engineer's mistake, and in either case it may be subject to change or elimination on a moment's notice.

Even when the necessity for his task and its meaning are apparent to him, he cannot feel fully secure in his function. Experience has taught him that technological progress refuses to admit the necessity of any job. A dozen key men today may be replaced by a machine tended by a single semi-skilled worker tomorrow. Progress has a price; and part of that price is the gnawing suspicion of the industrial worker that he is performing a function that is either worthless to begin with or that may be made so at any time.

This feeling is heightened by his general lack of acquaintance with the scientific and engineering principles that lie behind the actual division of labor itself. Since it is often difficult for him to appreciate the logic of the division, he is likely to feel that his whole industrial environment has been set up on a whimsical and capricious basis that is meaningless from his point of view and thus subject to meaningless and unpredictable change. Not only is his feeling of security challenged, but his understanding of the context in which he works as well.

Finally, the repetitious tasks to which he is assigned deny his need for new experience, for the element of novelty that must be present in his world to provide the necessary challenge of a positive sort that keeps him human. On every count, the division of labor hinders rather than facilitates establishment of the conditions necessary for a human way of life.

High Capital Investment and the Industrial Worker

Since we have emerged as human beings, we have relied upon tools to help us prepare to meet the future. We have come to regard our tools as extensions of our selves. The hunter's rifle, the woodsman's axe, the mason's trowel, these artifacts add to their possessors' confidence that the future can be met and mastered even though it may be seen only dimly at the moment. With tools our self-reliance and our self-confidence are increased. We feel that by their use we can command the future and bend it to our will when we cannot predict it otherwise; we will be able to make a way for ourselves in the world, carve out a niche in society with our tools.

But modern industrial processes have taken tools away from the individual and lodged their ownership with the enterprise. The industrial worker cannot possibly hope to purchase them for himself. As a result, his maintenance of the conditions necessary for a human way of life is challenged in two respects. Since he may be denied access to the tools in the first place, he may not even be permitted to demonstrate his ability to perform the function that he depends upon to earn the group membership necessary to his existence. Having secured the opportunity and the membership, he cannot depend upon his ability to retain it; the use of the tools that make possible his performance of his function may be taken from him for reasons that have nothing to do with the quality or usefulness of his work.

In addition to the insecurity which he feels with regard to his status in the society of the enterprise, his concept of self suffers. His lack of ultimate control over the tools he uses diminishes his self-confidence and his self-reliance. He finds it difficult to picture himself, as an industrial worker, being able to command the future by means of them. Even if he were to own them, their value to him would be dependent, not upon his own ability in their use, but upon the continued operation of the whole enterprise. This is a situation which is completely out of his reach as an individual. The handicraft worker commands his tools; but the industrial worker is likely to feel that he is commanded *by* them.

Skill Requirements and the Industrial Worker

Some few industrial workers are able to feel that even though they do not own the tools with which they work, the tools cannot, nevertheless, be operated without them. They possess skills of a sufficiently unique nature so that they are not easily replaceable, the roller or second helper in a steel mill, for example, the loom fixer, the skilled operator in a finishing plant, the weaver who works with fine count fabrics. These men and others in the same category can feel that they are as necessary to the operation of the enterprise as the operation of the enterprise is to them. The difficulty in this case is that though their skills are high, they are also highly specialized. Their possessors are still not their own men in the sense that the cabinet maker is, for example. Their fortunes are irrevocably tied in with that of the enterprise; the roller can hardly set up a rolling mill in his back yard to carry him through a layoff, nor can the weaver of silk brocade tide himself over by doing custom work for the neighbors while the mill is down.

Unfortunately for his peace of mind, the much more numerous semi-skilled worker, the machine tender in mass production industry, lacks even this dubious assurance. He is well aware that the level of skill required to perform his function can be so easily acquired in a short time by such a large number of people that he cannot in any sense be regarded as indispensable. He is readily replaceable and he knows it. The result is still further loss of self-confidence on his part. The knowledge that the work he is doing could quite as easily be performed by almost anyone between the ages of sixteen and sixty-five—or even by a well-trained chimpanzee—is not likely to inspire confidence in the future on the basis of his estimate of his own abilities.

In addition, he is more convinced than ever of the unimportance of the function he performs, and he is concerned with the status that it is likely to earn for him. Despite his reluctance to admit it in his own case, he is aware that logically status must be assigned to him, not on the basis of the total ability he possesses as a person, but rather on the basis of the minimum level of ability required for satisfactory performance of his function. "The rate goes with the job" is a ruling that he himself agrees must be adhered to for the good of all.

Enforcement of the ruling, however, means that the only way by which he can achieve what he regards as a satisfactory balance between ability and status is to progress up the job hierarchy by means of promotion, but he is likely to doubt that he will receive recognition for his possession of capabilities beyond the requirements of any particular mass production job on which he happens to be placed. Initially he is likely to suffer from anxiety as to the possibility that he will be given an opportunity to perform a function and possess a status commensurate with his own estimation of his ability. Eventually, partly because of the lack of stimulating novelty in his routine work and partly because his initial judgement of himself is not sustained and reinforced by the demonstrated judgements of others through promotion to more demanding and important tasks, his self-concept may shrink to the point where he privately doubts his ability to undertake a more important function. Self-doubt may progress to the point that he refuses the promotion when it is finally offered to him.

The Managerial Structure and the Industrial Worker

Still further difficulties are introduced into the situation of the industrial worker by the necessity for a managerial superstructure to coordinate and oversee the various production operations going on within the plant. It is of course important that the machine tender be able to understand his fellow workers for the sake of his personal relationships with them as well as to enable him to cooperate with them. It is even more important that he be able to predict the probable courses of action of various members of the managerial group, be able to assume their points of view, and be able to anticipate their value judgements. It is this management group that can grant or deny him access to the tools with which he works, that allocates his function and assigns his status, and that sets up the conditions under which he works. It is this group whose recognition he must continue to receive if he is to maintain his membership in the industrial society of the plant. Above all, he must be able to predict the future actions, decisions, and judgements of this group if he is to have any reliable preview of his future in the plant society.

Yet despite the paramount importance of his relationship with the people in management, the industrial worker by the very nature of things finds it difficult to maintain them in a satisfactory fashion. He finds it difficult in the first place to assume the managerial point of view even in a general sort of way. Not only are there differences of education, background, status, and often of nationality and even language, but the very function of management is in itself such as to give items completely different meanings when viewed from that vantage point. There is the matter of wages, for example; the worker defines them as income and seeks to maximize them, whereas management defines them as expense and seeks to minimize them. There is also the fact that management is aware of much that is unknown to the worker, and the worker is acquainted with facts that have escaped the attention of management. Not only is management likely to define differently those things which it sees in common with the worker, but, looking at the same situation, it is likely to see a different set of things to define.

Even if the worker is able to master the general point of view of management, it is still with individual members of management that he must deal, with real persons rather than with an abstract idea of Management or with a stereotyped image of the Top Brass. The physical and social distance that separates managerial people from himself makes it difficult for the worker to predict how they as individuals are likely to vary from the typical managerial viewpoint. He may become fairly well acquainted with his foreman and be able to make reasonably accurate predictions about the probable responses of his department head. Yet while these people play an important role in his day-to-day experiences, they have little control over the more important aspects of his work life so long as he is reasonably diligent and skillful in the performance of his function. Of the people who may or may not adopt a new production process that will throw him out of work, who may or may not grant him a pay increase, who may or may not change the whole system of production, he knows very little. He can rely only upon a vague, unsatisfactory, and generally inaccurate picture in his mind of what top management is like; and inaccuracies are inevitably introduced into his predictions because of it.

There is also the fact that as the worker scans the managerial ladder, he is aware that these people in the ascending scale who have more and more control over his ultimate industrial destiny have less and less knowledge of him as an individual; and finally, at the level where decisions of the utmost importance to him are finally reached, he has shrivelled to the status of a statistic, a unit of labor for which a certain price must be paid. If his own idea of what Top Management is like is vague and inaccurate, so also is he very often on the receiving end of policies that are based upon an equally vague, inaccurate, and generally unrepresentative picture of The Industrial Worker. He is likely neither to understand nor to be understood by the people at the top.

Behind the management of his plant he sees the impersonal and finally controlling element of the Market; he is aware that no matter how sympathetic his employers may be toward him and how aware they are of his abilities and his problems, they must themselves answer to the inexorable voice of the laws of supply and demand. The plant may be owned, manned, and managed in the Georgian Piedmont, but it cannot detach its destiny from the mysterious gyrations of the price of print cloth as determined on Worth Street in New York City. The worker sees himself, then, losing his personality, shrinking to a unit of labor producing for a mass market the actions of which he can neither control nor predict. His concept of self, measured against this impersonal and imponderable background, diminishes to the point that he loses even the feeling of his own identity.

PART TWO

THE CONTEXT OF THE RELATIONSHIP

CHAPTER II

The Piedmont Region and Its People

WHEN WE ASSUME a correlative relationship between the natural features of man's environment and the fundamental patterns of his life processes, we are using the concept of *regionalism*.[1] The concept by no means implies the further and incorrect assumption that man is completely a creature of his environment, that he is an inert, plastic, passive lump of protoplasm shaped without protest into an organic complement of the physiographic characteristics of his *milieu*. Man not only responds to action, he initiates it; and while the nature of his activities may be modified by the features of his region, his activities in turn modify its natural features.

A three-way process of interaction takes place, out of which emerges a regional way of life. (1) The natural features of the region may be modified; but they remain present as limiting factors that can be pushed back or ameliorated, but not removed. (2) The human nature of man himself will set further limits within which his life problems must be solved if he is neither to perish nor cease to be what we have come to regard as "human." (3) Within these limits his cultural inheritance, which may well have been developed in some other region and with regard to some other way of life, will play a role in the emergence of new life patterns, of new cultural traits. In a regionally oriented study of human institutions, then, there are at least three sets of factors that are of interest to us:

1. The natural features of the physical environment
2. What man has done about and with those natural features
3. The life patterns he has employed and developed in the process

1. See Howard Odum's *Southern Regions of the United States* (Chapel Hill: The University of North Carolina Press, 1936), pp. 4 ff.; also his "Folk Sociology as Subject Field for Historical Study," *Social Forces*, XXXI (1953).

The Piedmont Region

The most common point of view fails to differentiate the Piedmont from a much larger region, generally referred to simply as "the South" or "the Southeast." There is no denying the fundamental homogeneity of the Southeast, including the Piedmont, along many lines of culture, tradition, and experience.[2] Yet a single glance at a map of the textile towns of the Southeast shows a remarkable concentration of the industry. The map is black with names in a great sweeping curve from lower middle Virginia, through the Carolinas and Georgia, into Alabama. Only a few names, thinly scattered, lie east or west of its unmistakable boundaries. Since our study is grounded in the assumption that the natural features of the land set limiting conditions that enter fundamentally into the patterns of man's socio-economic behavior, we seek an explanation for this phenomenon first in the physiographic characteristics of the Southeast.

There is no natural homogeneity except that of climate tying together the broad sweep of land south of the Ohio and the Potomac that lies east of the Mississippi. Isiah Bowman, in his monumental work on the *Forest Physiography* of the United States, identifies not one but six "physiographic provinces" in this area.[3] He differentiates the Mississippi Valley, the Appalachian Plateaus, the Great Appalachian Valley, the Appalachian Mountains, the Piedmont Plateaus, and the Atlantic and Gulf Coastal Plains as regions distinctive from each other, in terms of natural attributes that are reasonably capable of affecting the life patterns of their inhabitants.

Comparison of these natural regions and the locus of the textile industry shows the latter to be almost entirely confined to the Piedmont Plateaus (more commonly called simply "the Piedmont"). This, the region that lies "at the foot of the mountain" and west of the Coastal Plain and that is the industrial heart of the Southeast for more than textiles, will command our principle attention throughout our study. Yet much of what we will say with regard to its essential style of

2. See Odum, *Southern Regions*. See also Rupert Vance's *Human Geography of the South* (Chapel Hill: University of North Carolina Press, 1935), p. 20; and Carl O. Sauer's *Geography of the Pennyroyal* (Chicago: Geographical Society of Chicago, 1920), p. 5.

3. The account in this chapter of the physiographic features of the Piedmont and its neighboring regions is drawn entirely from Bowman's comprehensive and exhaustive treatment of the *Forest Physiography of the United States* (New York: Wiley, 1911), pp. 498-635.

living can be applied with equal validity to the entire southeastern upland region of mountain, mountain valley, and plateau; and the natural endowments of all six provinces have played their role, by indirection or directly, in shaping the Piedmont way of life.

The rich alluvial soils of the Mississippi Valley were at first a diversion that helped draw the rolling tide of plantation culture away from the Piedmont. Later, the glut of cotton from its fertile plantations forced prices downward to a level that proved ruinous for many of the upland farmers east of the Appalachians. On the other hand, the thin and scanty soil cover of the elevated Appalachian Plateaus, relieved only by the lime-rich Blue Grass and Nashville Basins, held out little attraction to the stream of population pouring out of the Middle Colonies into the high-lifted system of river valleys that collectively make up the Great Appalachian Valley. When the fertile river bottoms, coves, and basins of the latter were pre-empted, a considerable share of the population made surplus within it by birth and continuing immigration preferred to turn back eastward across the mountains into the Piedmont, joining there those other settlers coming directly from the North who were already threading their tortuous way into the Piedmont along the headwaters of its numerous streams, within the shadow of the eastern escarpment of the Blue Ridge.[4]

The Shenandoah, the Tennessee, and the other major and tributary streams that collectively make up the Great Valley system thus served not only as a back door but as a continuing reservoir of population for the Piedmont. Later, the human and hydrodynamic resources of the lower reaches of the valley would encourage a manufacturing development that would add this section to the region of industry already outlined by the boundaries of the Piedmont; and the pulsing energy from the integrated system of dams that was necessary effectively to curb its rivers would feed into the network of transmission lines that tie the whole industrial Southeast into a great curving crescent of super-power.

The Appalachian Mountains, dominated by the Blue Ridge, fall easily toward the west; but their eastern slopes are precipitous. Thus, while cutting the Piedmont off from travel directly westward into the interior, they permitted an eastward movement into the Piedmont from the Great Valley, as pioneers made their way up the streams that angled easily up the western slopes and broke through high-lifted gaps

4. See Vance, *op. cit.,* p. 45.

to see the undulating swells of the Piedmont forests stretching without apparent limit toward the east. The shadow of the Blue Ridge kept the Piedmont a backwater of rutted clay roads long after the balance of the Southeast was criss-crossed by the tracks of burgeoning rail systems. Yet in addition to their wealth of hardwood and the coal and iron at their southern base, the mountains possessed another resource that by itself was to outweigh their disadvantage to the Piedmont— the rushing streams, falling by the most direct route down the eastern slopes, that would one day channel mountain rainfall through numerous mill wheels and hydro-electric turbines lining deep Piedmont valleys.

Eastward of the Piedmont lies the Atlantic Coastal Plain. Its original forest cover of pine laid down only a scanty blanket of organic material; and heavy rainfall, plus lack of an adequate subsoil, soon leached this after the region was deforested. Yet the virgin fertility of the plain remained long enough to encourage the development of a slave-based plantation agriculture that advanced steadily westward, leaving behind it devoured fields and desolation, and infecting the Piedmont with the virus of a one-crop economy. The swift currents of the rivers that hurry proudly across the Piedmont spend their last energies in a foaming dash through rapids and shoals that mark their emergence into the Coastal Plain; and then, after rolling torpidly through broad, shallow valleys, they struggle listlessly through tidal estuaries to the ocean.

The weathered crystalline debris of the ancient Appalachian system that is the Piedmont is separated from the ocean-born sands of the Coastal Plain by a geological fault known as the "fall line." The name derives from the steepened stream descents, low falls, and rapids that quite commonly mark the transition of rivers from the "old" land of the highlands to the "new" land of the Plains. Since this boundary marks also the practical head of navigation for southeastern rivers, it is the site of many of the large cities of the Southeast. Richmond, Raleigh, Camden, Columbia, Augusta, Macon, Columbus, Montgomery, and Tuscaloosa were founded at points where it was necessary to transfer goods from barges to overland transportation; and they have continued to serve as centers of distribution for the back country. The fall line is additionally outlined through the Carolinas and into Georgia by a belt of shifting sand hills that have never been able to support anything more valuable than their original cover of jack pine and scrub oak.

The Piedmont in its entirety swings southwestward from New Jersey until it disappears under the sandy loams of the Coastal Plain in east central Alabama; but its width is negligible in the North. It is narrow in Virginia, crowded between the mountains and Chesapeake Bay with its outflung tidal estuaries. It reaches its greatest width of more than 150 miles measured perpendicular to the Blue Ridge in North Carolina, averages something like 100 miles in South Carolina and Georgia, and tapers to a point south and east of Birmingham in Alabama. From an altitude of 1,000 to 1,200 feet at the west, its surface declines rather uniformly to reach an altitude of 400 to 500 feet along the fall line.

The soils of its rolling surface are loams of red clay or grayish sands over clay subsoils. Its original forest cover of deciduous hardwood and shortleaf pine contributed enriching humus, and its clay subsoil prevents extensive leaching. Its growing season places it within the cotton belt, and its forty or fifty inches of rainfall well-distributed over an average year is sufficient to sustain a wide range of vegetation —but it has also been sufficient to expose the red clay subsoil of countless slopes that have been improperly cropped and that lie bare and vulnerable, without the protection of frost, to washing winter rains. Erosion is the mortal enemy of the Piedmont farmer.

The profusion of streams that cross the Piedmont from west to east have invited hydro-electric development. Their swift descent within the confines of steep and narrow valleys that forbid a river-bottom agriculture have enabled their power resources to be developed initially on a modest scale, without the necessity for the large capital investments required to utilize streams of lesser fall flowing through more shallow and tillable valleys—those of the Great Appalachian Valley, for example. But while the channels of the Piedmont streams encouraged use of their power potentialities at an early date, they made north to south travel within the region difficult except along their headwaters.

This was the Piedmont in its natural state. A region of rolling hills shrouded with hardwood forests, with soil fertile enough, but difficult to till and difficult to keep. It was virtually isolated by its own physiography and that of its neighbor regions. There were mountains to the west, forbidding sandhills to the east, and rivers flowing between the two that could be easily forded only near their sources— rivers that speedily carved out valleys in the middle and lower Piedmont, their swift currents so swollen by tributaries from the plateau that they discouraged primitive attempts to be bridged. Yet just as the Piedmont slopes could be thriftily tilled if one worked with their contours, so could these rivers be broken to harness through exercise of ingenuity and determination. It was a region that was easier to settle in than to pass through, which was no great drawback—for it was, after all, not a gateway to anywhere; but it had considerable possibilities in its own right. It was a region that would not be bullied but that would, if one worked intelligently with what it had to offer, yield up its resources in a kind of gracious and modest plenty.[5] The combination of challenge and reward presented by it was something like that of ancient Greece. One could live decently within it by dint of moderate toil, and one had to toil moderately to live decently; but not even the most frantic endeavor was likely to cajole or force it into supporting one lavishly.

THE PIEDMONT PEOPLE

If we are to understand the development of the Piedmont way of life, we need to know something of the cultural traits—the characteristic ways of attacking those life problems amenable to classification—that its settlers brought into the region with them; and our best clue in this respect lies along the line indicated by the heading immediately following.

Who They Were and Where They Came From[6]

The Southeast was not settled entirely by a movement directly westward from the coastal areas, as is commonly supposed by those not familiar with its history. There was an interlacing of westerly

5. For an excellent portrayal of a style of life that might be thought of as based on optimum use of the natural features of the Piedmont and growing out of them, see Ben Robertson's *Red Hills and Cotton* (New York: Alfred A. Knopf, 1942).

6. For a documentary account of the settlement of the Southeast, see Ulrich B. Phillips' *Documents of the Plantation and Frontier* (2 vols., Cleveland: A. H. Clark, 1910). See also Vance, *op. cit.*, for a good summary discussion. Thomas J. Wertenbaker's *The Old South* (New York: Charles Scribner's Sons, 1942) presents the settlement of the northern Piedmont in some detail. See Ellen Semple's *American History and its Geographic Conditions* (Boston: Houghton Mifflin, 1903), for an account of physiographic influences on the settlement of the Southeast.

and southerly movements. The former was predominant in the Coastal Plain and the latter in the Appalachian Valley. The two met and mingled in the Piedmont.

There was not any important immigration from the Coastal Plain into the Piedmont until after 1800, except in Virginia and the northern tier of counties in North Carolina, where tobacco planters sought new land in the plateau well before the Revolution and pressed on even into the Shenandoah Valley. Further south, rice and indigo culture would tie the plantations to the sea islands and the coastal lowlands until cotton came into the picture; while the slave-based plantation system with its one-crop economy discouraged the plebian immigration directly from Europe that would have built up sufficient population pressure to have burst through the forbidding pine barrens into the Piedmont.

Yet the back country did not remain empty. The western march of tobacco planters, noted above, met a determined tide of population sweeping down from Pennsylvania and Maryland (or from Europe via those states) even before 1730, bringing with it the intensive agricultural practices of Ulster and the Palatinate. Germans, English, Scotch, Scotch-Irish, Irish, Swiss, Quakers—for the most part they were people who had come late to the Middle Colonies, and finding their best land already settled, had tarried for a generation in the western counties of Pennsylvania or Maryland before turning toward the south and the rich loams of the southeastern back country.

This stream from the north, as it pressed on into the Carolinian Piedmont, was augmented by a considerable number of English from Virginia itself—not a few of which were members of impoverished Virginia planter families who preferred to take their chances on the frontier rather than resign themselves to a life of impecunious gentility. It penetrated into North Carolina before 1740. Staying close to the Blue Ridge in its southern march, where the headwaters of the Piedmont rivers could be easily forded, it fanned out between the rivers as far east as Raleigh well before the Revolution.[7]

Another portion of the stream that funneled into the Shenandoah Valley from the north continued on into the lower and middle portions of the Great Valley. Many of these pioneers, as we have noted,

7. See Wertenbaker, *op. cit.* See also John Spencer Bassett's "Regulators in North Carolina," *American Historical Reports* (1894).

broke eastward through mountain gaps with the Piedmont as their original objective or followed the Tennessee until the valley of the French Broad at the southern base of the Blue Ridge offered easy access to the back country of lower North Carolina, South Carolina, and north Georgia.[8] Within a generation, the valley itself would be a prime source of population for the region across the mountains.

This southern and eastward flow into the back country did not populate it overnight; yet by the eve of the Revolution only the Georgian Piedmont, which was still Indian country, remained to be settled. Not until after a good portion of the Piedmont wilderness was at least partially brought to heel by pioneer farmers from the north would an event occur that would finally result in a surge of population into it from across the fall line.

The cotton gin was invented in 1793; and the hardy upland cotton, that the English had found already growing in the region when they first arrived, became a practicable cash crop. The huge profits inherent in cotton culture as a means of translating soil fertility into cash had been brought to the attention of the Coastal Plain when the sea islands had begun raising an Egyptian variety in 1786; and now commercial culture of the staple was no longer restricted to the areas capable of raising an easily ginned but delicate strain. The tidewater planters abandoned rice and indigo for cotton; but its culture was most avidly seized upon by those yeoman farmers whose holdings had come to ring the Charleston-Savannah district as they had pushed out beyond the plantation area to practice subsistence farming. More aggressive, more willing—and often more able—to pay top prices for good cotton land, they usually won out in the mad scramble for acreage that marked the extension of the cotton kingdom; and the "cotton aristocracy" came into the picture, modeled after that of the tidewater but only occasionally in the direct line of descent from it.

The initial sweep forward into the Coastal Plain, as the new planter class sought more and more land upon which to employ field hands purchased from the slave-surplus areas of Virginia and the tidewater, had hardly slowed before the necessity for a new surge westward arose. Cotton had already drained the thin soils of the plantations nearest the coast, and a process of leap-frogging began that left behind depleted

8. See Harold Underwood Faulkner, *American Economic History* (6th ed., New York: Harper and Brothers, 1949), p. 106. See also Vance, *op. cit.*, pp. 45-46.

fields and a beginning class of poor whites. The cotton planters would
by preference have swung around the southern tip of the Piedmont
and gone directly westward to the Gulf Coastal Plain of Alabama and
Mississippi; but even as late as 1820 the Creeks and the Cherokees
held the land west of the Altamaha and the Ocmulgee Rivers in
Georgia. They would not be completely removed until 1833; and so
the planters pressed on across the fall line, and the lower Piedmont became plantation country.[9] After 1833, the migration of the planters
into the region halted. Though the soils of the Piedmont were more
fertile than those of the Coastal Plain, its rolling contours were not
only more difficult to work with slave labor, but they eroded rapidly
under the heavy rainfall of the region when they were planted to row
crops. There was, in addition, the problem of transportation. Roads
varied from poor to impassible, the Piedmont streams were not suitable
for floating the crop out, and rail lines were non-existent in the upper
and inadequate in the central Piedmont even as late as the eve of the
Civil War.[10] A yeoman farmer might essay the task of getting his
modest crop out to market; but the great plantations were necessarily
tied to transportation that could move large quantities of goods with
ease and dependability.

Thus finally, after 1800, the streams of population into the Piedmont
from the North and East met and mingled along its eastern and its
southern borders. Along the fall line, plantations were predominant.
Further inland, plantations and small farms intermingled. The central
and western Piedmont remained a region of small, family-owned and
operated farms, still practicing a diversified agriculture and largely
self-sufficing in its economy. The difference between the two streams
of settlement was not as great as might have been supposed, however;
for the cotton aristocracy had largely sprung from the yeomanry of
the Coastal Plain. In his ways of thinking and behaving, and in his
general approach toward life, the cotton planter was closer to the
Piedmont pioneer than to the tidewater aristocrat after whom he
consciously modelled himself.[11]

9. For an eye-witness account of the western march of the cotton planters, see
Frederick Law Olmstead's *The Cotton Kingdom* (original edition 1861), A. M. Schles-
inger, ed. (New York: Alfred A. Knopf, 1953).

10. See Robert C. Black's *The Railroads of the Confederacy* (Chapel Hill: The
University of North Carolina Press, 1952), Chapter One.

11. See Olmstead's account, *op. cit.*

What They Brought to the Piedmont

Statistical evidence as to the original ethnic diversity of the Piedmont people is notable mainly for its absence; but even on the basis of the brief investigation into their origin we have just completed, it is apparent that three racial strains with diverse cultural heritages—Anglo-Saxon, Celtic, and Teutonic—met and mingled in the Piedmont. Yet despite their differences, there were important similiarities to begin with even before a process of cross-cultural fertilization could take place. All were north European in their origin. Presbyterians, Baptists, Lutherans, Moravians, and Quakers, each of them was powerfully influenced by a rigorous interpretation of the Christian ethic that put considerable emphasis upon industry, thrift, frugality—and individual responsibility for self-discipline.

But even more important than the existence of these and other initial similiarities between them that would encourage the development of homogeneity on a region-wide basis was the fact that ethnic origins were not to be completely determinative of what these people were to become. The overburden of "customary behavior" is burned off in the crucible of the frontier. The human way of life is reduced to a kind of least common denominator. Under the stress conditions which face the pioneer and the pioneer farmer, elemental human nature is divested of the veneer of civilization. Complete dependence upon traditional ways of doing things becomes not only impracticable but foolhardy. Old ways, devised to meet the problems of other worlds, must go by the board if they do not stand up to the test.

And yet the way in which the pioneer solves the problems of the frontier is necessarily colored by the point of view that he brings to them initially. He does not start completely from scratch in the wilderness; he brings with him a certain basic orientation that may be modified, but that is not wiped out. He would not have become a pioneer, as a matter of fact, had he not possessed a certain way of looking at the world and himself—a point of view without which he could not have survived long under pioneer conditions. If we are to understand the developing pattern of the Piedmont way of life, the ground against which we must view the play of human relationships in Piedmont industry, we must first concern ourselves with discovering the nature of what the people brought to the Piedmont—the characteristic attitudes, points of view, and ways of doing things that not only survived the rigours of the frontier, but that perhaps enabled their possessors to face up to those rigours and conquer them in the first place.

The Christian Ethic.—Except in the case of certain groups such as the Moravians and the Quakers, these people who came down the Great Valley into the Piedmont were no more assiduous in their practice of Christian ways than any of the rest of us. The Reverend Charles Woodmason, as a matter of fact, on the evidence of his visits to *The Carolina Backcountry on the Eve of the Revolution,* was inclined to believe that they were even less so.[12] They brought the Christian ethic into the wilderness with them, nevertheless, simply because they were the heirs of western civilization like the rest of us.

We are inclined to overlook the tremendous impact of Christianity upon the mind of western man. The Christian ethic in its essential core can be defined as the marriage of two great ideas—the Greek idea of the dignity of the individual human spirit and the Hebrew idea of the brotherhood of man. These ideas, transformed to the status of ideals, have formed the ethical basis of the Christian religion; and in the words of Alfred North Whitehead,

> They have constituted an unrivalled program for reform, which has been one element in the evolution of Western civilization. The progress of humanity can be defined as the process of transforming society so as to make the original Christian ideals increasingly practicable for its individual members. As society is now constituted a literal adherence to the moral precepts scattered through the Gospels would mean sudden death.[13]

Certainly no one would claim that anyone has at any time lived to the letter of even his particular version of the Christian ethic; nor have societies or nations in western civilization since the birth of Christ come even close to realizing them—but these ideals embodied in the ethic constitute an asymptotic rather than a modal norm. We may not observe them, but we are under a driving compulsion to explain and justify our departure from them. "So long as the Galilean images are

12. Edited by Richard J. Hooker and published by the University of North Carolina Press at Chapel Hill in 1953. See Parts One and Two, *passim.*

13. Alfred North Whitehead, *Adventures of Ideas* (New York: The Macmillan Company, 1933), p. 18.

but the dreams of an unrealized world, so long must they spread the infection of an uneasy spirit," Whitehead goes on to tell us.[14]

That they oriented their lives on the basis of an ethical code in turn based on the ideas of the brotherhood of man and the dignity of the human spirit did not differentiate the settlers of the Piedmont from the balance of the western world. What is significant is that it was an orientation that was reinforced by the conditions of pioneer life. The formal structure of pioneer worship may have been crude when it was not totally absent. Penitence in church on the Sabbath may have been reinforced by over-indulgence in raw liquor on Saturday night. Pioneer life was crude, raw, elemental; and it evoked behavior patterns that were equally earthy. Yet the lesson of man's responsibility to others and to himself, wrapped in hellfire and brimstone sermons delivered by itinerant preachers, was powerfully seconded for the pioneer by the conditions of his daily life.

As for brotherhood, it was never a particular man against the frontier—it was always man against the wilderness. In no other situation could the essential dependence of man upon his fellows have been quite so vividly brought home. The frontier could not be conquered except on the basis of co-operative effort. Though human contacts might be infrequent, when they occurred they were highly significant. The frontier is the birthplace of the voluntary co-operative association—from log rollings, house raisings, and husking bees to Regulators and Vigilantes.[15] And there is far more than mere dependence upon others involved. The fact that all face common danger and hardship, that the conditions of frontier life play no favorites, greatly facilitates the implicit process of role-taking upon which human associations are built. It was not only easy—it was virtually an impossibility to avoid putting one's self in the place of the other fellow. What happened to one happened, to a degree, to all. Whether Presbyterian Scot, Lutheran German, or Baptist English, "the frontier met each and all alike, with the same need and the same menace, and molded them after one general pattern. . . . The spirit of the frontier was modelling out of old clay a New Adam to meet the needs of a

14. *Ibid*, p. 21.
15. See Frederick Jackson Turner's *The Frontier in American History* (New York: Holt, 1921), p. 4. Also Vance, *op. cit.*, p. 69.

new earth."[16] The Piedmont was building socio-psychological homogeneity among its people even while its rugged terrain forbade any
considerable degree of intra-regional communication.

As for the dignity of the human spirit—in practical terms this
means nothing more than recognition of the importance of such attitudes as self-respect, self-reliance, self-confidence, and so on. If one
respects the dignity of the human spirit, one respects the rights of
others to maintain the attitudes necessary to that dignity, one fights to
maintain them for oneself. The vital importance of such self-concepts
on the frontier goes without saying. In the unknown wilderness, on
the frontier farm far separated from neighbors, anxiety for the future
can be allayed and faith put in one's predictions only on the basis of an
implicit belief in one's own ability to master the problems of the
future whatever they might be.

Thus the conditions of pioneer life, in the Piedmont as on all
frontiers, powerfully reinforced the essential elements of the Christian
ethic—which were the same no matter what creed might have enshrined
them. The brotherhood of man and his essential dignity as an individual were not theoretical points in philosophy or theology. Ob-
servance of them was a practical way of life.

The particular interpretation of the Christian ethic that provided
a basic orientation for the Piedmont settler is worthy of note. Whether
Presbyterian, Baptist, Methodist, or Lutheran, he had been reared in a
militant protestant faith that emphasized man's own responsibility for
his destiny, his obligation to do good works upon earth, the stewardship over God's bounty with which he was vested, and the essential
equality of all mankind in the sight of God. It was an orientation that
encouraged industry, frugality, and thrift. It did not discourage the
accumulation of wealth, but it suggested that such accumulations
ought to be usefully employed rather than merely hoarded or used to
surround oneself with luxury and comforts.

Idealism.—This may seem a strange quality to credit to the Piedmont pioneer or to any frontiersman. Yet idealism is implicitly
grounded in the way of western man in the mere process of his subscription to the Christian ethic—for he is committed to the "realization" of ideal norms of conduct in his daily life. Max Weber, in his

16. Constance Lindsey Skinner, *Pioneers of the Old Southwest* (New Haven: Yale
University Press, 1919), pp. 47-49.

work on comparative religions, has pointed out that a basic influence of Christianity upon Western man has been to move him to alter conditions when they would deny right patterns of conduct—whereas the Indian tendency is to withdraw from such situations and the Chinese is to adapt the code to the situation.

The pioneer, in his role as pioneer, must be an idealist in the basic sense of the word. He must be a man for whom the power of an idea can be so great that he will follow it into a situation where he is virtually certain of undergoing privation, danger, and hardship not only for himself but for his family. There were some few who plunged blindly into the wilderness, fleeing from conditions they could no longer contend with; but they were in a minority. The typical pioneer who abandoned the shelter of civilization may have left debts behind him, neighbors with whom he could not get along, a nagging mother-in-law, a society intolerant of his religious beliefs—but his was an advance into the wilderness, not a route from the settled company of his fellows. Certainly he was dissatisfied where he was, or he would not have left; but by the same token he saw the possibility of bettering his condition by leaving. Whatever he sought on the frontier, he was a man willing to face real and tangible dangers to realize an ideal.

To a high degree it was this ideal image of the world he was seeking that enabled the pioneer to face up to situations that might well have been expected to crush his spirit. He was what Mannheim would have defined as "utopian" in his thinking. ". . . the utopian mentality . . . guided by wishful representations and the will to action, hides certain aspects of reality. It turns its back on everything which would shake its belief or paralyze its desire to change things."[17] The pioneer saw the wilderness not as what it was, but as what it could become; and he refused to recognize those aspects of "reality" that would seem to label as impracticable the "realization" of his hopes and goals.

This strange combination of practicality and idealism, this drive of the pioneer to realize his visions, is perhaps best exemplified by the careers of some of the men who might be considered as demonstrating in their own lives a kind of distillation of the essential spirit of the Piedmont. Among its first settlers were Daniel Boone, John Sevier, and James Robertson. John C. Calhoun, Jefferson Davis, Stonewall

17. Karl Mannheim, *Ideology and Utopia,* translated by Louis Wirth and Edward Shils (New York: Harcourt, Brace and Company, 1949), p. 36.

Jackson, James K. Polk, Sam Houston, and Andrew Jackson were born in the Piedmont. The parents of Abraham Lincoln were born and reared there, and Thomas Jefferson had his home on the edge of the Blue Ridge. "These men," Turner remarks after listing their names, "represent the militant expansive movement in American life."[18]

Democracy.—It was not so much democracy as the seeds of democracy that the pioneer brought to the Piedmont. Turner has pointed out that democracy was a product of the frontier. "In the long run the effective force behind American democracy was the presence of the practically free land into which men might escape from oppression or inequalities which burdened them in the older settlements."[19] Yet it is difficult to see how free land can do more than facilitate a democratic way of life. Turner himself was aware that the pioneer settlers of the Piedmont brought with them certain well-defined ideas that must have played an important role in the usage to which they put the free land. Speaking of the Ulster Scots who were the most important ethnic group coming into the Piedmont, both in point of numbers and of influence on its developing institutions, he says, "They were brought up on the Old Testament, and in the doctrine of government by covenant and compact."[20] Constance Lindsay Skinner, recounting the history of the Ulster Scot, decides that on the basis of his actions both in Scotland and Ireland "the Scots of Ulster had already declared for democracy" before they set out for the New World.[21]

Perhaps as important as any positive set toward democracy that the pioneer might have brought to the frontier, however, was a negative attitude that he was likely to possess initially—a distrust of constituted authority. Either his own experiences or those of his fathers were likely to have been such as to convince him that it was not likely to be used to his advantage. On the frontier, this mistrust which in the beginning had been highly colored by resentment slowly changed into something else. The Piedmont farmer continued to distrust authority —but on the basis of a positive rather than a negative conviction. The conditions of his life were such as to demonstrate the practicality of relying upon his own efforts. He knew more about his affairs than did anyone else, he was in a better position to orient them toward the future than was anyone else.

18. Turner, *op. cit.,* p. 105.   19. *Ibid.,* p. 274.
20. *Ibid.,* p. 103.   21. Skinner, *op. cit.,* p. 3.

Yet his very distrust of authority, whether it be "constituted" or "expert," had the seemingly paradoxical effect of emphasizing the necessity of co-operative action and the wisdom of following demonstrated leadership ability wherever and in whomever it might be found. If one would not accept coercive direction of one's efforts in a situation where joint activity was a factor in survival, then one had to learn to work with others and to accept informal leadership in co-operative situations. This distrust which ripened into lack of awe extended into political situations. The settlers of the back country felt themselves under no particular allegiance to England nor to extensions of its authority in the new world. They thought of themselves not as Pennsylvanians or Virginians or Carolinians or Georgians. In a quite literal sense they thought of themselves as Americans.[22]

The facilitating aspect of the frontier, in this matter of democracy, was that its expansiveness gave the pioneer an opportunity to indulge himself in the desire to run his own affairs without having to deny the same right to some one else in order to do it. The chances were there for all. One man's success did not imperil that of another—actually, it enhanced it. When the chips were down, it was what a man could do that counted, not who he was or where he came from. Belief in the inherent superiority of family or class did not stand up to the demonstrated fact of the frontier, yet undreamed-of potentialities might be demonstrated by the most humble under the stress conditions of pioneer life. The result was, "An optimistic and buoyant belief in the worth of the plain people, a devout faith in man prevailed in the west. Democracy became almost the religion of the pioneer. He held with passionate devotion the idea that he was building a new society, based on self-government, and the welfare of the average man."[23]

Skills and Crafts.—There were few manufacturing artisans among the people who settled along the seacoast and populated the Coastal Plain. They were not attracted to the region, for it traded its agricultural surpluses to England for manufactured articles and never generated any real demand for a home industry. The region had the typical rural distrust of and contempt for manufacturing as a way of life.

The situation was quite different in the Piedmont. All the trades

22. See Robert Riegal, *America Moves West* (New York: Holt, 1930), p. 6.
23. Turner, *op. cit.*, p. 275.

and crafts were represented among the people who came down the Great Valley or across the Virginia Piedmont from the Middle Colonies. These craftsmen might take up land and farming to begin with, but as soon as they were able they turned to their higher skills—as indeed there was need for them to do. The Piedmont had neither agricultural surpluses nor the opportunity to trade them for manufactured goods. It had to be self-sustaining, which had the practical effect of helping to create opportunities for those people who could help it to achieve that state. The region was a magnet for the journeyman artisan who had visions of setting up his own workshop.

The presence in the region of so large a group that labored with its hands at occupations other than farming, and the obvious dependency of the region upon them, had an important effect upon regional thinking. The antipathy against industry and manufacturing that formed in the Coastal Plain never became typical of the Piedmont. An important part of its original and continuing population was made up of people who earned their place in society by creating "value added by manufacture" and who quite understandably saw nothing degrading in the process.

Those people who were not artisans were pioneer farmers. They were, in addition, farmers who had been trained in the practices of intensive rather than extractive agriculture, who viewed the wasteful methods of slave culture with professional scorn even when they did not object to it on moral grounds. Like all yeoman farmers, they had a smattering of numerous handicrafts in addition to agriculture; and thus their attitude toward the artisan was more likely to be the respect of the amateur for the professional than any measure of contempt.

Both artisans and yeoman farmers are notoriously independent and self-reliant people. Their command of tools and skills of fundamental importance and considerable versatility encourages them to believe that they can meet and master the future, no matter what its shape may be. Thus the practical cultural equipment of the people who came into the Piedmont had two significant effects. It made them self-confident, self-assured and independent; and it insured against development of a prejudice against manufacturing or against people who practiced it. Manufacturing was more than a part of the Piedmont heritage; it was a necessary part of its way of life from the very first.

THE PIEDMONT WAY OF LIFE

Out of the interaction of human needs, physiographic limitations
and possibilities, and cultural endowments and developments arose
the Piedmont way of life. We can consider the results of this interaction separately under the headings "economic," "political," and "social"
—bearing in mind that these are merely convenient analytical abstrac-
tions and that in actuality their development was mutually interde-
pendent.

The Economics of the Piedmont

The topography and soil conditions of the Piedmont were well
suited to the cultural background of the people who settled it. This
should hardly be regarded as coincidental—they were, after all searching for something; and we ought not be surprised that they stopped
when they found it. A region of small, family-owned farms with
numerous hamlets and villages in which a mill and forge industry
supplied neighborhood needs on a custom basis was not only logically
indicated but developed on a flourishing basis. Charles Eastman, in
picturing the development of the Piedmont in *The South in the
Building of the Nation,* tells us that

These settlers brought with them a large degree of knowledge and skill
in manufacturing. All along the Piedmont and even in the mountains from
Pennsylvania to Georgia, they not only followed agriculture, but developed
varied household manufactures in the period between 1750 and 1800. Here
also, the materials and water power for manufacturing were abundant, and
the health conditions were better. In 1800 many charcoal blast furnaces
making pig iron and many catlin forges and rolling mills making wrought
iron bars, and other products of iron, indicate that a manufacturing development throughout the Piedmont region of the South might have continued parallel with that which had taken place in Pennsylvania, except
for the circumstances of the combined influence of the cotton gin, the institution of slavery, and the checking of this immigration. As late as 1810
the manufactured products of Virginia, the Carolinas and Georgia exceeded
in variety and value those of the entire New England states.[24]

This balanced economy, almost a hundred years in the building,
was swept away when the hysteria of cotton culture burst into the

24. "The Mountain Whites as an Industrial Labor Factor in the South," in *The
South in the Building of the Nation,* J. A. C. Chandler, *et al,* eds. (13 vols., Richmond:
The Southern Historical Publishing Company, 1909), VI, p. 59. See also Harriet
Herring's "The Early Industrial Development of the South" in the *Annals of the
American Academy of Arts and Sciences,* CLIII (1931), p. 5.

middle Piedmont after 1840. Only scattered plantations penetrated so far inland; but the lure of the cash crop, cotton, turned the attention of its independent farmers from diversified agriculture to a one-crop economy. Even more serious, interest in manufacture was halted; the Piedmont as well as the Coastal Plain now began to barter an agricultural surplus for manufactured goods made abroad or in New England. What might eventually have happened had the Civil War not intervened, we do not know. What did happen was that its effect was disastrous to the Piedmont. With the highest proportion of able-bodied white males in the South, the region furnished a disproportionate share of the manpower for the Armies of the Confederacy.

These men left their farms in the hands of their women and children and the men too old to fight. Those who returned found their livestock commandeered or slaughtered, their fields overgrown with weeds, their seed stock gone, and in many cases their buildings burned —it was the southern Piedmont that caught the brunt of Sherman's raids. There was nothing left but the land; and twenty years of cotton culture had reduced that to the state that it could no longer raise a crop without the aid of artificial fertilizer. The region had some cash, in the hands of the middle class that had been developing in its many towns and villages since the Revolution, but the cash was sterile where it was. The economy was founded on an agricultural basis; and if it was to recover, the farmers had to be refinanced by the non-farmers who had the money.

The effort was attempted and it failed. Titles to debt-burdened farms passed over to creditors who faced financial ruin themselves. The price of cotton fell and continued to fall. In its desperate need for cash, the region planted cotton up to the doorsteps of its farmhouses, and kitchen gardens were sacrificed to the staple. But the eroded and worn-out soil was not up to the burden placed upon it. It became apparent at last that the salvation of the region did not lie along the lines of a one-crop agriculture, and the hope for political rescue suffered with the defeat of Hancock in 1880. The Piedmont did not *turn* to manufacturing after 1880; it *re*turned to it. From the perspective of the present, it appears that it was its experiment with a completely agricultural economy rather than its excursion into the manufacture of cotton textiles in 1880 that was a deviant.

Yet it was not a revival in the sense that the Piedmont picked up and returned to a pattern of behavior of an earlier day, discounting a lapse of some forty years or so. "There was," an interviewee told Broadus Mitchell, "in the South a quiet element of business and professional men who did not approve the course of the leaders of the section, and who, smothered under, so far as public attention was concerned, kept up activity and stood forth when a liberal industrial and commercial program became the order of the day."[25] The embers from which the flame of industrial expansion burst had been smoldering since an earlier day, "smothered under"—but the wind that fanned them into life, and the fuel upon which they fed, were new.

There had always been an undercurrent of industrialism in the Piedmont even in the days when the fever of cotton culture was at its height before the war. There had been cotton mills of considerable size built at Columbia, at Graniteville, at Augusta, at Columbus; and small mills were scattered throughout the back country. But there was an important difference between the ante-bellum industry of the Piedmont and the emphasis which came to be placed on it after 1880. The motivation for the earlier industry had been almost entirely economic and private in nature. The mills brought into being by the Cotton Mill Campaign of the 1880's were expected to make profits— very high profits, for that matter—and in the immediate instance their building was the work of private individuals: *but taken in its entirety, their building and their operation was caught up in the sweep of a tremendous social movement, classic in its proportions and development.* This topic will be treated in detail in the following chapters. For the moment we will content ourselves with noting that the industrial development of the region could not have taken place as it did without three enabling agencies:

1. The hydrographic resources of the region.

2. The capital resources of the middle class that had developed in its numerous small cities and villages—for the mills were not built by the North, but out of such resources as the region itself could scrape together. Northern money for mill building would not come south in important amounts until after 1923.

25. Broadus Mitchell, *Rise of the Cotton Mills in the South* (Baltimore: Johns Hopkins Press, 1921), p. 100.

3. The extension of railroads into the Piedmont—in this case, with the help of northern capital.

The renascence of industry in the Piedmont, which in recent years has become increasingly diversified and which has been accompanied by a return to the earlier pattern of diversified agriculture and owner-operation of farms, has been accompanied by a particular and highly significant variety of urbanization. In speaking of piedmont regions in general, Ellen Semple remarks that they "tend toward urban development even when rural settlement is sparse."[26] This categorical judgment has been well borne out in the Piedmont of interest to us. Of the eighteen cities of over 50,000 population in the four Piedmont states of North and South Carolina, Georgia, and Alabama, all except three (Charleston, Savannah, and Mobile) are located within or on the edge of the Piedmont Plateau. But the urban population of the region is not concentrated in fifteen large cities. In analyzing the pattern of its population growth, Vance notes that the Piedmont is "the region in which, to use Geddes' phrase, the rustic type has assumed its urban disguise. . . . There are no great cities if one excepts Atlanta, but the area is one of the country's few places where small towns are flourishing."[27]

The increasing industrialization of the Piedmont has not destroyed the small towns and cities that grew up about settlements that were at first a protection against marauding Indians or centered around a sawmill, gristmill, or foundry. Part of this has been due to the human factor, since the small towns themselves were often the moving spirit behind reviving the industry of the Piedmont and thus decentralized its location to begin with—but this decentralization would not have been possible had it not been for the hydro-electric development afforded by the topography of the region. It was the availability of an abundant supply of electrical power, the development of which actually outstripped the needs of the region and created a buyers' market, that made possible the later stages of the Cotton Mill Campaign along the lines it took and that facilitated a decentralized industry and the continued importance of the small town in the Piedmont. ". . . the trend of the South is toward the growth of small cities rather than a few gi-

26. *Influences of Geographic Environment* (New York: Holt, 1911), p. 327.
27. Vance, *op. cit.*, p. 26. See also his *All These People* (Chapel Hill: University of North Carolina Press, 1945), pp. 306-17.

gantic metropolises. . . . The region's urbanization has been delayed until the perfection of the technology of transmitting electric power which permits a regional development of industry."[28]

In explaining the decentralization of its industry we must give credit also to the railroads, financed largely with northern capital, that extended their main lines into the Piedmont from the north (the Southern bridged the gap from Charlotte to Atlanta soon after 1870) and sent out feeder lines between the region's rivers. The Southern Railroad particularly tied the Piedmont together with a network of steel, providing not only virtually express service to the New York market for countless Piedmont hamlets and villages as well as its cities, but an intra-regional system of communication and transportation as well that emphasized and augmented the socio-psychological homogeneity already present in the province.

Thus the economic way of life of the Piedmont was originally and is once more one of intra-regional balance between industry and agriculture. Though it is no longer self-sustaining in the sense that it once was, since its industry is tied into national markets and dependent upon them, it has retained or recaptured much of the essential style of life of the self-sustaining region—an industry of considerable total importance, but widely dispersed over the landscape in small operating units; numerous hamlets, small towns and small cities, but few metropolises; and a small-scale agriculture that is swinging back toward diversification and emphasis on regional markets. The pattern of economic development can be seen as springing logically out of the cultural traits of its people and the natural characteristics and resources of the region. The difficult task would have been to have explained how it could have developed in any other fashion, given the particular boundary conditions that maintained.

The Piedmont and Politics

As early as 1676, under Nathaniel Bacon, the primitive democracy of the Piedmont defied the aristocratic power of Governor Berkeley. In 1769 in South Carolina and in 1771 in North Carolina, under the banner of the Regulators, the region clashed again with the aristocracy of the Coastal Plain. Political convictions born and nurtured in the Piedmont "broke down the traditions of conservative rule, swept away

28. Vance, *Human Geography,* p. 506.

the privacies and privileges of officialdom, and . . . opened the temple of the nation to the populace."[29]

The struggle between the Piedmont and the Coastal Plain has never abated. It persists as a political schism to the present day in the Piedmont states. It is no longer a struggle between democratic and aristocratic ideas, but rather now one between the cautious and provincial conservatism of an almost completely agricultural area on the one hand and the needs of an industrial region for national and international perspectives on the other. The most liberal politically of the Piedmont states is North Carolina—which possesses the greatest ratio of Piedmont to Coastal Plain. The famous "county unit" system of voting in primary elections in Georgia, on the other hand, is a political technic by which the Coastal Plain, outnumbered in direct voting strength but superior in area, manages to retain some degree of political power over the more thickly populated Piedmont area of the state.

The economic development of the Piedmont along the line of small farms and decentralized industry has facilitated its continuance as a region of the "common man." An important factor in its political outlook can be traced to the relationship existing between the Piedmont farmer and the Piedmont industrial worker. They are not, as is so often the case, likely to be found on opposite sides of the fence politically merely by virtue of their differing roles. Often they are the same person. When they are not their common origin is so recent as to be determinative. The industrial worker has a rural background; the farmer is in close contact with relatives in the factory.

The Social Structure of the Piedmont

If we have, in the preceding discussion, appeared to place undue emphasis upon the frontier phase of the development of the Piedmont, it has been for a reason. The frontier, Odum tells us, is "definitive of the southern heritage and prophetic of the days to come."[30]

The Frontier Heritage of the Piedmont.—Professor Odum goes on to say, "The South was nurtured in the frontier world perhaps no more

29. Turner, *op. cit.,* p. 268.

30. Howard Odum, *The Way of the South* (New York: The Macmillan Company, 1947), p. 19. The writer owes much of his understanding of the southern scene to this work. Crystallizing in its pages conclusions based on long years of patient and illuminating research, it goes beyond data and objective fact to become a kind of voice of the South. It is not the objective marshalling of data of *Southern Regions;* it is rather the socio-psycho-analysis that makes the data meaningful.

than the West of America; but, more than the rest of the nation, it
retains in its fabric of folk culture threads of the frontier struggle and
reflects the costs that went into the building of a frontier society."[31]
He voices a further judgment that is particularly pertinent to our
later discussion: "For the frontier has been powerful not only in its
earlier character-forming influence upon the region, but in the conflict between frontier folkways and the technological, psychological
foundations of modern society. . . ."[32]

But why this persistence of the frontier heritage in the South?
There is first of all the time element. We tend to think of the South
as old. Actually much of it, particularly the Piedmont region with
which we are concerned, is comparatively new in terms of settlement.
We must remember that the Creeks and the Cherokees barred the advance to the Gulf Coastal Plain along the line of the Ocmulgee and
Altamaha in Georgia until after 1820 and that the Cherokees were
not removed from north Georgia until after 1838, seven years after the
Sacs and Foxes had been driven out of southern Wisconsin during the
Black Hawk War. Atlanta was not founded until 1836, and it was not
incorporated until 1847—the same year that Salt Lake City was founded, and only two years before gold would be discovered in California.
Turner tells us that "Georgia belonged at least as much to the West
as to the South. From colonial times the Georgia settlers had been
engaged in an almost incessant struggle against the savages on her
border, and had the instincts of a frontier society."[33] And even with
regard to that section of the Piedmont that was settled earlier, Cash
remarks, "Men who, as children, had heard the war-whoop of the
Cherokee in the Carolina backwoods lived to hear the guns at Vicks-
burg."[34]

But more than the time element explains the persistence of pioneer
traits in the Piedmont. A way of life emerged in the region that was
well calculated to preserve many of the most definitive of pioneer
characteristics. ". . . the frontier did not recede so quickly in the
South," Vance tells us.

31. *Ibid.*, p. 21.
32. *Ibid.*, p. 31.
33. Frederick Jackson Turner, *Rise of the New West* (New York: Harper and
Brothers, 1906), p. 57.
34. W. J. Cash, *Mind of the South* (New York: Alfred A. Knopf, 1941), pp. 10-11.

When it did recede it gave way to a rural society which contains many elements in common with the frontier. . . . The South still possesses the largest number of practically self-sufficing farms to be found in any comparable area in the nation. Its rural life is characterized by isolated farmsteads in the open country. If southern conditions of living have often appeared crude to the critics, it is for the reason that they have retained not only the usages but often the conditions of the frontier. More than any other section except perhaps the sparsely settled western range, it has remained a pioneer belt, and the common man living in the open country faces much the same situation with the cultural heritage left by the frontier. While they were formative, the folkways of the South got the stamp of the frontier. From the frontier, part of the area passed to the plantation, but the plantation area retained many of the frontier traits. Institutions and customs are still tinged with the shades of the forest, whether as survivals or as adjustments to ruralism.[35]

Vance is speaking here of the entire Southeast; but if "the plantation area retained many of the frontier traits," then what he has to say is emphatically true of the Piedmont which was never a plantation area of any consequence.

There is also the fact that no new strains of thought that might have diluted the pioneer-based culture of the region have been carried into it by immigrants for over a century. Immigration into the Piedmont, except for the movement of tidewater people across the fall line as the plantations rolled on into its lower reaches, virtually ceased after 1820.[36] Henceforth there would be only population movements within the region itself, like that which settled the north Georgian Piedmont after the removal of the Indian tribes and a continuing trickle of excess population from the Great Appalachian Valley across the Blue Ridge—a kindred region and even more pioneer in its life conditions than the Piedmont.

For all the way from six to ten generations, then, the people of the Piedmont have been living and working together under conditions that when they have not actually been frontier in nature have been strongly influenced by the frontier—with no alien strains coming into the region to break the developing "cake of custom." Whatever deviations there have been from the pioneer ideals have been functions

35. Vance, *Human Geography*, p. 76. See also Turner's *Rise of the New West*, pp. 56-57, and Cash, *loc. cit.*

36. Harold Underwood Faulkner, *American Political and Social History* (5th ed., New York: Appleton-Century-Crofts, 1948), p. 301.

of the region itself. They cannot be laid to the intrusion of outside ideas, except as the region has seen merit in them and adopted them of its own accord, or adapted to inter-regional conditions Yet these very adoptions and adaptations must necessarily have been colored by the past history of the region, as it has arisen out of the interaction between the basic needs of its people, its own natural features, and the cultural patterns of its settlers. The result has been vividly stated by Odum:

When we come to apply this measure [of the general influence of the frontier upon American culture] to the southern regions, it must be very clear that the task is almost synonymous with the cataloging of many of the main traits of southern culture. For here was a regional culture which featured strong individualism, great religious influences, strong sense of honor and personality, strong allegiance to the family and morals, quick tempers and emotional reactions, impatience with organization and formal law and control, love of freedom and the open spaces, and not too much emphasis upon finished standards of art, education, work. There were the frontier patterns of all earlier America as reflected in the homogeneity of native white, northern European stocks, Protestant church-going, Sabbath observing, patriarchal folk, abounding in the spirit of honor, fighting politics, liquor drinking and little love of the law.[37]

Elsewhere Professor Odum has defined the American ideals fixed by the frontier as "work, individual love of freedom, religious faith, the fighting spirit, the philosophy of neighborliness and mutual help."[38] *These are ideals that must be taken into account not only in the Piedmont but throughout our nation if one is to understand the behavior patterns of its industrial workers.* The frontier ideals are the heritage of all Americans, just as the frontier has figured in the history of all our nation. It is not with regard to what he seeks but rather in the manner of his seeking that we are likely to find interesting variations in the case of the Piedmont textile worker—for *it is only in the Piedmont that we find the attempt on a major scale to realize the pioneer ideals in an industrial society that has remained oriented along the lines of the culture that developed them.*

Typology of the Piedmont Society.—The term "pioneer," like the term "industrial," is descriptive rather than analytical. Neither are suitable for classifying a society as to its basic typology, for they divert

37. Odum, *The Way of the South*, pp. 29-30.
38. *Ibid.*, p. 21.

one's attention from the truly definitive characteristic of any society—
the nature of the interpersonal relationships maintained within it and
by means of it. Once more we can turn to Odum's sensitive and in-
sightful portrayal of *The Way of the South* for a clue as to the fundamental nature of the Piedmont society:

> . . . the way of the South has been and is the way of the folk, symbolic
> of what the people feel, think and do as they are conditioned by their
> cultural heritage and the land which Nature has given them. . . . This is
> an elemental reality definitive of most of the South's culture and economy.
> The folk society of the South is well-nigh inclusive and is reflected on many
> levels of time and class and in the organic nature of the folk-regional
> society as definitive of how all societies are formed and grow up.[39]

The term "folk society" is descriptive also, of course, but in so
fundamental a manner that its analytical connotations are dominant.
In explaining the basic nature of a folk society to his students, Professor Louis Wirth used to ask them to consider what they meant when
they used the term "the folks" in everyday speech. "You mean the
people you know well," he told them. "Your relatives, your intimate
friends. A folk society is made up of 'the folks' in just that sense. It
is a society based on the intimacies of ordinary, everyday life."

The term "urban" is often used to describe the antithesis of a folk
society. The usage is unfortunate, however, for it encourages us to
think of the physical context of the society rather than of the people
who make it up or of the nature of the relationships by which they
order their lives together. In addition, we run into confusing con-
tractions when we employ it, for an urban context does not always contain an "urban" society in the sense that it is diametrically opposed to
a folk society. Nor is the term "urban" semantically antithetical to
the term "folk."

If a folk society is intimate and personal, then its opposite number
must be detached and impersonal—and what kind of society is described by these terms? One which is used to achieve order, regulation, and unified action among the individuals who constitute a mass
—a mass meeting or a mass audience for example—any grouping of
individuals, whether in physical proximity to one another or not, who
are acting with regard to common objects of attention but who remain
anonymous, detached, and alienated from one another in the process of

39. *Ibid.,* p. 61.

their concerted or often merely simultaneous action. We will use the term "mass society" to describe that orienting device for interpersonal relationships that is antithetical to the folk society.[40]

The most fundamental distinction that can be made between the two is in terms of the manner by which each enables the individual to integrate himself with the group whose collective activities are of importance to him. On this basis the following significant distinction appears: *The folk society is based upon the possibility of achieving social order, social integration and joint social action through sympathetic identification, basing predictions as to the probable actions of others upon information gained by looking at situations "through their eyes";* whereas, *the mass society is based upon the necessity of achieving social order, social integration and joint social action by predicting that others will conform to established and objectively defined roles or abide by objective and deliberately derived rules or regulations, under conditions such that sympathetic identification and thus reliable social prediction based upon it is not possible.*

The distinction can perhaps be more simply made.[41] The individual in the folk society orients his participation in joint activity on the basis of his knowledge of the participants while in the mass society he orients it on the basis of his knowledge of some over-riding system. There is admittedly a "system" in either case, as those familiar with the folk society will be first to point out—but even the role of the sys-

40. See Herbert Blumer's "The Mass, the Public, and Public Opinion," in *New Outline of the Principles of Sociology,* Alfred M. Lee, ed. (New York: Barnes and Noble, 1946), p. 186.

41. The existence of this fundamental dichotomy has been noted in one form or another that can be subsumed under the distinction we make by practically all sociologists who have given serious thought to the structuring of social action. To name only a few, and to cite but a single example for each: Odum in his *Way of the South,* p. 85; Robert Redfield in "The Folk Society," *The American Journal of Sociology,* Vol. LII; Robert Park, "Culture and Civilization" in *Race and Culture,* E. C. Hughes, *et al.,* eds. (Glencoe: The Free Press, 1950), p. 29; William Graham Sumner in his *Folkways* (Boston: Ginn and Company, 1911), p. 56; Charles Horton Cooley in *Social Organization* (New York: Charles Scribner's Sons, 1920), pp. 23-31 and 135-48; R. M. McIver in *Community* (New York: The Macmillan Company, 1928), pp. 23-47.

Ferdinand Tonnies' famous work *Gemeinschaft und Gesellschaft* (1st ed., 1887), translated and edited by Charles P. Loomis as *Fundamental Concepts of Sociology* (New York: American Book Company, 1940) makes the distinction its basic premise. The distinction is implicit in Sir Henry Maine's differentiation between *status* and *contract* in his *Ancient Law* (London: J. Murray, 1861), as it is in Durkheim's analysis of *The Division of Labor in Society,* translated by George P. Simpson (Glencoe: The Free Press). Herbert Blumer developed the distinction into a graduate course at the University of Chicago, calling it "Folkways and Fashions."

tem is definitive of the one type or the other. In the folk society it is internalized and implicitly held; the participant may be aware of its lack but seldom of its presence. In the mass society it remains external and is explicitly held; the participant is aware of its presence as well as its absence.

The folk society is familial in nature. Essentially the same technics are used to order the overall society as are used to maintain social relationships in its intimate groups based on kinship and friendship. Its most important goal is maintenance of the human way of life. Its technics are socio-psychological in nature, and its end product is *culture*—which has been quite correctly described as a "design for living." The mass society is built around and extends outward from the market place. An entirely different set of technics from those used in its primary groups must be used to order its overall relationships. Its most important goal is man's survival and the maximization of his satisfactions as an intelligent animal. Its technics are politico-economic in nature, and its end product is *civilization*—which consists of the impedimenta that embellish and enrich a culture but do not constitute it. We are speaking of a "civilized" but not "cultured" person when we say, "He has everything in the world, but he doesn't know what to do with it!"[42]

The possibility of extending the social technics of primary groups beyond the boundaries of their intimate, face-to-face relationships is dependent upon the possibility of making accurate predictions about the attitudes, feelings, intentions, and probable responses of people whom we do not know with some degree of intimacy. But if others tend to think along the same lines that we do, to look at the world from essentially our point of view, to respond to its problems in much the same fashion as we, we can predict rather accurately as to how they will think, feel, and respond in particular situations even though we have never met before.

42. For an excellent short discussion of the basic typology of the folk society, see Redfield's paper, cited above. For penetrating discussions of the essential contrasts between folk and mass societies, see Howard Becker's "Sacred and Secular Societies" in *Social Forces*, XXIII (1950); Park's paper on "Culture and Civilization" in *Race and Culture;* Edward Sapir's paper on "Culture, Genuine and Spurious" in the *American Journal of Sociology*, XXIX (1924); and Louis Wirth's paper on "Consensus and Mass Communication" in the *American Sociological Review*, XIII (1948). See also Wirth's "Ideological Aspects of Social Disorganization," *American Sociological Review*, V (1940); and his "Urbanism as a Way of Life" in the *American Journal of Sociology*, XLIV (1938).

Thus folk relationships are not necessarily based upon the possibility of face-to-face contacts in the society. One assumes that the other has much in common with oneself and goes ahead on that basis—but only after identifying him as "one of the folk—one of *us*." The size of the society that can be effectively oriented with folk technics, in other words, is dependent upon the degree of homogenity within the society, where homogeneity is defined as primarily a matter of similarity in ways of thinking, feeling, and responding, rather than primarily a matter of origin, background, and custom. These latter help to achieve homogeneity, but they do not by any means guarantee it.

Thus also our identification of the folk society as essentially familial in nature does not preclude our identifying the Piedmont or the entire Southeast as a folk-regional society, and it does not prevent our describing a city the size of Atlanta or Milwaukee as essentially folk rather than mass in its underlying social organization.[43] On the other hand, though we ordinarily think of the mass society as large, a very small group may be basically mass in its relationships if there is no homogeneity as between its members. The essential determinant as to type is neither size nor density of population; it is the nature of the relationships themselves that effect the basic organization of the group in question. A rural society is likely to be of the folk, while an urban society is likely to be of the mass; but there is no necessary correspondence. The reverse may be true without constituting a paradox.

No society is completely a folk or a mass society.[44] There are elements of the massways in the simplest and most primitive of folk societies—particularly as they may be displayed by certain formalized and stylized patterns of behavior that survive after the conditions that originally produced them as a matter of necessity have disappeared—blind adherence to tradition and custom is characteristic of the mass rather than of the folk. The folk society may, and in nearly all cases does, adopt certain technics of the massways—formal government at any level supported by taxation, for example; and the ubiquitous traffic signal is a device of the mass society wherever it appears. On the other hand, folk relationships are characteristic of the primary groups within and may develop in other aspects of a mass society. The mass

43. See Odum's "Folk Sociology as Subject Field for Historical Study," *Social Forces, XXXI* (1953).

44. See Robert Redfield's "The Natural History of the Folk Society," *Social Forces, XXXI* (1953).

society of a nation may encompass numerous folk-regional societies. That individual is rare whose life is not ordered to some degree by folkways and massways alike. The mass controls of federal legislation, for example, extend into the most isolated of rural communities nowadays. The Piedmont textile company that is an integral part of the folk society of its community is also an integral part of the mass society of the national textile market.

Yet with regard to any aggregation of individuals or primary groups living in contiguous and reasonably permanent physical association, one or the other system will predominate in the necessary task of bringing about order and establishing the basic pattern for collective action; and one or the other will give the resulting society its tone— which will be pretty much a derivative of the tendencies of its members with regard to carrying on social relationships with people who are not included within their circles of intimacy.

It is possible for a society of either type to transform itself or to be transformed into the other. The folk society becomes a mass and must be brought under mass relationships whenever, for any reason, the socio-psychological elements of its homogeneity are broken down. It is possible, on the other hand, eventually to establish sufficient rapport among the individuals in a mass society to transform them into a folk society. The Piedmont has not always had a folk society. It was not a society of any kind at first but merely an aggregation of individuals and primary groups—and the Regulators of South Carolina, for example, saw the need for the mass agencies of constituted law and order to be brought into the back country to hold it steady, as it were, until the folkways could develop.[45] The very instruments of "mass communication" that are developed in an efficient mass society are potentially capable of developing sufficient rapport among its originally detached and alienated individual members to knit them into a common folk. We note this occurring even on a national scale during times of stress or danger, as for example during a war.

Folk relationships may degenerate until only their empty forms remain, devoid of the content of sympathetic identification and understanding upon which they must be based. In cases of this sort there may for a while be no effective social organization of any kind, either folk or mass; there may be only an aggregation of individuals re-

45. See Woodmason, *op. cit.*, Part Three.

maining, with every man for himself. The intricate patterns of control that administer and integrate a mass society may break down, leaving an aggregation of detached individuals and primary groups without any effective total organizational pattern.

Folk relationships are essentially the same the world over, since they are functions of basic human nature. Mass relationships present a bewildering variety, since they are, to a much greater degree, functions of particular environments and their special problems. Folk relationships are natural, while mass relationships are synthetic. When they are given an opportunity, groups and societies will replace mass relationships with those of the folk. The increasing complexity of the total pattern of human interdependency, however, has brought about increasing emphasis upon the overtly coercive power of the massways to achieve social control in our modern world.

A Folk-Mass Check List.—So far we have dealt in generalities. It may be useful toward later understanding if we can be somewhat more specific in outlining the essential differences between the folkways and the massways. Students of social phenomena for many years and in many countries have noted the fundamental differences existing between the two types of social organization we have been discussing and have called attention to particular differences between them that appear to be fundamental.[46] We can arrange the results of their observations in a kind of check list that will identify a model folk society on the one hand and a model mass society on the other. (It should be kept in mind that no real society will exhibit completely folk or completely mass characteristics from any point of view and that as we shift our point of view we will change the overall pattern of the rating. With regard to a particular distinction from a particular

46. No attempt is made toward an item-by-item documentation of the folkmass checklist presented in this chapter. It begins with the famous distinction made by Tonnies between a society based on "fateful" relationships (*Wesenwillen*) and one based on "willful" relationships made by deliberate choice (*Kurwillen*). For the balance of them, so far as the writer's orientation as well as his sources are concerned, major credit must be given to the sociologists Robert Park and Louis Wirth, and the anthropologists Howard Becker, Robert Redfield, and Edward Sapir. They can be validated by the reader himelf, however. He need only recall that the folkways are essentially familial and that formal government is perhaps the most common example of the massways, and then he should contrast his relationships within his family with, for example, those he has with the Bureau of Internal Revenue. Given the general orientation presented in this chapter, the reader who has lived for any length of time both in a small town and in a great city should not only find the distinctions familiar, he should be able to supplement them with additional sets of his own.

point of view, perhaps the most we can ordinarily say is that it is more one way than another. No high degree of objectivity is claimed for the check list, and it certainly does not lend itself to quantitative measurement.)

Fateful-Willful: The relationships of the folk society are typically determined by fate, whereas we think of the relationships of the mass society as involving a certain degree of choice. We cannot cease to be Irish, for example—but we can disavow our allegiance to the Irish Free State if we wish.

Homogeneous-Heterogeneous: The folk relationships are typically between people who share certain enduring situations together and thus are likely to develop a common point of view, whereas mass relationships are thought of as arising out of a relatively transient mutuality of interest which does not necessarily lead to mutuality of points of view.

Understanding-Conforming: The folk relationships are based upon subjective understanding, whereas the mass relationships are based upon objective conformity.

Personal-Anonymous: The contacts of the folk society are between whole people, person to person, whereas those of the mass society are between agents of institutions—the "shopper" meets the "clerk," "employer" deals with "employee."

Intimate-Reserved: The contacts of the folk society are intimate and revealing of basic traits of personality, whereas people wear the masks of "customary behavior" in mass contacts and conceal personality.

Closed-Open: The folk society integrates the stranger slowly since it must know him as a person. The mass society integrates the stranger as quickly as he can become acquainted with its objectively prescribed pattern of conduct.

Enduring-Transient: The relationships of the folk society are enduring, existing apart from and over-riding the situations that call for joint action; those of the mass society are transient. They are called into existence by the needs of particular occasions and do not survive them.

Oral-Written: The routine relationships of the folk society are based upon the body of orally transmitted tradition, custom, and mores that are known as the folkways. The routine relationships of the mass society are based upon the formally developed and written regulations, rules, ordinances, directives, and laws we will call the massways.

Sentimental-Rational: The folkways are based on sentiments and feelings; they need not be logically justified. The massways are based on "objective fact" and must answer to logical justification.

Spontaneous-Calculated: The folk relationships are spontaneous, arising out of the nature of a situation itself. Mass relationships are calculated, planned in advance. They are never improvised.

Intuitive-Empirical: The folkways are based upon and concern themselves as much with attitudes as with acts—the intimacy of the relationship makes it often possible to identify the attitude before it has resulted in action. The massways are in general based upon and concern themselves with matters of demonstrated or demonstrable fact—there is not sufficient intimacy in the relationship to facilitate looking beyond the act to the attitude.

Categorical-Contingent: The folkways are all-embracing; there is nothing that they do not cover. If a situation cannot be brought under the folkways, they will be modified to cover the situation. Massways are contingent. They operate only in those situations that meet strictly and previously defined conditions.

Unspecified-Specified: Obligations are unspecified and may be un-limited under the folkways—they depend upon circumstances. Who can list the nature of the obligations one owes to a friend? Obligations under the massways are specified and limited—one does what has been formally determined in advance as one's obligation, and that is all. The mass society interprets the law to the letter, the folk society seeks its spirit.

Adaptive-Rigid: The folkways are dynamic and adaptive. They change with the changing times, imperceptibly and without attracting attention, since they have never been formally derived or committed to writing. They become frozen only when the conditions of the society itself become static. The massways are formally derived, they must be as formally changed. They must be amended, repealed, and rescinded —and all this to the accompaniment of debate which attracts attention. While they are in force they must be adhered to even though they may no longer be pertinent to the situation as it has developed.

Asymptotic-Modal: The changing patterns of the folkways attempt to realize in a changing world certain asymptotic norms—ethical standards, value systems, ideas of right and wrong—that remain stable and that are never completely attained. The massways attempt to realize normative standards that are modal in nature, built up in the form of precedents and bodies of jurisprudence. Their norms are "practical" and "realistic," and deviations from them are expected in both directions. The massways tend to idealize the mass society's concept of reality.

Consensus-Contract: The folk relationships are regulated by consensus, by the actor's estimation of "what people will think." The deviant is controlled by opinion, a sense of honor, fear of ridicule. Judgements are felt rather than objectively realized. The mass relationships are regulated by contract, enforceable by formally appointed agencies. One does not rely upon another's honor or shame him if he deviates; one gets a contract that can be taken into court.

Restrictive-Restitutive: Since they deal with attitudes as much as with acts, the folkways attempt to prevent deviation by correcting the attitude that would result in it. Since they concern themselves mainly with acts, the massways must content themselves more generally with obtaining restitution after the deviation has taken place. Corrective measures can be taken only after the necessity for them has been revealed by overtly deviant action.

Ends-Means: The relationships of the folk society can be ends in themselves, rich in response and responding. The relationships of the mass society are means to an end. They are purposive, seeking something through the relationship rather than regarding it as satisfying in itself.

Other distinctions between the folk and the mass society come to mind. The folk society is, in general, poorly set up to serve the detached individual, whereas the mass society makes elaborate provisions for him with mass entertainment and mass communication. A town that is organized after the way of the folk is likely to be regarded by the service man as a poor "liberty" town; there is little for the casual visitor to do. The folk society is very curious about the stranger while at the same time it maintains an attitude of reserve toward him; it can eventually fit him into the fabric of social life only in terms of its knowledge of him as an individual. The mass society, on the other hand, is deliberately not curious, though it may maintain an easy, surface familiarity.

The Folk Society and the Individual.—What is perhaps most important to the individual, the folk society develops, sustains, and reinforces one's image of one's self through its intimate contacts, thus carrying on the function of the primary group in this respect. The innumerable human contacts of the folk society are conducive to the development of personality. In the mass society, particularly when one possesses no compensating memberships in primary groups, one's image of one's self shrinks. Paradoxically, it is in the folk society that the quality of so-called "individualism" flourishes, rather than in the mass society where the individual is apparently free from subjective control—where no one is concerned with what an individual thinks or feels so long as he follows the rules. It is the small town, rather than the great city, that produces "characters" and not only tolerates but prizes them. In the folk society, the technics of getting along with others have been so thoroughly internalized that one can devote one's conscious attention entirely to the substance of the on-going relationship. In a social situation under the massways, one must devote one's conscious attention to the mechanics of fitting in one's actions with those of others. "Self-consciousness"—and thus correspondingly less consciousness of others—and "manners" mark relationships in the mass society. Park has noted this:

> In the little world where people come close together, human nature develops. . . . The definite personalities that we know grow up in intimate groups. In the larger society we get etiquette, urbanity, sophistication, finish. . . . We don't ever get to really know the urbane person and hence never know when to trust him. It is more or less fundamental traits of personality which arise in the intimate group which enable us to act with definiteness toward others. Manners are of secondary importance.[47]

The feeling of freedom in interpersonal relationships that one has under the folkways is the freedom of knowing intuitively what the limits of action are, of being able to "act with definiteness and assurance toward others." It is the freedom of the concert pianist who has so thoroughly internalized the technical possibilities and limitations of his instrument that he seems somehow to rise above them and free himself from them. There are powerful constraints under the folkways, as anyone who has attempted to defy convention in the small town has

47. Park, *op. cit.*, p. 22.

discovered. But they lie lightly, bonds of silk, that go unnoticed unless one struggles against them—and then they cut deep and cruelly.

The nature of these restraints defy analysis in any formal fashion. One cannot sit down and write out a list of them. They are implicit and intuitive; and though everyone may be in agreement that a certain situation ought to be handled in a certain way, yet no one could have outlined the way before the occasion. In noting this, Sapir remarks, "The mores of a people are its *unformulated* ethics as seen in action."[48] (The italics are the writer's.)

We are reminded once again of Whitehead's description of the Christian ethic that lies behind the mores of the western world—which Odum defines as its "matured folkways ripened through folk wisdom into morals and morality."[49]

It is a hidden driving force, haunting humanity, and ever appearing in specialized guise as compulsory on action by reason of its appeal to the uneasy conscience of the age. The force of its appeal lies in the fact that the specialized principle of immediate conduct exemplifies the grandeur of the wider truth arising from the very nature of the order of things, a truth which mankind has grown to the stature of being able to feel though perhaps as yet unable to frame in fortunate expression.[50]

Though the Christian ethic, as a "hidden driving force," cannot be postulated as the ultimate source of the mores for those great hosts of people who have not come under its influence, yet it is possible that the two great ideas upon which it is founded may be a universal source for the mores. We have seen that the human way under any and all circumstances is dependent upon maintaining a balance between the essential brotherhood of men and the essential dignity of their persons. The mores and the folkways, in the final analysis, can be seen as nothing more than patterns for action that have demonstrated their usefulness in enabling *homo sapiens* to maintain a human way of life—to remain in communion with his fellows without losing his identity and his individuality. The folkways manifest—but they do not state—the implicit principles that differentiate the human way of life from all others.

48. Sapir, *op. cit.,* p. 366.
49. Odum, "Folk Sociology as Subject Field for Historical Study," *Social Forces,* XXXI (1953), p. 201.
50. Whitehead, *op. cit.,* p. 19.

CHAPTER III

Origin and Development of the Piedmont Cotton Textile Industry

THERE ARE TWO SCHOOLS of thought as to the date that should be assigned to the origin of the modern cotton textile industry in the Southeast. One points to the obvious fact that the manufacture of cotton textiles on an industrial basis started almost as early in the Southeast as in the New England states and would put the origin of the modern industry no later than 1815. The other, admitting the presence of cotton mills in the ante-bellum South, stresses the fact that they were relatively unimportant in its pre-war economic structure and concludes that they represented a deviant rather than a normative phenomena for the region before 1860. They contend also that the wave of mill building that began in the early 1880's was much more than the fanning into flames of embers that had been smoldering for half a century. The ante-bellum industry, they point out, like the New England industry, was the result of private venture for profit; while the Cotton Mill Campaign that ushered in the post-war phase of the development represented the collaborative effort of the whole Piedmont region.

There is no fundamental quarrel between the two points of view. The Cotton Mill Campaign could not have succeeded as well as it did had it not been for the industrial acumen developed in the region before the Civil War. We have already voiced our opinion that it was its preoccupation with a predominantly agricultural way of life, between 1830 and 1860, that represented a deviant pattern of economy for the Piedmont. On the other hand, the establishment of the modern industry could never have been achieved in the manner in which it was had not the full weight of the regional society been behind it—as was surely not the case for the ante-bellum mills. If there were the smoldering embers of a pre-war industry (and the raiding Union Armies under Sherman made this a particularly apt figure of speech), it was a post-war society that seized upon them to rekindle the spirit of the Piedmont.

THE ANTE-BELLUM MILLS[1]

It would appear that there was a tendency toward a balanced economy in the Piedmont that was never quite overcome by the reign of King Cotton. We recall that the pioneers who came into the Piedmont had brought skills and crafts with them and had put them to such good usage that "as late as 1810 the manufactured products of Virginia, the Carolinas and Georgia exceeded in variety and value those of the entire New England States." This was the output of a household economy, however.

The original impetus to what can really be thought of as a factory economy in textiles in the South seems to have been the Napoleonic Wars, which resulted in serious disruption of our foreign trade and finally in the War of 1812. Discontinued trade with England indicated the desirability of a domestic industry that would consume our raw materials despite the nature of the international situation. The initial spurt of mill building occurring in the Southeast between 1813 and 1820 was soon over, however. After the latter date the importance of cotton culture overshadowed its manufacture. It seemed to the bulk of the people in the Piedmont as well as in the Coastal Plain that the practical thing to do was to trade the raw staple for manufactured goods from England and New England.

The textile industry was to play only a minor role in the southeastern economy during the balance of the ante-bellum years—but it remained a latent force until 1853 when the shadow of the coming war took precedence over everything else in the minds of southern people. Despite the general lack of interest in the Piedmont as well as the Plain, men such as William Gregg, J. H. Hammond, and R. W. Roper urged that if the South was to prosper, it must process the staple that it raised. *De Bow's Review,* which was to preach the gospel of cotton manufacturing with missionary zeal, was founded in 1848. As

---

1. This account of the ante-bellum mills is drawn from Harriet Herring, "The Early Industrial Development of the South," *Annuals of the American Academy of Arts and Sciences,* CLIII (1931), Chapter Two. See also Victor S. Clark's "Manufacturing During the Ante-bellum and War Periods" in *The South in the Building of the Nation,* VI, pp. 250 ff.

Harriet Herring remarks in speaking of the efforts of these early apostles of industry, "There has hardly been a major argument or device set forth since that was not presented in those years."[2] Anything that tended to shake the confidence of the Piedmont in its future with the raw staple, such as the blockades and embargoes of the War of 1812, the fall of cotton prices in the 1820's, the Panic of 1837, and the depressed cotton market of the 1840's provided an opportunity that was seized upon by the protagonists of the industry to enlist capital support for cotton manufacturing.

Their efforts were not completely without results. By 1860 North Carolina, according to the United States Census for that year, had 39 mills averaging 1074 spindles each. South Carolina had 17 with an average spindleage of 1817, and Georgia had 33 averaging 2561 spindles; Alabama was already under way with 14 mills with an average spindleage of 2553. Together, these four Piedmont states that were to be the principal location of the modern southern industry had 193,700 out of the total of 324,000 southern spindles in 1860. (The balance of 131,300 southern spindles represented a purely local industry in such states as Tennessee, Kentucky, and Mississippi that would not play an important role in future commercial developments.)[3]

For the most part these mills were small, located in the back country and supported by local custom; but even as early as 1850 there were Piedmont mills that depended on the national market—Vaucluse, Saluda, Graniteville, for example, and the mills at Augusta and Columbus. These larger establishments were all located on the fall line, where the changing character of the rivers as they crossed the steepened descent from the Piedmont to the Coastal Plain afforded ample power at the mill site and safe and dependable transportation to seacoast shipping ports.

These initial ventures into the national market were not without their attendant problems. As Miss Herring points out, they were hampered by lack of marketing experience, by insufficient working capital, and by the concentration of capital generally in the North—all of which resulted in their falling too much under the control of com-

2. Herring, "The Early Industrial Development of the South," *Annals*, p. 5.
3. Unless otherwise credited, statistical data throughout the study concerning cotton textile manufacture is based on information furnished by the Bureau of the Census, either through its own publications or as abstracted from them by the *Statistical Abstract of the United States*.

mission houses even at this early date. In addition, their lack of ex-perience with manufacturing and business enterprise and their limited technical skill were weaknesses that resulted in the failure of some of the most prominent ventures, which had the effect of discouraging in-vestment in textile manufacture generally.

The Piedmont's ante-bellum establishment of 193,700 spindles repre-sented only 3.7 per cent of the total national spindleage in 1860; and the output of all the 324,000 spindles in the cotton-growing states in 1860 amounted only to $12,600,000 in value as compared with a cotton crop for that year worth in excess of $243,000,000. Yet the continuing presence and slow growth of the industry, particularly as represented by the larger mills along the fall line, substantiates our surmise that there was a strong tendency toward industrialism in the region that would not be stifled though it might be overshadowed. The tendency is rather difficult to explain when we think of the South as one region. On that basis, the ante-bellum industrial development seems truly in-significant so far as any later events were concerned.

When we think of the South as made up of coastal lowlands and interior highlands we see the phenomena in a different perspective. The strain toward a completely agricultural economy was the product of the lowlands; the strain toward industry was the product of the highlands. The natural features of the two regions were such that it was possible for the highlands to be influenced by the lowlands, but not the other way around. The lowlands possessed none of the re-sources in population or power that favored an industrial economy; while the highlands had resources in land that permitted it for a time to go along with the agricultural lowlands. But we noted that when-ever the price of cotton fell, the natural tendency of the highland area toward a balanced economy reasserted itself.

THE WAR AND RECONSTRUCTION

With its productive resources stretched to the limit by the demands of the Confederacy for textile products of all kinds (not only for the armies in the field, but to clothe the people at home, for they were no longer able to get manufactured goods from England or New Eng-land), the industry labored valiantly to bear its share of the burden of the war. During the latter part of the war many of the mills went down under the torches of the Union raiders of Sherman, Stoneman, or Wilson. Those at Columbus were burned, for example, along with 60,000 bales of cotton. Those that came through were in poor shape physically and financially. Their machinery had depreciated from driving usage and want of repair until much of it was worthless; and their financial resources were nonexistent. Graniteville, which had escaped destruction and had been one of the soundest of the ante-bellum mills, is reported to have been in economic difficulty in 1867; it was in debt and paying 12 per cent interest on its loans. Other mills that had survived were generally in worse shape.[4]

One effect of the War, however, had been to revive interest in the small mills of the back country. They had suffered during the decade of the 1850's, many of them going out of business as the price of cotton revived and cotton culture extended further into the Piedmont. During the war the people who had begun to look to Savannah, Augusta, Charleston, and other large centers for goods which they purchased with the cash income from their cotton crop found it necessary to return to an earlier semi-barter stage of economy and to depend once more upon a local product they had for some time been in the habit of scorning. These small, locally-owned mills suffered less from the war than the large mills along the fall line, and they were partially able to fill the breach caused by the destruction of many of the latter.

Industrial Recovery of the Piedmont South

When we consider the extent of the destruction it had suffered during the war and its apparent lack of resources, the beginning industry of the Piedmont showed remarkable recuperative power. Somehow the mills were re-equipped or rebuilt and put back into operation. By 1870, the United States Census reports, there were 92 mills with a total of 188,485 spindles operating in the four Piedmont states of North and South Carolina, Georgia, and Alabama—only 5,215 less than their pre-war total. Two states—South Carolina and Georgia—had actually increased their spindleage by small amounts.

The rehabilitation begun immediately after the war was extended into the decade of the 1870's. Victor Clark reports that

In spite of the panic and depression that introduced the following decade, between 1870 and 1880 every important Southern manufacture was

4. For an account of the impact of the Civil War on the economy of the Southeast, see Holland Thompson's "The Civil War and Social and Economic Changes," *Annals of the American Academy of Arts and Sciences*, CLIII (1931). See also Clark, *op. cit.*

completely rehabilitated, and most industries made positive progress beyond any earlier development. . . . Cotton manufactures, though as yet giving but faint promise of their subsequent development, were better established than ever before.[5]

This power of recovery displayed by the industrial South is difficult to understand so long as we cling to the stereotyped image of the ante-bellum South as a land consisting solely of aristocratic planters, disinherited poor whites, and Negro slaves. With the planters hopelessly in debt and the poor whites and Negroes as penniless as ever, it is difficult to understand on the basis of the stereotype how the South could ever have recovered on its own. The explanation is that the stereotype leaves out of the reckoning the substantial middle class of the South that the war had not impoverished to the extent that it had affected the planters, a middle class that possessed the initiative and vision that were lacking among the poor whites and the Negroes.

Much of the glory that was the South and of the grandeur that was *not* was found in the experiences of the millions of middle folk not commonly recorded in the annals of the heroic or in the stories of submerged groups. . . . the culture of the Old South and of the New was found exclusively neither in the romanticism of its aristocratic gentry nor in the tragedy and comedy of the much-described poor whites, but in the living drama of its common folks. . . . in their life and labor particularly were to be found not only the fabric of the New South and its civilization, but much that was in the Old as well.[6]

These were to be the people who, as Dr. Odum suggests, were to be the backbone of the New South. "To say that there was no middle class in the South is just as silly and as untrue as to deny the existence of such a class in England in the early nineteenth century. To be sure, it was no more articulate in the South in 1860 than in England fifty years earlier; but it existed nevertheless," says Holland Thompson.[7]

To this "inarticulate" middle class—professional people, merchants, independent farmers, small manufacturers, and skilled craftsmen—fell the greater share of the task of rebuilding the South. This is not to say that the planters did not help; but there were neither enough of them, nor did they possess the experience that was needed for the

5. Clark, *op. cit.,* pp. 258-59.
6. Howard Odum, *The Way of the South* (New York: The Macmillan Company. 1947), p. 147.
7. Thompson, *op. cit.,* p. 16.

major part of the work. Many of them clung grimly to the land. They still had it, though it might be ridden with mortgages, and it was the only way of life they knew.

Cotton Culture under Reconstruction[8]

Southern agriculture was far from showing the same healthy recovery that was typical of its industry during the fifteen years following the War. The institution of slavery upon which the dominant agricultural pattern had been based was gone. The complicated credit structure that had financed the operation of the plantation system was almost nonexistent. Livestock resources were severely depleted. The land was still there, but its virgin fertility had long since been mined over the greater part of the South. Erosion had taken its toll of the Piedmont farms during the last few decades before the war. There was abundant manpower, but how to utilize it was a problem that had to be worked out. The long growing season, the generally abundant rainfall, and the specialized knowledge of cotton culture was about all there was left that could be depended on.

Thousands of plantations or parts of plantations were thrown on the market for whatever they would bring during the first few years after the war. Many of the young men who had returned to the land after Appomattox migrated to the West or Southwest, or they decided to try their fortunes in New York, which had always been hospitable to Southerners. The plantations did not disappear, however. There was a stubborn determination to adapt the system to the new circumstances. It became apparent after 1866 that a wage system would not work, and the various forms of tenantry and sharecropping that are familiar today sprang into being almost spontaneously on the Coastal Plain. It is difficult to see how the region could have survived the period of Reconstruction without them, but tenantry has never been a satisfactory long-range method of land use in the United States. It customarily results in minimum returns to landlord and tenant alike, whether it is practiced in Wisconsin or Georgia.

To make matters worse, the price of cotton was to fall steadily for the next thirty-five years. Between 1865 and 1900, there would be only five years when it would advance over the previous year's price by as much or more than a cent a pound. Worth 31.59 cents per pound on

8. This discussion is drawn from Thompson, *op. cit.*

the average on the New York market in 1866, it fell to 15 cents by 1874 and would remain below that price until 1916. It averaged only a little over 10 cents for the decade of the '80s and less than 8 cents for the decade of the '90s. Cotton culture was unprofitable at such prices even for the rich lands of the Delta. It was ruinous on the depleted soils of the Atlantic Coastal Plain, where commercial fertilizer had become a necessity after the war.

Tenantry came into the picture in the Piedmont region as well, but from a different direction. In the lowlands it had resulted from the splitting up of huge landholdings. In the highlands, it was the result of a largely undesired and unpremeditated amalgamation of small landholdings into larger units. For the first time in its history, the Piedmont suffered desperately for cash after the war. Mortgages were the only answer. The small-town merchants of the Piedmont, its professional people, and of course its bankers, were beset with pleas for loans from the farmer. The latter went chronically into debt, and as the price of cotton fell steadily his chances of getting out grew less and less. Formerly cotton had been only one of a number of crops he had planted, now he grew nothing else. He had to have cash to pay the interest on the mortgage, to pay for seed, to buy the fertilizer that every year was becoming more of a necessity. Cotton was cash; and if he got less per pound, all he could do was try to raise more of it.

Farm after farm passed over to the mortgagee. The owner became a renter, the merchant or the banker, a landlord. The latter were no happier about the arrangement than was the farmer. The whole web of circumstances that was impoverishing the farmer was wrecking havoc with those who had advanced him money, for in the long run their prosperity was dependent upon his. They were still not out from under the necessity of advancing him money, even though they now owned his farm. He still had to have seed and fertilizer; he needed food for himself and his family until the crop was harvested. His livestock went under chattel and finally the growing crop itself. The upland farmer who operated under this system assuaged his self-respect with the thought that he was at least a tenant, with legal title to (though seldom any equity in) his mules and his tools; he was at least not a sharecropper like the poor white of the Coastal Plain who owned nothing but the ragged clothes on his back. Financially he was but little better off. There was no money in growing cotton on worn-out, eroded soil, no matter how it was done.

The position of agriculture grew steadily worse in the Piedmont as well as in the Coastal Plain. There had already been a "landless proletariat" in the lowlands—those individuals who had been crushed by the advancing plantations and were eking out a miserable existence in the Piney Woods and the Sand Hills, on the leached acres of abandoned plantations and in the shanty towns of the few large cities. There had not been such a group in the Piedmont before the war, but the difficulties of the post-war period were fast creating one. The small farmer found it impossible to maintain title to his land. It passed into the reluctant hands of those who had granted him credit on the basis of their trust in the future of cotton culture. The self-sustaining and independent yeomanry of the Piedmont was being forced into surrender to the same one-crop economy that had spelled disaster for the lowlands.

The End of Political Reconstruction[9]

In 1870, North and South Carolina, Georgia, and Alabama had possessed among them 187,125 of the total of 328,000 spindles in the entire South, leaving 140,025 in the balance of the southern region. In 1880, the four states had among them 422,897 of the total of 561,000 spindles for the entire South—the balance of the South had actually lost ground by almost 2,000 spindles, dropping back to 138,103. Between 1870 and 1880 the nation as a whole had increased its cotton system spindleage by 50 per cent, the Northeast by 57 per cent, and the entire South by 70 per cent—but spindleage in the four Piedmont states had grown by 135 per cent. The tendency already in evidence during the closing years of the previous decade toward larger mills was becoming significant. There had been an average of 2,050 spindles per mill for the four states for 1870. In 1880 the average was 3550—for South Carolina it was over 5,800, and for Georgia it was almost 5,000.

Yet despite the rapid growth of textile manufacturing during the 1870's, the Piedmont as a total society was not yet ready to turn to industry as the means for its salvation. The increase in cotton manufacturing during the decade continued to be for the most part, as it

9. See Broadus Mitchell's *Rise of the Cotton Mills in the South* (Baltimore: The Johns Hopkins Press, 1921), pp. 77-99.

had been before the war, the result of an aggregate of unrelated individual ventures. The people as a whole had yet to realize either the
possibilities of, or the necessity for, a balanced economy for the region.

Political problems engaged popular attention almost to the exclusion of anything else. The South was still under military government and carpetbag rule. Because the source of its most vexing ir-
ritation lay in Washington, the South felt that the key to all its
problems would be found there. They looked to Washington not only
for political, but also for economic, relief—a lower tariff, easier credit.
The whole gamut of political panaceas was held out by their political
leaders as the answer to their difficulties if only the South could achieve
again the power it had once held in national politics.

There were high hopes for the outcome of the Hayes-Tilden campaign of 1876. A Democratic majority had been returned to the House
in 1874, and as a consequence the burden of military rule over the
South had been somewhat lessened, though not removed. This seemed
proof that the salvation of the South lay in the political arena. The
disputed election of 1876 which resulted finally in the seating of the
Republican candidate was a bitter blow to the common men of the
South. Rancor was somewhat lessened by Hayes's withdrawal of
Federal troops from the former Confederate States. This brought
about the immediate collapse of the carpetbag governments and the
end of political reconstruction; but this further demonstration of the
power for good or evil which the Federal government held over the
southern states only strengthened their determination to win national
political control in 1880. It was not until Garfield defeated Hancock
in the fall of that year, and a Republican majority was returned to
Congress along with him, that the South, including the Piedmont, reluctantly gave up its vision of working out its destiny via the political
route.

THE PIEDMONT TURNS TO INDUSTRY

The results of the election of 1880 could have plunged the people of
the Piedmont into despair. Both of the traditional remedies of their
region—cotton and politics—had failed them. The increasing poverty
and desperation of the bulk of the common people cried out for action,
but conventional lines had proven ineffective in relieving their dire
need. The people as a whole were unsettled and restless. Their hopes

in the election of 1880 were destroyed. Reluctantly they were concluding, in the Piedmont, that the way ahead could not be through
cotton culture, for it was destroying the little capital the region still
possessed. The people felt out of context. As it stood, they could
neither analyze their present situation satisfactorily, nor could they
make adequate predictions as to what the future would bring. There
was, in effect, a rejecting of certain aspects of an existing order of life,
to the extent that those aspects had proven themselves to be ineffective
in dealing with circumstances that were new and strange. To the
degree that the people of the Piedmont felt out of context and filled
with anxiety because of their inability to foresee what the future would
bring, they were susceptible to suggestions. They were searching for
some new definition of their situation that would make the past once
more meaningful and the future something that could be depended
upon.

The definition was not long in coming. It was not revolutionary.
The mode of action for the future had already been outlined in the
past. It was all there, for example, in Gregg's "Essays on Domestic
Industry" that had appeared in the *Charleston Courier* in 1846.[10]
Gregg had been a prophet crying in the wilderness, a forerunner of
what was to come but not a leader in his time. His pleas and warnings had fallen on deaf ears. Now the people of the Piedmont were
ready to listen. It was almost as if the strain toward a balanced
economy for the Piedmont, that was logically its destiny, had been in
solution in the very air of the region all during the years when cotton
was king. Now it was ready for crystallization.

The Cotton Mill Campaign

The press and the pulpits of the Piedmont and of those large cities
of the Coastal Plain that depended on the upland region for their
wealth reflected and reinforced this new spirit—or more correctly
this revival of an old spirit—that was abroad in the region. The following from the *Raleigh News and Observer* for November 9, 1880,
was a typical editorial response to the challenge of political defeat:

We have been defeated in the national contest. . . . What, then, is our
duty? It is to go to work earnestly to build up North Carolina. Nothing
is to be gained by regrets and repinings. No people or State is better able

10. Collected and republished under the same title at Graniteville, S. C. by the
Graniteville Company in 1941.

to meet emergencies. . . . But with all its splendid capabilities it is idle to talk of home independence so long as we go to the North for everything from a toothpick to a President. We may plead in vain for a higher type of manhood and womanhood among the masses, so long as we allow the children to grow up in ignorance. We may look in vain for the dawn of a new era of enterprise, progress and development, so long as thousands and millions of money are deposited in our banks on four percent interest, when its judicious investment in manufacture would more than quadruple that rate, and give employment to thousands of now idle women and children.

Out of our political defeat we must work . . . a glorious material and industrial triumph. We must have less politics and more work, fewer stump speakers and more stump pullers, less tinsel and show and boast, and more hard, earnest work. . . . Work for the material and educational advantages of North Carolina, and in this and not in politics, will be found her refuge and her strength.[11]

This was the editorial theme that swept the Southeast. F. W. Dawson of the Charleston *News and Courier* took up where Gregg, an earlier contributor, had left off. Henry Grady of the *Atlanta Constitution* took as his text, "If the South can keep at home the $400,000,000 it gets annually for its cotton crop, it will be rich beyond comprehension. As long as she sends it out for the supplies that make the crop, she will be poor."

Editorials in every little country newspaper took up the cudgel for industrialism—which meant cotton mills, for the two were synonymous in the minds of the southern people. The clergy added their powerful voice to the importunities for a balanced economy. The idea that the future of the region lay in its own hands, and was to be achieved through hard work, was one that could be preached fervently from pulpits where man's responsibility for his own salvation through good works had always been emphasized. The theme made sense to the business men, the merchants, and bankers, and they added their considered urgings to the more impassioned oratory of the press and the pulpit.

The oratory of Grady, the editorials of Dawson, the exhortations from the pulpit, the reverberating chorus up and down the Piedmont that took up the cry "Bring the mills to the cotton fields!" was climaxed by an international cotton exposition held in Atlanta. This occasion memorialized the return of the cotton states to full stature in the

11. Quoted by Mitchell, *op. cit.,* p. 89.

union and demonstrated the identity of interest existing between northern textile manufacturers and southern cotton planters.

Originally proposed by Edward Atkinson of New England as primarily an agricultural exposition, with examples of the latest machinery for cleaning and ginning cotton, the idea expanded and developed in the hands of Piedmont men into a full-fledged exhibition of the whole process of cotton manufacture, from the raw fibre to the finished material.[12] The exposition drew together for the first time those in the Southeast who had been crusading for the new industrial order. It gave them an opportunity for mutual reaffirmation of their purpose and for an exchange of views. It furnished them with a realization of the degree to which their thinking was paralleled by others equally sincere and capable, but somewhat less vocal. The exposition was by no means the beginning of the industrial idea in the Piedmont, but it made concrete and tangible the whole spirit of the crusade that had been going on for better than a year. It was sufficiently important as a symbol so that the *Baltimore Journal of Commerce and Manufacturing* said, "When the Atlanta Exposition closed it began to be realized that the South was awakened to a new life."

The Cotton Mill Campaign as a Social Movement.—If we have created the impression that the Cotton Mill Campaign was a matter of a few leaders and many led, of newspaper promotion and oratory from pulpit and platform, we should hasten to correct it before going further. It was a true social movement, a phenomenon participated in actively by a whole society that found itself faced with the necessity for action and without traditional and familiar patterns of action that it could follow. It was this whole-hearted participation of the entire region in mill building, beginning in 1880, that marks the difference between the ante-bellum industry and its immediate post-war revival, on the one hand, and the textile industry in the Southeast following 1880, on the other. Students of the industry such as M. T. Copeland, V. S. Clark, and Broadus Mitchell have recognized the essential change in the whole spirit of the development of cotton textiles in the Piedmont after 1880, and for that reason they have chosen it as the date to mark the beginning of the modern industry. Their analyses have been economic in nature, and for this reason they have not been able to throw into sharp relief the facts that justify their conclusions. However, they

12. See Mitchell, *op. cit.,* pp. 122-25.

have sensed that despite the economic continuity that carried over from the ante-bellum industry, through the 1870's into the 1880's, something significant was present after 1880 that made the whole picture different from what it had been before.

Their intuition was sound. To the student of sociology the Cotton Mill Campaign is a classic example of a full-fledged social movement.[13] There was the failure of traditional lines of behavior, the consequent turning from old ways of doing things, the restlessness, the anxiety of a people who cannot see into the future, the search for leadership, the emergence of leadership, the redefinition of the problem in the light of new perspectives, voluntary co-operation in the initial stages of the movement, the emergence and institutionalization of new behavior patterns, and the organization of life activity on the new basis. There was the creation of *esprit de corps,* the building of morale, the formulation of a rationale. The campaign offers intriguing possibilities for study from this point of view; and to the knowledge of the writer its significance in this respect has so far escaped the attention of sociologists—though it has been sensed by economists like Mitchell and journalists like Cash.

Those people who were the leaders of the campaign were leaders because they were able to analyze the situation that existed and present it in a way that made sense; but the people who put vitality into the movement were the folk. The editors, the pastors, and the business men were saying what the common folk felt but could not put into words. "Through the procession of years while the South was convalescing from its tragic wounds and sickness, from hunger and fear, and from grief and bitterness after the Civil War, there was again this universal power of the middle folk and the common man as Nature and Society were growing a new generation of men. Buttressed by the great middle class of the prewar era, the destruction of much of the old planter aristocracy, and the merging of all the folk elements of a new and mingling South, the 'rise of the common man' in the nation was being recapitulated in the South again."[14] Thus Howard Odum reminds us of where the power lay that was to rebuild

13. See C. F. Dawson and W. E. Gettys, *Introduction to Sociology* (New York: Ronald Press Company, 1935), Chapter 19. See also Herbert Blumer's paper on "Social Movements" in *New Outline of the Principles of Sociology,* pp. 199-219.

14. Odum, *op. cit.,* p. 145.

the South and particularly the Piedmont South—which had been the birthplace of the common man in America.

Acting, striving, seeking humans, in a shifting and incalculable world they were calling for a leadership that was able to sense the nature of things, to discriminate, to take advantage of circumstances that puzzled and perplexed. As Professor Herbert Blumer would say, a collectivity of acting individuals was attempting to carve out a line of behavior. *They were seeking out the leadership.* As it emerged they used it, to solve the problems that faced them.

The leadership of the Cotton Mill Campaign was truly an emergent leadership. It was born out of the nature of the times themselves. It crystallized and gave direction to the restless searching of the common people. It was the kind of leadership that identified the nature of the goal that could mean the way out, but that made no attempt to enforce any specific pattern of activity to be followed in achieving the goal. Once the objective was delineated, the consuming energy of the folk would be channeled under their own initiative into positive action. The frontier heritage, the pioneer traits that had carved the region out of the wilderness little more than a century before, manifested itself again in the collective action of a homogeneous people. "No people less homogeneous, less one family, knit together and resolute through sufferings, could have taken instant fire, as did the South, at such appeals," says Mitchell.[15] One of the effects of the anxiety that introduces a social movement is to achieve homogeneity. In the South it reiterated and reinforced a homogeneity that was already in existence.

Cash, speaking of the campaign in his *Mind of the South,* says of it, "It acted upon the South of the time as the sermons of Peter the Hermit acted upon Europe of the eleventh century. It swept out of the minds of the men who had conceived it, to become in the years between 1880 and 1900 the dream of virtually the whole southern people. . . . a mighty folk movement which already by the turn of the century would have performed the astounding feat (in a land stripped of capital) of calling into existence more than four hundred cotton mills."[16]

The campaign put the people of the Piedmont back into context in their world—once more the past became meaningful and the future predictable, from the new point of view that it presented. That it

15. Mitchell, *op. cit.,* p. 90.
16. W. J. Cash, *Mind of the South* (New York: Alfred A. Knopf, 1941), p. 176.

should have succeeded so quickly, that it should have been accompanied by such phenomenal results, we can explain partly by this homogeneity that enabled the folk to act so efficiently and effectively as a unit under a pattern of voluntary co-operation. We can explain it partly by the presence of the frontier heritage, by its refinement and its re-affirmation during the trying days of Reconstruction. We can explain it partly by referring to the strain toward industrialism, toward self-sufficiency and a balanced economy that had never quite been defeated in the region. In this latter respect, we can think of the campaign as offering to the Piedmont the protection of a comfortable old garment, somewhat renovated and refurbished, a garment that had been put aside for a while in favor of more glittering but less substantial raiment. The garment had never really been discarded, but for a while it had hung far back in the closet.

The Folk Build the Mills[17]

It is doubtful if the people of the Piedmont realized the enormity of the task when they undertook it or after they had accomplished it. A region without capital and without industrial experience was setting out on a way of life that required both. Certainly the pioneer quality of idealism demonstrated itself as still powerfully present; here was the refusal of the idealist to recognize those aspects of what others might define as "reality," that which would have the effect of deterring him in his quest for his goal.

The Piedmont people were not without numerous warnings as to the impracticability of their proposed project. Northern manufacturers in particular sought to deter them—and not, at this early date, out of selfish interest. They were genuinely concerned over what they regarded as the certain failure of a foolhardy undertaking. They overlooked two factors. They assumed the Piedmont to be without experience in the industrial arts, not aware that as late as seventy years before the Piedmont states were exceeding New England in the value and variety of their manufactured products. And they also failed to take into account the determination and the ingenuity of the people themselves. Their indecision in the fall of 1880 had not been for want of ability, but for want of an objective toward which to apply it. Ad-

17. See Mitchell's chapter on "The Rise of the Mills," *op. cit.*, for a much more detailed account of this phenomenon.

vice that they continue a kind of provincial relationship with New England did not sound to them like the kind of advice they were looking for.

In the matter of capital, southern pride did not stand in the way of soliciting aid from the North. "Willingness to welcome help of Northern money in Southern mills was a test of earnestness in the new program, the characteristic mark of conquest over hurtful pride and estranging rancor," Mitchell tells us on the basis of his extended research into the history of the early mills.[18] Concessions were offered in the way of tax reductions to northern firms that might wish to locate in the South. Men like Grady made trips into the North, pointing out the rich resources of their region and the opportunities it offered for those who wished to assist in its industrialization.

There was however very little response from the North except from two sources—the commission houses and the machinery manufacturers. Pure investment capital did not come south, nor did northern mills. Grady regretted that "our brothers from the North have not taken larger part with us in this work"; but it became apparent that the industrialization of the Piedmont was going to have to be a task for its people alone, plus such help as they might get from the few large cities of the Coastal Plain.

The people did not wait for northern capital. They wanted it, and with Grady, they regretted that they did not have it. But they did not defer the building of the mills until it should arrive. "Nothing stands out more prominently than that the Southern mills were conceived and brought into existence by Southerners. The impulse was furnished almost exclusively from within the South, against much discouragement from selfish interests at the North, and capital was supplied by the South to the limit of its ability," says Mitchell.[19] "The great majority of cotton mills in the South represent the sacrifices and great efforts of the communities in which they are situated. In the East the cotton mill is built from the capital of the rich; in the South it is built from the combined capital of many of little means." Thus Lewis W. Parker explained the rise of the southern mills before the House Committee of Judiciary in 1902.[20]

All at once it seemed that every little town and city wanted a cot-

18. *Ibid.*, p. 237.   19. *Ibid.*, p. 102.
20. *Ibid.*, p. 233.

ton mill. The new spirit behind their building is demonstrated by the changing nature of their location. Before 1880 individuals had built mills, and they had sought out the best site for their location—along a stream which gave them water power and a somewhat more humid atmosphere to facilitate manufacturing. Now the mills began to locate without regard to water power. Communities built them, and they wanted them at home whether they had water power or not. The merits of steam versus water power had been debated for quite some time, but now the debate was over. It became a matter of expediency. If a community had water power, it used it; if not, there was steam and plenty of coal in Alabama and West Virginia. Soon, as a kind of by-product of the campaign, the Piedmont would seize upon new developments in the generation and transmission of electrical power; and numerous small hydro-electric and steam generating plants would spring into being and criss-cross the region with a network of electric power lines.

The motivation behind the building of particular mills was different now than it had been. Before 1880 the mills had been built to make profits. The profit motive was certainly not absent after 1880; but the small investors who contributed to the fund for starting a mill in their community did not think of their stock certificates primarily as instruments entitling them to a share in its future profits. They were something that would help get the mill built, that would help give employment to men who were idle, that would bring a payroll into the community. They wanted the mill to make a profit, but not so much for the sake of the dividends they would personally receive as to insure that the mill would stay open. Many of them sold their stock as soon as they conveniently could—they had seriously crippled their meagre capital resources to purchase it in the first place, and once the enterprise was assured, they were not interested in dividends. Their purpose in purchasing stock had been achieved when the mill began operating.

"This was not a business, but a social enterprise," says Gerald W. Johnson. "Any profit that might accrue to the originators of the mill was but incidental; the main thing was the salvation of the decaying community, and especially the poor whites, who were in danger of being submerged altogether. The record of those days is filled with a moral fervor that is astounding. People were urged to take stock in the mills for the town's sake, for the South's sake, literally for God's sake."[21]

It should certainly not be argued that even a significant minority of those who purchased stock did so out of altruistic purpose, with no idea in mind but to furnish employment for the idle. Merchants hoped to see some cash in their tills once more as payrolls were distributed—perhaps even to collect some long overdue accounts. Doctors and lawyers saw an opportunity for receiving cash payment for their services. Fathers saw the opportunity of employment for their sons. Bankers saw increased deposits and more liquid assets in store for them. Doctor, lawyer, merchant, chief, butcher, and baker, and candlestick maker—all of them saw in the advent of the mill in their community not nearly so much the possibility of dividends from its operation as of revitalization of the whole economic and social life of the community.

The stories of how particular mills got started are as varied as the number of mills themselves. Quite often some individual was a moving spirit behind the enterprise—though we must not forget that he was himself very often responding to the whole tendency of the campaign, that he was unconsciously an agent of a larger movement. More often a committee of business and professional men would decide that a mill must be brought to their community and would delegate to one of their group the task of assuming the active leadership. Since none of them were likely to have had industrial experience, they chose him on the basis of his integrity and standing in the community. He might be a doctor or a lawyer. Often he was a cotton factor. He might be a member of the tidewater or the cotton aristocracy. He might be an ex-Confederate officer. He might be a minister or a school teacher. There was no pattern in the selection, except that the man chosen possessed certain qualifications that the community felt would be useful under the special circumstances that it faced.

Emulation and rivalry played its part. A successful mill seemed to beget a whole ring of mills about it, as other communities in the vicinity followed the example. The clergy often played an important role. The first mill at Salisbury, for example, owed its beginning to the powerful preaching of an evangelistic minister, who "declared that the great morality in Salisbury was to go to work, and that corruption.

21. Cash, *op. cit.,* p. 178.

idleness and misery could not be dispelled until the poor people were given an opportunity to become productive. The establishment of a cotton mill would be the most Christian act his hearers could perform."[22] The three resident ministers of Salisbury were active in the actual establishment of the mill, and one of them became its first secretary and treasurer, and later its president.

The first managements of these community-inspired mills were often of an interim nature. As they got into operation, talent for industrial leadership made itself evident among younger men who had begun with minor offices or who were salaried employees. They were elevated into positions more in keeping with their abilities, and their predecessors (often with a sigh of relief) went back to their banks or their law practices or their ministries. These younger men regarded cotton manufacturing as a career rather than primarily as something that one undertook as a community service, and often they invested every cent of money they could save or borrow in the stock of the mill as it came on the market, gathering blocks of it sufficiently large to give them an important voice in the control of the mill.

More often than not, no one had owned a sufficient amount of stock in the mill to begin with to give him a controlling interest. Stock subscriptions as large as $2,000 were rare. They were much more likely to be under $500. In many cases, stock was sold on an installment basis, with payments as low as 25 or 50 cents per week per share.[23] Sometimes construction of the mill would not be undertaken until all the capital, or at least a substantial portion of it, had been paid in; but more often a local bank would underwrite the venture on the basis of the subscription list, and construction would begin immediately that sufficient funds had been promised by people whose integrity satisfied the bank.

The average capitalization of the mills erected during the first years of the campaign was in the neighborhood of $100,000.[24] Local resources were likely to fail after about half that amount had been

22. Mitchell, *op. cit.,* p. 135.

23. See Holland Thompson, *From the Cotton Field to the Cotton Mill: A Study of Industrial Transition in North Carolina* (New York: The Macmillan Company, 1906), pp. 82-83. See also Liston Pope's *Millhands and Preachers* (New Haven: Yale University Press, 1942), pp. 14-15, for an account of the pattern of investment that built the mills in and around Gastonia, S. C.

24. See Mitchell's chapter on "The Role of Capital," *op. cit.,* for a discussion of the financial problems of the early mills.

raised, however. The community could generally be counted on for enough to erect the building, but not to equip it with machinery or to afford working capital. Having got assurances of perhaps $50,000 from their community, the promoters of the enterprise now went to the machinery manufacturers and the commission houses. On the strength of the subscriptions already received, the machinery companies would agree to take stock in the mill amounting to anywhere between a fourth and a half of the cost of the necessary equipment. The commission houses would usually take some additional stock, in return for a contract to handle the mill's output, and would in addition advance ready cash on a short term basis for the initial purchases of raw stock and initial payrolls.

The mill that began operations with working capital set aside out of its equity investment was rare. It was much more likely to start with indebtedness on the plant and its first run of goods already consigned to a commission house in return for a cash advance of from 75 to 90 per cent of its value. The result of this "shoestring" financing was likely to be very high return to equity capital, or severe financial embarrassment, or bankruptcy. All three results were common. On the whole, the new industry did much better with regard to profits than might have been expected when we consider the inexperience of its management and operatives.

It is difficult to make any generalizations as to the rate of return for the early mills since the basis for their calculation varies and often is not known. There was often no correlation between the dividend return of an early mill and its actual financial condition—a company might declare dividends of 20 per cent one year and be thrown into bankruptcy the next. High dividends were often declared when heavy indebtedness on the mill should first have been retired. Proper provision was seldom made to begin with for depreciation, nor was there likely to be any attempt to acquire independent working capital. Reserves were seldom set aside at first for future expansion. Thus it is impossible to make any categorical statement as to the real earning power of the early mills. One generalization can be made, however: no matter how high their dividends might be, and whether economically justified or not, they were almost certain to find their way into the building of more mills.

The Location of the Mills

Some of the initial impetus for the Cotton Mill Campaign had come from the large cities of the Coastal Plain, whose fortunes as centers of trade and distribution were tied in with the Piedmont as well as their own region. The grass roots strength of the campaign, however, was in the Piedmont and the lower reaches of the Appalachian Valley; and it was here that the mills were built. There were a number of reasons for this, many of which we have already mentioned, but it might be well at this point to summarize the factors that resulted in the Piedmont emerging as the manufacturing region of the Southeast.

1. It was the Piedmont that had a tradition of a balanced economy, a remembrance of a time when it had been self-sufficient. The appeals of the leaders of the Cotton Mill Campaign, though they had often been directed toward the whole Southeast, were heard most sympathetically by the people of the Piedmont after the false promise of cotton culture had been blasted. The completely agricultural Coastal Plain, however, retained all its earlier antipathy toward manufacturing as a way of life. Though Charleston, for example, furnished the money to build many up-country mills, its own venture in mill building was unsuccessful. The people whom it had depended upon to work in the mill refused to accept employment—they were sure that a factory of any kind was a den of iniquity and that only people of low moral character would be found there.

2. The Piedmont had what experience there was in the South with cotton mills. Those of the ante-bellum days were located either in the interior of the Piedmont or along the fall line. There were practically none in the Coastal Plain.

3. The principle reason for the location of the early mills in the Piedmont (in addition to the social and economic forces that favored their growth there) was the presence of water power. The Coastal Plain could not have developed the industry even had manufacturing been in its tradition until railroads were built that would connect it with the coal fields of Alabama or West Virginia. It had no power; its sluggish streams flowing through broad shallow valleys were of no value for turning spindles and operating looms. The electrification of the industry beginning in the late 1880's still tied it to water power;

early transmission lines were not capable of long-distance transmission of electrical power. The Coastal Plain could have used coal for power after 1880, as did certain areas in the Piedmont; but coal that had to be shipped in was not a positive argument for industrialization, as was water power which was on the spot and waiting to be developed.

4. The Piedmont possessed, in 1880, a surplus population of a character that could and would man the mills and that could operate them in a way that would insure their success. These impoverished and displaced farm people possessed a knowledge of household manufacture that was valuable. Though they had been crushed financially by the war, they were not poor in spirit. They were ambitious, anxious to better their circumstances. They saw the advent of the mills as opportunity. The Coastal Plain, on the other hand, had a surplus population of Negroes and landless whites. Experience with both groups demonstrated that they were not dependable as a source of industrial labor—nor were they anxious to work in the mills.

5. The movement toward the building of the mills was almost entirely a middle-class movement. It was the middle and the common folk who took hold of the campaign and translated its oratory into actuality. They had neither the aristocrat's adversion toward manufacturing nor the poor white's lack of initiative. A very important consideration, they were the people of the South who had sufficient capital, when it was pooled, to make the initial move toward mill building. The Coastal Plain had no substantial middle class—it was out of its acquaintance with this region that the North formed its stereotyped image of the South as a land of aristocratic planters, Negroes, and impoverished poor whites. The only areas in the Coastal Plain where a middle class existed in important numbers was in its large cities, and we have already noted that cities like Charleston and Savannah furnished financial support for building mills in the Piedmont.

6. The building of the mills was in large part the result of community activity. The Coastal Plain possessed relatively few of the towns and small cities of the Southeast. It depended upon its few large cities. There were not the nuclei of population in the Coastal Plain that could build mills through co-operative effort.

7. The planter class in the Coastal Plain was not lacking in leadership ability; but there were not enough of its members to have

furnished the practical, on-the-spot, day-to-day direction and guidance that was necessary to get the mills built and get them in operation. The upper-middle class of the small cities and towns of the Piedmont provided a necessary source of leadership in sufficient quantity as well as quality. An even more important factor, and one that is always overlooked, is that there was no element in the Coastal Plain that could have furnished enough supervisory people. Its population ran too heavily, to put it into military terms, to generals and privates. There was not the middle group that could furnish the lieutenants and the sergeants. The middle class and common folk of the Piedmont were able to supply the expanding industry with administrative and supervisory personnel.

8. There was finally the homogeneity of the people of the Piedmont that enabled them to co-operate as a whole society. It was a democratic society, perhaps the most democratic in the nation. There was a feeling of kinship between its highest and lowest elements that was lacking in the Coastal Plain—and the range of difference between the two was not so great as it was in the Coastal Plain. In this latter region, we can hardly speak of homogeneity as existing among its three principle groups—planters, disinherited whites, and freed Negroes. There was no such disparity of station or of outlook on life among the people of the highland region. It is important to remember that the extremes of individual financial status existing in the region in 1880 were of rather recent origin. The farmer who was a tenant in 1880 had been (or was the son of) an independent farmer in 1860. The differences in status had not become traditional, and it is noteworthy that an important purpose of the Cotton Mill Campaign was to reduce the gap between those who had and those who had not, rather than to continue or to increase it.

Thus it was the Piedmont that came to be dotted with cotton mills until in some parts of it one is never out of sight of a textile plant— by the time the water tower of one has disappeared over one's shoulder, another has loomed up in the foreground. The nature of this impetus toward the building of the mills in 1880 instituted a trend toward decentralization that has never abated. The Piedmont became a manufacturing region without becoming an urban region in the usual sense of the word. The independent spirit of its small communities insured their survival. It has remained one of the few regions in the United States where small towns still flourish.

The Communities and the Mills

A relationship grew up between the communities and their mills that was and has remained unique in an industrial region. The communities built the mills, and the mills saved the communities. The mills "belonged" to the communities. Either community initiative to begin with or community approval of an individual project brought them into being. It did not matter a great deal who owned the stock certificates that gave legal title to them—they remained "our mills" from the point of view of the community even after their initially widely distributed stockholdings had gravitated into the possession of a few people or a family who were interested in the mill as a primary source of income. The purpose for which the mills had been built and the return that the communities had expected to get from the mills had not altered. The purpose was to furnish payrolls.

The net result of this feeling of possession on the part of the communities was that they took rather an active role in the affairs of the mills. Not in their actual day-to-day management, but rather through the implicit development of a pattern of expectations to which the mills were expected to conform. The mill, for example, was expected to remain open and furnish employment as long as it could borrow money to meet its payrolls. If it was necessary to forego profits in order to accomplish this, it was regretable and unfortunate—but from the community point of view, the important purpose of the mills was to furnish payrolls. The mill management that would have attempted to operate in conformity with hard-headed business practice, and close the mill down temporarily when prices were off and demand was slack, would immediately have found itself in bad repute in the community. The stockholders were welcome to their high profits when business was good; but they were expected to approve continued operation even at a loss when business was bad.

Other expectations developed, of which we shall speak later, with regard to the way in which worker-management relationships should be maintained in the mills. What is important for us to note is that the building of this pattern of expectations which bound the mills to the communities was implicit. The folk built the mills, and in the building of them they wove them into the folkways. It was not a matter of the mills "adopting" the folkways or even of adapting to them. They were built upon the foundation of the folkways to begin with. Even more than that—they were themselves a way of the folk; the solution forged by a vital and dynamic folk society in the face of circumstances that threatened its survival. The implicit controls to which southern mill managements were thus submitted dwarfed in their power and inclusiveness the explicit and limited controls of legislation and ordinance. They were beyond the reach of special interest groups, impervious to the persuasive tongue of the lobbyist. They represented the natural, intuitive adjustments of a folk society to industrial technics which they themselves adopted and fashioned into an institution.

Results of the Cotton Mill Campaign

The growth of spindleage in the Southeast during the 1880's bears out the contention that a new element had entered the picture. United States Census figures show the lead that was being assumed by the Piedmont in the national expansion of cotton system spindleage. The nation as a whole increased the number of its cotton spindles by 35 per cent between 1880 and 1890. The South as a whole showed a growth of 162 per cent over the 1880 figure during the same period—but the greater share of this increase was due to the activity of the four Piedmont states of North and South Carolina, Georgia, and Alabama, which increased their combined spindleage by 182 per cent during the 1880's, going from 119 establishments with a total of 422,957 spindles in 1880 to 191 establishments with a total of 1,195,246 spindles in 1890.

The trend toward larger establishments continued. In 1880 the average number of spindles for the four states had been 3550; now it was up to 6250. The small, local mill that had depended upon neighborhood custom, or at the most upon regional trade to dispose of its product, was being replaced by a mill that had to depend upon the national market. A mill at Columbus already had 45,000 spindles and 1500 looms. The new mills were not merely distributing local money. They were bringing it in from outside the region.

Another practice was also entering the picture—that of combining two or more small mills into a larger company. Thus the increase in the number of establishments in 1890 over 1880 does not give the whole picture as to how many mills were built during the decade since the census was quite likely to count two mills in the same locality, belonging to the same company, as only one "establishment." A depression lasting from the summer of 1884 until the autumn of 1885 was disastrous for a number of the new mills that had not provided reserves for such contingencies. "This was a period of reorganization and improvement in individual establishments, and of centralization through the absorption of weaker plants by stronger competitors," says Victor Clark.[25] Such reorganization did not result in a regional loss but actually, in many cases, through strengthening of credit facilities and improvements in managerial practices, in a regional gain. The effect of the recession of 1884 upon the Piedmont mills indicates, however, that though they might be a product of the region, their fortunes were nevertheless tied in with the national economy. The mills strengthened and sustained the folk society of the Piedmont region; but at the same time they integrated it more firmly than it had ever before been into the mass society of a national market. Thus though the Piedmont was through the agency of its industry able to retain and reinforce its own distinctive character, it was henceforth to be under the necessity of fitting that individuality into the activity of the total society of the nation.

25. Clark, *op. cit.*, p. 281.

CHAPTER IV

The Piedmont in the National Market

IF THE PIEDMONT folk society sought and found its salvation through the offices of an industry that depended upon a national market, then perhaps we should digress for a few pages and consider the nature of that industry and that market. What was the Piedmont letting itself in for? In our first chapter we made certain generalizations with regard to the impact of the basic industrial process upon basic human nature. Can we make somewhat more specific generalizations with regard to the textile industry as the locus of industrial relationships?

THE COTTON TEXTILE INDUSTRY

The textile industry in its modern form was born in England during the latter half of the 1700's—the first major industry to emerge in modern dress. The great demand for coarse cotton cloth to be used as an article of commerce in the expanding British trade empire encouraged a flood of inventions that took the manufacture out of the cottages of the crofters and put it into the factory—and took the crofters out of their cottages and lodged them in huge industrial slums, to bear company with the many already there who had been forced off the land by the changing pattern of British agriculture. The essential processes of its manufacture, though refined and accelerated, have not changed in their essential details since the perfection of the power-driven loom during the first decade of the 1800's.

Technology and Industrial Relations in Textiles

In two respects the processes of textile manufacture are intrinsically less disturbing to the industrial worker than those of any other major industry with the exception of primary metals.

The first derives from the fact that a raw material is processed in logically reasonable steps that derive from the nature of the raw stock itself.[1] The division of labor that is employed, as a matter of fact, was first developed for the handicraft industry and merely mechanized in the course of transferring it to the factory. It is not a mass production industry of the usual type, in which individually meaningless components are separately manufactured and become meaningful only in the final end product. The whole product is worked upon at every stage in its manufacture. The reason for each operation is readily apparent to those who perform it, and its importance to the following stages of manufacture and to the final end product can be visualized by the operative; he need not be a process engineer to understand the fundamental importance of the function he performs. In addition, the successive operations have remained essentially the same through so many generations of industrial processing, subject to modifications and improvements but never in danger of elimination, that the mind of the operative is at rest with regard to the continued importance of the function he performs.

The second characteristic of textile manufacture that ameliorates somewhat its impact upon the industrial worker derives also from its relative antiquity. The status relationships between the various tasks have, during the course of five generations, been worked out and adjusted to the point that the worker has little doubt as to their equity. Given the opportunity to perform a certain function, the textile worker has no question in his mind as to the status it will earn for him, nor does he in general question its justice.

But to offset the feeling of security that arises through being aware of the essential importance of his task and of its relative worth is the fact that though the worker is assured of the continuing importance of his function, he has no such assurance that *he* will continue to perform it. On the basis of a survey made in 1940, the Bureau of Labor Statistics reported that 56.2 per cent of the textile workers in the nation were semi-skilled. The balance were almost equally divided between unskilled and skilled.[2] Thus better than 84 out of every 100 textile workers are aware of the fact that they can be replaced by others with little or no training. Textile manufacturing in its technological aspect

1. For an excellent brief account of the processes of textile manufacturing, see A. F. Hinrichs, "Wages in Cotton Manufacturing," Bureau of Labor Statistics, *Bulletin No. 663,* 1938.

2. U. S. Bureau of Labor Statistics, "Hours and Earnings in Manufacture of Cotton Goods, September, 1940 and April, 1941," *Serial No. R. 1414,* p. 4.

offers the worker little protection against the inherent anxiety of the industrial worker that he may be replaced in his job. He is fairly well assured of the importance of his function—but not of his own importance, which, among other things, is injurious to his self-confidence and self-respect.

The Managerial Superstructure and Industrial Relations

The textile worker is potentially somewhat better off with regard to his relationships with management than is the typical industrial worker, as a result of characteristics inherent to the industry. The usual textile plant is small, relative to those in other major industries. The Bureau of the Census in their Annual Survey of Manufactures for 1951 found only 24 textile establishments out of a total of 7,758 of all kinds that employed more than 2,500 workers; only 208 employed more than 1,000. The average number of employees per establishment in the broad-woven cotton textile industry in Georgia in 1952 was 692. Not only are textile plants generally small, but their managerial structure is simple and uncomplicated, as are their lines of communication. Thus the textile worker is potentially better able to become acquainted with and take the role of people in management; and there is potentially more possibility that he will be recognized as an individual by significant people in management.

This advantage is somewhat watered down, however, by the fact that the textile plant is more tightly bound to the vagaries of a national market than is that of any other major industry. The management of the plant must answer to the market; and though the worker may be able to understand and predict the probable patterns of action of his top executives, it is unlikely that he can predict the market. He is aware that managerial recognition of his worth is powerless to insure the continuance of his status as an employed worker in the face of unfavorable market conditions.

Economic Aspects of the Textile Industry[3]

With regard to their impact upon industrial relations, two characteristics of the economics of the cotton textile industry are of major importance:

3. A good summary discussion of this topic is given by Jules Bachman and M. R. Gainsbrugh in their *Economics of the Cotton Textile Industry* (New York: National Industrial Conference Board, 1946).

1. Of all major industries, it pays out the highest proportion of "value added by manufacture" in the form of wages—52 per cent in 1947, according to the *Census of Manufactures* for that year.

2. It is the only major employer of industrial labor that continues to sell its product in what can be regarded as a freely competitive market in the classic sense of the term.

Labor Costs in Textiles.—Because of the great importance of labor cost in establishing the price of the finished product, the textile industry is known as "labor-oriented." This does not mean that it automatically gravitates to those sections where workers are willing to work for the lowest wage—the lack of correlation between "cheap labor" and low labor cost as a factor in production has been so thoroughly exploded that there is no need to go into it here—but it does mean that the textile industry is very interested in areas where it can find and depend upon an *efficient* source of labor. The question of importance in the manufacture of textiles is not "For how little will these people work?" but rather "Will the quantity and quality of their production at the price they are willing to work for result in the lowest possible price per unit of output?"

Merely "cheap" labor may prove in the long run to be expensive even when the worker is on a piece-work basis and it would seem that the labor cost per unit of product is thus definitely fixed. The textile plant, like all others, has certain fixed costs for non-productive labor, capital charges, and taxes that do not vary with the amount produced; and when cheap labor results in low production, even though the wage bill itself may be low, the amount of this overhead that must be charged against each unit of production to recover it may be so high that the total unit cost is greater than the product can be sold for. The high cost of inefficient labor was not so apparent in the national textile industry before World War I, during the period when an expanding market resulted in prices sufficiently high to enable the moderately inefficient producer (from whatever cause) to survive.

Since World War I supply has often exceeded demand; and efficiency of operation, including efficient labor, has become the first requisite for staying in business. It is only by keeping its wage bill at the optimum low point that the industry finds any important possibility of reducing its unit cost of operations. We must caution once more than the "optimum low" does not mean "the lowest possible wage bill"; it does mean that point at which the balance between wages paid and labor efficiency results in the lowest unit cost of production including *all* factors. The importance of this becomes even more apparent when we consider the nature of the market in which its product is sold.

Competition in the Textile Industry.—The theoretical requirements for a free competitive market are usually stipulated as being some variation of the following:

1. No one supplier or purchaser, or combination of suppliers or purchasers, can be large enough to influence the market by its own activities.

2. There must be ease of entry into the market, so that high prices for any period of time will be followed by the entry of new suppliers.

3. The product must be of a standard nature, produced according to standard specifications, so that there will be no choice as to quality between producers.

4. There must be a central market in which prices are established by competitive bidding; and information as to its condition must be freely and immediately available to all suppliers and purchasers.

Examining these conditions one by one as they apply to textiles, this is the situation:

1. Solomon Barkin discovered that as late as 1948 it took the 42 largest southern textile companies to account for 50 per cent of the total southern cotton system spindleage.[4]   The *Statistical Abstract of the United States* for 1953, basing its figures on the *1947 Census of Manufactures*, reports that for that year the four largest textile companies making broad-woven cotton textiles accounted for only 13.1 per cent of the total production in that field. Only 6 of the 38 industries listed showed less concentration—"sawmills and planing mills," "commercial printing," "men's and boys' suits and coats," "dresses, unit price," "heating and cooking apparatus," and "women's suits and coats." The first 8 textile companies in point of size accounted for 22.2 per cent of the broad-woven cotton goods output, the first 20 for 40.4 per cent of it and the first 50 for 63.2 per cent. Obviously there is little possibility here for any one company or workable combination of them to influence the market by their own efforts. The

4. Solomon Barkin, "The Regional Significance of the Integration Movement in the Southern Textile Industry," *Southern Economic Journal,* XV (1949), p. 406.

importance of the very small, family-owned textile mill is declining, but the trend appears to be toward a considerable number of companies of moderate size, rather than one toward a market divided between a few huge companies.

2. Ease of entry into the cotton textile market is facilitated in three ways. To begin with, the large producer enjoys no economies of operation over the small producer; he is, as a matter of fact, likely to increase his overhead costs disproportionately.[5] The small mill, well managed, can hold its own with the best of them; and it need not worry about the high cost of national advertising campaigns or promotional expense. If it can manufacture a satisfactory product, it can sell it as easily and for as good a price as the large producer. In the second place, not only is a small plant economical, but the investment per worker is low relative to other major industries. The National Industrial Conference Board discovered that in 1942 the net capital investment per worker was smaller for the textile industry than for any of the other nine industries for which they collected data.[6] The investment necessary for a modern broad-woven cotton textile mill will still run into millions of dollars; but it is not so high that it will prevent large purchasers of cotton textiles, for example, from building or purchasing their own plant if prices climb.

Finally, we must remember that the "textile market" is actually many related markets: one for print cloth, one for denim, one for corduroy, one for sheeting, one for shirting, and others. But the versatility of the typical mill is such that it can switch from one product to another with little difficulty. A. F. Hinrichs of the Bureau of Labor Statistics estimated in 1938 that 75 per cent of the cotton goods output could be produced on the type of equipment that tends to be standard in a cotton mill.[7] This means that if the price gets out of line on any one item, there is an immediate adjustment of production within the industry itself. The Office of Price Administration discovered during World War II, for example, that it had to use extreme care in setting prices on cotton goods; a price a fraction of a cent too high or too low resulted either in cessation of manufacture or in a

5. See Stephen Jay Kennedy's *Profits and Losses in Textiles* (New York: Harper and Brothers, 1936), pp. 185-86. See also Hinrichs, *op. cit.*

6. Unpublished data collected by the National Industrial Conference Board and quoted by Buchman and Gainsbrugh, *op. cit.*, p. 20.

7. Hinrich, *op. cit.*, p. 15.

flood of production.[8] It is noteworthy also that the smaller mill, because of its shorter lines of communication and generally more flexible structure, is able to switch into profitable lines of production more readily than the larger mill.

3. The bewildering variety of cotton products that faces the purchaser in the piece goods department of a large store appears to indicate that the textile industry manufactures anything but a standard product. What the consumer seldom realizes is that this variety has been introduced after the product has left the mill. Under the camoflauge of modish prints, colors that "everyone" is wearing this year (and "no one" may be wearing next year) and special finishes are a relatively few standard constructions of cloth. The typical cotton textile mill produces a standard product that meets standard specifications and sells it "in the gray" before it has been washed, bleached, dyed, printed, or subjected to any of the other numerous finishing operations required to prepare it for the consumer. A finishing plant, to be economical, is the one textile installation that must handle a large volume of goods (except for certain special finishing, such as for towelling); the output of the average Georgian mill of 700 employees would not keep a modern finishing plant busy one day a week. This is not the principle reason why the integrated spinning and weaving plant prefers to sell its goods in the gray, however. A standard product, while it is still in the gray, can always be sold at the market price; but a styled product based on an inaccurate estimate of the vagaries of fashion represents almost a complete loss. The textile producer is generally content with a modest manufacturing profit. He prefers to sell his standard product to the converter, who is a specialist in predicting consumer trends, and let him enjoy the large profits and risk the equally large losses of the style market.

4. There is finally the matter of the central market. What the Chicago Board of Trade is for grains, or the New York Stock Exchange is for stocks and bonds, Worth Street in New York City is for textiles. Here lots of standard fabrics are offered for sale and bid upon, and prices for all standard constructions of cotton textiles are established and continually revised in line with supply and demand.[9] This

8. See *Report of the Senate Committee on Banking and Currency*, Report No. 325, June, 1945, 79th Congress, 1st Session.
9. See Bachman and Gainsbrugh, *op. cit.*, p. 117.

information is widely and immediately disseminated. The office of the little mill in the Georgian Piedmont may still be using the furniture with which it was originally equipped when it was built in 1890—with the exception of one item: the teletype machine that is busy tapping out the latest information on sales transacted a thousand miles away.

The net result of all this is that cotton textiles are sold in a market that is still highly competitive in the classic sense of the word. The producer has no chance to set prices. He produces *for* a price, and he can sell all he can make at that price, if he is willing to accept it, without affecting the market by his own efforts. As a consequence, falling textile prices are for a while likely to be accompanied by an increase in production, just as in the case of an agricultural product in an uncontrolled market. Other industries curtail operations when demand falls and prices weaken. But the single textile plant, like the single wheat ranch, will not affect the market by its own operation. Demand will continue to be no worse than it has been, and prices will fall no further or no faster whether either of them produce much, little, or nothing at all. The wheat rancher and the textile producer both have fixed costs that must be met whether they produce or not; and knowing that what they do will not affect the market, they often see only one practical answer when unit prices fall—produce more units. If they are able to increase production significantly without a corresponding increase in overhead costs, they may be able to reduce their unit costs below even the depressed market prices.

With many mills attempting this at the same time, the overall result is obvious. Total production increases, prices do fall further and faster, inventories that have been accumulated hoping for an upturn in the market must eventually be sold for whatever they will bring to keep the mill solvent (thus depressing prices even more), and disaster results for many producers.[10] This has happened so frequently since 1920 that most textile men are likely to regard it rather morosely as the normal state of the market. Yet the play of supply and demand that brings the situation about is so impersonal in its operation that except for certain specialty manufacturers, there is little feeling that a competitive situation acually exists. The textile mill manager does

10. See Claudius Murchison, *King Cotton is Sick* (Chapel Hill: University of North Carolina Press, 1930), pp. 71-107. See also Reavis Cox, *The Marketing of Textiles* (Washington, D. C.: The Textile Foundation, 1938), pp. 291-92.

not regard his neighbor as a competitor. He sees both himself and his neighbor as producing for the same impersonal market; he neither profits by the other's disaster nor suffers as a result of his success. A New York banker once remarked that he liked to attend conventions of textile manufacturers. He enjoyed what was to him the amazing spectacle of men who were actually in direct and ruthless competition displaying a high degree of neighborliness and good fellowship in their personal contacts!

Profits in Cotton Textiles.—The textile industry, classic in its competition, has fulfilled the predictions of such men as Adam Smith and John Stuart Mill with regard to the eventual state of its profits. As long as the population of the country continued to increase faster than the number of cotton system spindles, the industry was prosperous. This condition lasted until 1900. The artificial stimulus of World War I brought up the curve of profits just as the industry was about to dip into the red in 1914; but they declined steadily all during the boom years of the 1920's. The industry had over-expanded during the war and immediate post-war boom, and so it had a productive capacity greater than the actual ability of the nation to consume.

Dr. Clair Wilcox, examining the condition of the industry between 1919 and 1939 for the Temporary National Economic Committee and reporting his findings in *Monograph No. 21* on "Competition and Monopoly in American Industry," concluded cautiously that "profits in the industry as a whole have been something less than moderate."[11] For the years 1929 through 1938, he discovered that the industry experienced an aggregate net deficit of $32,815,000. Backman and Gainsbrugh in their *Economics of the Cotton Textile Industry* calculate that the industry went into the red to the total amount of $64,000,000 during the fourteen years beginning in 1926 and ending with 1939.[12]

The industry was partly able to recoup its losses during World War II—yet even here it found itself at a disadvantage compared with other industries. Because of its low earnings during the 1936-39 period, upon which wartime excess profits taxes were based, it found itself paying an unduly high proportion of wartime income to the federal government as excess profits tax—50.6 per cent as compared with 44.1

11. Clair Wilcox, "Competition and Monopoly in American Industry," Temporary National Economic Committee *Monograph No. 21,* p. 33.

12. Bachman and Gainsbrugh, *op. cit.,* p. 143. See also Kennedy, *op. cit.,* and Murchison, *op. cit.,* for analyses of the profit picture in cotton textiles.

per cent for all industry in 1943. Including normal as well as excess profits taxes, the industry paid out nearly 65 per cent of its income to the federal government in 1942, and almost 68 per cent in 1943.[13]

For a short time after World War II, the industry enjoyed high profits. In 1949 it went into a recession, recovered to some degree in 1950, went into recession again in 1951, and has been fluctuating about its "normal" condition of no profits ever since. What its future profit situation will be is open to question. It is obvious that an automatically expanding market can no longer be counted upon to compensate for low labor productivity, technological obsolescence, or managerial inefficiency. Or, to put the statement in reverse, textile profits are no longer partly a reward for developing an immature industry. The industry has come of age in a highly competitive market. There seems little possibility that the degree of competition will be reduced; therefore, its profits from now on will be largely compensation for managerial astuteness in utilizing technological improvements and obtaining efficient co-operation from its work force.

Marketing of Cotton Textiles.—We have already noted briefly the role played by the commission houses in the building of the southern industry. The relationships between the mills and their commission houses, for the greater share of the southern industry, remained virtually unchanged from 1880 until World War II. The commission houses continued to advance operating capital against stock in manufacture and inventory. When the mills were making money in the years before 1920, they preferred to use undeclared dividends for expansion rather than to set up independent working capital. After 1920, few of them made enough money to acquire financial independence. The mills were not in general happy with the arrangement, particularly during those depression periods when they could do nothing about it.

Three principle causes of contention seem to have arisen. The southern mill operators, themselves a part of the folk society that regarded the principle function of the mills to be that of furnishing employment, felt there was something shameful about closing a mill down short of its actual bankruptcy; but the commission houses were reluctant to advance working capital against unsold goods when sound business practice would have suggested a temporary shut-down. In the second place, the southern mills felt that the commission houses

13. Bachman and Gainsbrugh, *op. cit.,* pp. 149-53.

were not as aggressive in their selling as they might have been during periods of slow demand; they seemed too content to play the role of order takers when the mills thought they should have been attempting to create a market. And third, since one commission house might handle the accounts of dozens of small mills, each of them was likely to feel that at best its business was being neglected in favor of others, even when it had no reason to suspect that the house was playing off one client against another to its own advantage, forcing prices down to buy for its own account and resell later at a profit.[14]

As a result, the majority of southern mills used a substantial part of their profits during and immediately after World War II to build up sufficient operating capital to free them from financial dependence upon commission houses. Many of them went even further and set up their own selling houses—so many of them, in fact, that a number of commission houses bought mills of their own in order to stay in business. In other cases, mills bought controlling interests in their selling houses.

This integration of sales and production has had the effect of increasing even more the competitive nature of the market since it increased the number of sellers. It also resulted in more aggressive marketing. The mill-owned selling house does not sit and wait for orders when business is slow; it gets out on the road and promotes them. The commission houses, to retain the accounts they have, have followed suit. As a corollary, the past several years have seen aggressive publicity campaigns, carried on by individual firms and on a collective basis through trade associations, to increase the consumption of cotton in every conceivable area.

Impact of Economic Factors Upon Industrial Relations.—As the classic economists predicted would happen in such a case, the profits of the cotton textile industry "have tended to a minimum." With higher labor costs relative to value added by manufacture, and lower profits than any other major industry, it is in no position to buy labor peace. By the same token, labor productivity is of more consequence to it than to any other major industry.

Because of its highly competitive nature, wage rates must be fairly

14. See Broadus Mitchell, *Rise of the Cotton Mills in the South* (Baltimore: The Johns Hopkins Press, 1921), pp. 250-55, for a discussion of the relationship between the mills and their selling houses. See also Murchison, *op. cit.,* pp. 63-66.

uniform throughout any competitive area within the industry. Neither labor peace nor a superior competitive position can be long maintained by the individual firm through manipulation of its wage rates. If they are set significantly above the "going rate," the firm soon prices itself out of the market. If set significantly below, it finds itself unable to attract and hold a work force capable of achieving competitive standards. Thus the individual firm finds a primarily economic approach to the solution of its labor problems impracticable. Wage levels are set by factors for the most part outside its control. It must depend on socio-psychological factors, over which it has some measure of influence, to call out the kind of attitudes within the people in its work force that will insure the degree of co-operation necessary between themselves and with management necessary for high productivity and low unit cost.

THE PIEDMONT INDUSTRY COMES OF AGE

After this brief survey of certain characteristics inherent in the manufacture and marketing of cotton textiles that are significant to our understanding of it, we return to the story of the emerging Piedmont textile industry.

It would be difficult to say when the Cotton Mill Campaign ended. Its greatest intensity in terms of exhortation and appeal was during the early years of the 1880's; but as we might expect with a movement of this sort, there was a lag between the original impetus and its realization in the concrete evidence of textile plants. The spectacular increases in spindleage were to continue during the decades of 1890 and 1900; and the momentum that was achieved had not been spent by the time we entered World War I. There would, indeed, continue to be an increase in the number of spindles in place in the four Piedmont states of North and South Carolina, Georgia, and Alabama until 1934; but we cannot attribute the latter part of this growth to the same factors that lay behind that part of it arising out of the Cotton Mill Campaign.

In terms of the continuity of the impetus arising during the 1880's, we might define the first phase of the modern Piedmont cotton textile industry as coming to a close in 1923. During the previous year, in 1922, the Northeast would have reached its maximum figure of 18.9 million spindles in place. It would not be until 1925 that the Southeast would surpass it in active spindles, nor until 1926 that it would forge ahead in terms of spindles in place; but from 1923 on, an ever-increasing proportion of the growth in southeastern spindleage would represent northern rather than southern investment. Northern operators began thinking about the advantages of a southern location during the depression of 1920. They put the idea aside as business picked up during 1921 and 1922; but when profits in the textile industry dropped sharply in 1923 and did not recover, while other industries were enjoying the boom of the 1920's, the shift of emphasis to the Southeast began in earnest. This invasion of the South in strength by the northern manufacturers, plus certain changes that were taking place in the southern industry itself, can be thought of as setting off another phase of the industry that is still working itself out.

We shall think of the period from 1890 to 1923, then, as being the years of expansion of the Piedmont industry along the lines laid down by the Cotton Mill Campaign. It continued to be an indigenous industry, along regional lines; there was no important contribution to the effort from outside the Piedmont. Even as late as 1931 a study by Lemert would show only 12 per cent of the spindles and 15 per cent of the looms in North and South Carolina, Georgia, and Alabama to be northern owned.[15]

Beginning in the 1890's there was less deliberate community effort in the building of mills and more that was on the face of it individual in its nature—but by this time the pattern had been established, and individually built mills were no less a part of their communities than were those that had been erected as the result of the work of groups of public spirited citizens. The money that mills already established were bringing into the Piedmont made it easier to raise capital for later mills; but it was still local capital in good part, supplemented as it had been in the past by assistance from machinery manufacturers and commission houses. Perhaps the main difference, in addition to the greater availability of capital, was the fact that the mills had demonstrated themselves as practical ventures. It no longer required the combined efforts of the most influential and respected members of a community, appealing for funds on much the same basis that might now be used to seek support for a new community hospital, to put across the idea that

15. Ben F. Lemert, *The Cotton Textile Industry of the Southern Appalachian Piedmont* (Chapel Hill: The University of North Carolina Press, 1933), p. 155.

a mill would be a good thing for all concerned. Its value to the community had become an accepted fact.

The relationship of the mill to the community had become established. Even though the prime impetus behind its erection might now be the expectation of profit on the part of those who promoted it—profit, that is, from the sale of the product of the mill—the promoters operated within the framework of expectations of the community. They received community support, both financially and morally, because it was assumed that the mill would be operated as an integral part of the community. The textile mill had become an institution of the Piedmont.[16] There was an institutionally defined role that it was expected to play in the community. So long as that role was satisfactorily discharged, the community was quite happy to let individuals assume the worry and trouble of building and operating the mill, and it was not particularly envious of the profits that accrued to them from its operation. Since a figure in the neighborhood of 50 per cent of the value added by manufacture was immediately paid out in wages by the mill, the community rather than the investors was still getting the lion's share of the money that the mill was bringing into the region.

While the manufacture was a touch and go matter, a major part of the energies of the people had been devoted to the task of getting it under way; but now that the issue was no longer in doubt, they passed the stewardship of it over to those who were willing to compete for it within the pattern of free enterprise and centered their energies once more upon their own personal problems connected with being butchers and bakers and doctors and lawyers. But though title to, and direction of, particular mills became concentrated in the hands of small groups, families or individuals, *title to and control of the institution of the manufacture of cotton textiles as a way of life for the Piedmont was retained by the folk*. It was woven into the folkways and answerable to the mores, a part of the social fabric of the region. It operated within the constraints of a folk society.

Between 1890 and 1900 spindleage in the four principle Piedmont states increased at the rate of almost 20 per cent per year. During the next decade, the rate of growth slowed down to an average of ap-

16. See Everett Cherrington Hughes' section on "Institutions" in *New Outlines of the Principles of Sociology*, pp. 225-80, for an excellent discussion of the development and role of an institution, and its relation to the community.

proximately 16 per cent per year. Between 1910 and 1920, there was an average growth of not quite 4 per cent per year. The combined increase for the four states brought their total spindleage from 1,200,000 in 1890 to 14,600,000 in 1923, better than a twelve-fold growth.

During this same period the nation as a whole had increased its spindleage from 14,400,000 to 37,400,000; a growth of 160 per cent over the 1890 figure—but a good share of this growth had taken place in the Piedmont. The nation *without* the four Piedmont states showed only a 70 per cent increase over 1890. The Southeast, *not including* the four Piedmont states, had increased its spindleage from 800,000 to 1,900,000, or by 140 per cent during the period—but the Piedmont states, on a percentage-wise basis, had increased by 1120 per cent over the 1890 figure!

The spindleage in the four Piedmont states grew better than seven times as fast as it did in the nation between 1890 and 1923. The figures usually quoted contrast spindleage in the cotton-growing states with those in the nation as a whole or in the Northeast. On this basis we find that the Southeast, between 1860 and 1923, had increased its share of national spindleage from 6 per cent to 44 per cent. What is often overlooked, however, is that there was a definite concentration of spindleage *within* the Southeast itself. In 1860, the four Piedmont states had contained 60 per cent of the total southeastern spindleage. Hardest hit by the devastation of war, they dropped to only 48 per cent of the southeastern total in 1870—but by 1923, 88 per cent of all the cotton system spindles in the Southeast were located in North and South Carolina, Georgia, and Alabama. In these states, it was located almost entirely within their Piedmont sections. No figures are readily available showing the spindleage distribution on a year-by-year basis as between the Piedmont and Coastal Plain areas of these four states; but computations by the writer for the year 1952, based on information in Davison's *Textile Blue Book,* showed the Georgian Piedmont to contain 95.2 per cent of the state's total spindleage. The ratio of highland to lowland spindles in the other three states is likely to be greater rather than less than this figure.

The size of the Piedmont mills increased between 1890 and 1923. The *United States Census of Manufactures* for 1927 reported the average spindleage per mill for North and South Carolina and Georgia to be 15,193 in 1899. By 1919 it had grown to 28,833, and by 1927 it had reached 29,598. A tendency toward leveling off in the size of the mills may be noted here. By contrast, the same source reports the New England mills to have averaged 50,374 spindles in 1899, 69,286 in 1919, and 80,008 in 1927.

Certain other significant differences between the northern and the Piedmont mills that appeared between 1890 and 1923, in addition to the smaller size of the latter, can be noted. The Piedmont mills were new. They represented the latest developments in mill machinery, which at the turn of the century were of rather an important nature. After 1895 the greater share of the southern mills were equipped with the Northrup automatic loom which reduced labor costs in weaving considerably, while the New England mills hesitated to scrap old-style looms that were still in good working order. Of approximately 322,000 looms that were added to the national industry between 1900 and 1914, the South took 153,000 and New England only 81,000. In 1919, according to *Senate Document Number 126*,[17] 71.5 per cent of the plain looms in the South were automatic, but only 38.5 per cent of those in the New England states. By 1927 New England had modernized to the extent that 56.8 per cent of its plain looms were automatic— but the South had in the meantime increased its proportion to 88 per cent. The southern mills, in addition, were all equipped with the labor-saving ring spindles that could be tended by women; whereas many of the New England mills still cling to the mule spinning frames that unquestionably turned out a finer product but which required more highly skilled operators, could not be easily tended by women, and produced much less yarn per hour of operation.

Thus the Piedmont, which in 1890 had only 8.3 per cent of the productive capacity of the nation in cotton textiles, by 1923 had more than quadrupled its share, possessing at that time 39 per cent of the nation's spindleage. Not only were its factories newer than those in the Northeast, but they were filled with machinery that permitted more economical operation. The greater share of southern production was still in coarse and medium count yarns and fabrics; but its production of the former had reached the point that the Northeast was no longer attempting to compete with it in this area. New England mills had virtually ceded the production of coarse fabrics to southern mills

17. Cabinet Committee, *Cotton Textile Industry,* 74th Congress, 1st Session, Senate, Document No. 126, Washington, 1935.

and were concentrating on medium and fine count goods. The Piedmont had, in addition, outdistanced New England in the production of sheeting, shirting, ducks, and drills by 1900. By 1905 it led in ticks, denims, and stripes as well; and by 1919 it also led in the important field of print cloth.

North and South

The indigenous nature of the Piedmont cotton textile industry should be apparent by now. It was not, as so many people unfamiliar with its history are inclined to believe, a creature of northern capitalists taking advantage of cheap labor. By 1923 the Piedmont, under its own power and out of its own resources, had built an industrial empire scattered throughout the length and breadth of its rolling countryside that was already a powerful competitive threat to the far more industrially sophisticated Northeast. It was so powerful a threat, indeed, that by 1923 many northern firms were beginning to wonder if it would not be the better part of wisdom to identify themselves with the Piedmont rather than attempt to compete with it. Yet we must caution that there was not, as is generally supposed, a wholesale migration of productive facilities in cotton textiles to the South.

"The flight of the spindles South" is a phrase that has a poetic ring to it; but it contains a great deal of poetic license as well. It represents neither the whole truth nor a substantial portion of it. There was definitely after 1923 a shift of emphasis in cotton textile manufacturing from New England to the Piedmont; but it was not completely or even primarily a migration of existing facilities from one region to another. There were a number of factors involved. (1) There was to begin with a continuing expansion of southern mills on a regional basis. The indigenous movement had not reached its zenith by any means. (2) There were many northern mills liquidated that did not resume the manufacture of cotton textiles anywhere. (3) There were northern interests, very often industrial users or merchandisers of cotton textiles that built or purchased southern mills as their first venture into textile production. (4) There were New England interests that maintained their existing northern mills in operation but that expanded their facilities by purchase or by building in the Piedmont. (5) There were northern companies that sold their northern properties, lock, stock and barrel, for whatever they would bring (very often scrapping antiquated productive machinery) and built completely new plants in the Southeast. (6) There were, finally—and these were in a minority—companies that disposed of their northern real property and moved their capital equipment bodily to new locations in the Piedmont.

How literally untrue the phrase "flight of the spindles south" actually is can be appreciated by the following statistical picture. The high point of New England spindleage was reached in 1922 when it possessed a total of 18,900,000. In that same year, there were already a total of 16,500,000 spindles in the cotton-growing states. The latter achieved their maximum spindleage in 1934, with 19,100,000 spindles, an increase over the 1923 figure of only 2,800,000 spindles—yet during the same period the New England states had lost 9,200,000 spindles. By 1952, the spindleage in the cotton-growing states had dropped from its 1934 high to exceed the 1923 figure by only 2,400,000 spindles, yet between 1923 and 1952 the New England states had lost a grand total of 14,900,000 spindles (with 27.5 per cent of those still remaining standing idle). Thus, during the twenty-eight-year period, there were 12,500,000 New England spindles permanently withdrawn from production without a corresponding replacement in the Southeast.

What was happening was regional competition in terms of production costs, largely by means of savings effectuated through greater production per spindle. To put it another way, there was a reduction in the amount of capital equipment necessary to produce a given volume of goods and thus a reduction in the amount of fixed charges that had to be paid out for each unit of production. In 1951, for example, the nation consumed 81 per cent more raw cotton than it had on the average between 1921 and 1925; and yet it had only 63 per cent as many active spindles as it had had on the average during the earlier period. This does not take into account the considerable production of synthetic fabrics that took place on cotton system spindles and looms in 1951 that did not enter into the earlier picture.

Between 1923 and 1952, North and South Carolina, Georgia, and Alabama increased their combined spindleage total from 14,650,000 to 17,150,000, or by 17.5 per cent over the 1923 figure. In the meantime, the balance of the South had dropped from 1,900,000 to 1,700,000 spindles for a loss of 10.6 per cent under the 1923 figure. The concentration of southern mills in the Piedmont was increasing. In 1923 the four Piedmont states had possessed 88 per cent of the total spindle-age in the cotton-growing states. By 1952, the ratio had grown to 91 per cent. In our figures so far, we have been leaving one Piedmont state out of the picture—Virginia, which possesses 650,000 spindles in its southern highland section. Adding these to our previous total, we find 94 per cent of the southern spindleage concentrated in the southeastern Appalachian Piedmont region. If we add Tennessee's 530,000 spindles, we find 97.3 per cent of the southern capacity for cotton textile production located in the interior highlands of the Southeast—almost 75 per cent of the nation's total capacity.

There was not any great increase in the total number of southeastern cotton textile mills after 1923. According to figures furnished by W. H. Simpson in his *Southern Textile Communities,* the four princi-ple Piedmont states had 752 mills in 1923.[18] In 1935, at the peak of southern spindleage, they had dropped back to 728 mills. By 1939, they had increased the total to 762—only ten more than in 1923. This does not mean that there was no mill building going on. It does mean that between 1923 and 1935, existing mills were liquidating or combin-ing a little faster than new ones were being built. It also means that a considerable amount of the growth of southern spindleage came about as the result of the expansion of existing establishments. Finally, it means that a considerable proportion of the northern investment that took place in southern mill properties after 1923 took the form of pur-chase of existing plants rather than the construction of new facilities.

Inter-Regional Competition

We cannot understand the expansion and increasing importance of the cotton textile industry in the Piedmont after 1923 unless we con-sider it in conjunction with what was happening in the North. What we have to investigate is why, in a competitive battle between the two regions, one of them lost out.

The North-South Wage Differential.—This is the factor quite com-monly offered in complete explanation of the shift in emphasis between the two regions. There is no question but that it was not only im-portant but necessary to the success of the early industry.

18. W. H. Simpson, *Southern Textile Communities* (Charlotte, N. C.: American Cot-ton Manufacturer's Association, 1948.) Figures quoted were compiled from data on pp. 19-23.

We should note to begin with that the differential was not, strictly speaking, a North-South differential. It was an urban-rural differential, arising from the fact that the northern industry was largely located in urbanized areas after 1880 while the southern industry was and continued to be largely rural. The low return from labor applied to the land in the Piedmont made industrial employment attractive at a wage level considerably lower than in the North; and the low standard of living—with its low protein, high carbohydrate diet, for example—to which the southern mill worker had been forced to accustom himself while attempting to make a go of it as a renter, and to which he tended to cling as a matter of custom after coming to the mill, had the effect of stretching his budget to the point that his low cash income seemed quite adequate to him. Mill-subsidized housing also had the effect of stretching his income; in general he enjoyed better housing for less money than did the northern worker.

It is doubtful that the Piedmont industry could either have got started in the first place or have grown as it did had not the differential existed. The infant northern industry had possessed the protection of an extremely high tariff to help it capture the home market. The beginning southern industry had no such protection. Its competition was at home, rather than from abroad, and the tariff was of no assistance. There were only two possibilities open to it for gaining a foothold in the national market—lower production costs and regional subsidies. The latter were afforded to begin with in an informal way by the very nature of the financing of the mills, and in a more formal fashion by advantages granted by local government units. Lower production costs were gained partially by the use of more efficient machinery (though not to the extent that they might have been; for until the mid-1920's the better southern equipment was offset con siderably by lower southern work loads). Partially it was gained by taking advantage of the competitive bidding for jobs among the members of the Piedmont labor force that resulted in a low wage level.

Wages merely low enough to obtain a competitive advantage in the national market were still not low enough for the needs of the infant Piedmont industry however, unless it was to be content with production and employment levels possible through the mills that could be built with the savings already available in the region in the late 1870's and 1880's. The first spurt of mill building had scraped the bot-

tom of the barrel of southern capital. If there was to be any more for
the building of more mills, it had to be created; and the mills were the
only agencies capable of creating it. The mills in existence had to build
the mills that were to come. They had to create new savings out of
which new capital investment might be made. Such savings could be
accumulated only if a substantial portion of the earnings of the mills
were diverted into the hands of people who were not likely to spend
them for consumer goods—and these people were not the mill workers;
they were still living too close to the subsistence level. High profits
and high dividends were necessary to provide a concentration of capital
that would be re-invested in production goods.

The net result of this early wage policy (arrived at in a completely
impersonal fashion and transcending the decisions of any individuals
or groups of individuals) was that though wage levels remained low,
employment mounted rapidly. Those people already employed in the
mills got less than they might have in order that more people in the
future might get at least as much. Rather than resulting in an elite
of textile workers, with high wages for a select few, the operation of
the system had the effect of sharing the increasing income of the region
among greater and greater numbers. The southern mill operative,
through his willingness to accept a wage that was lower than that
paid for comparable work in the North, was contributing his bit to
the economic and social regeneration of the Piedmont. Whether or
not he was aware of it is a question—Cash suggests that he was at
least intuitively so[19]—yet here we see another justification for the feeling still prevalent in the Piedmont that the mills belong to the people,
no matter what the corporation secretary's books may say. It was not
only the man who had money to invest who helped build the industry.
It was as well the men and women who worked in the mills, who
through their labor added to the store of southern capital. We can, if
we like, think of the operatives of these early mills as privates in an
army fighting the spectre of social and economic disaster. Like privates
in any army, they got little of the glory; but without them the whole
story would have been like the story of any war that was fought only
with commissioned officers.

The wage differential has steadily diminished since those early
days, until there is at present some basis for arguing that it is no longer

19. W. J. Cash, *Mind of the South* (New York: Alfred A. Knopf, 1941), p. 218.

significant.[20] Actually it became less and less important in the competitive picture after 1923. By and large, northern producers of fine
and high-count medium goods were competing with northern producers of fine and high-count medium goods, and southern producers
of coarse and medium goods were competing with southern producers
of coarse and medium goods. There was increasingly more intra-
regional and increasingly less inter-regional competition as time went
on, for any particular order. Northern producers of higher-count
medium fabrics who moved south or expanded their southern operations were not in general trying to meet southern competition; they
were trying to gain a competitive advantage over other producers in
their own region.

It was during the early years of the southern industry, when it was
engaging almost completely in inter-regional competition, that the
wage differential had a telling effect. Wages paid southern workers
today are not established with an eye to obtaining a competitive advantage over the North. They are set on the basis of what the rest of
the southern industry is paying. The wage rate for the total southern industry is largely a function of the rapidity with which the national
market will absorb cotton textile production at a specified unit price
and of the productive efficiency of the southern industry. It has been
this latter characteristic that has enabled Piedmont manufacturers to
maintain high wage rates and a high level of employment as well during the recessions that have followed World War II.

The Static Nature of the Northern Industry.—Highly significant
as a factor contributing to the decline of the northern mills was the
static nature of their management, which seems to have arisen out of
an implicit assumption on their part that they were dealing with an
unchanging world. To use a current slang expression, an hereditary
ownership appeared to feel that it "had it made"—that managerial
technics and industrial practices developed during the early days of

20. This argument is usually advanced by southern mill owners. They have
recently been backed up, however, from an unexpected quarter. As this is being
written, northern mill owners are requesting that the union agree to a cut amounting to
about ten cents an hour to enable them to meet southern competition. The following
is from the *Atlanta Journal* for April 15, 1955. "In a letter to management negotiators
Thursday, Emil Rieve, TWUA general president, said any North-South differential is
'not enough to affect your ability to compete.'" A ten-cent cut in the present (April,
1955) northern rate would virtually eliminate the differential for many jobs, particularly in the middle range.

the industry were completely adequate for all future occasions, to be
guarded as sacred by boards of directors insulated from the realities of
manufacture by hired executives with little authority for independent
decision. Wolfbein, in his excellent study of *The Decline of a Cotton
Textile City,* quotes Sanford and Kelly (a New Bedford financial
house that issued a yearly review of the state of the textile industry):
in 1927, "inefficiency of management in New England escapes un-
punished for . . . long periods, while capital and labor seek more
healthy conditions in other districts"; in 1930, "some of the exceedingly
large losses that have been experienced, particularly in the last year
or so, would have been prevented by an earlier change either of methods
or of management"; in 1931, "Before the textile business is entirely
restored to a profit basis, many who have never learned the lesson will
have to be convinced that in the operation of the industry many inefficient human elements will have to be removed and selection made
by men of trained judgment."[21]

"The New England mills had long traditions of operation and
family management which did not yield their places easily," says
Lahne in the *Cotton Mill Worker.* "Perhaps as a whole the early
Southern mill managers were behind their New England rivals in their
grasp of technical detail, but they were ahead in initiative and ambitious drive, and their technical excellence came later or was bought
in the market."[22] And Michl remarks in *The Textile Industries:*

The rapid growth of the South disturbed the complacency of the North
but it satisfied itself with the thought that, after all, the South would never
be able to manufacture any but the coarsest of materials and the manufacture of quality yarns and cloth, which brought the highest prices, would
remain a Northern monopoly. The growth in the market for cotton textiles
of all types made the industry prosperous and from a profit standpoint the
North did not feel any adverse effects from the Southern development.[23]

The static nature of the management of individual mills in the
North was buttressed by the high degree of inter-relationship between

21. Seymour Louis Wolfbein, *The Decline of a Cotton Textile City* (New York:
Columbia University Press, 1944), p. 97. This excellent study deals with the New
Bedford industry; but many of its conclusions can be generalized to other New England
centers of textile manufacture.

22. Herbert J. Lahne, *The Cotton Mill Worker* (New York: Farrar and Rinehart, Inc.,
1944), p. 98.

23. H. E. Michl, *The Textile Industries* (Washington, D. C.: The Textile Foundation,
1938), pp. 142-43.

northern firms brought about by interlocking directorates. An excellent analysis of this situation as it existed in the New Bedford area has been made by Wolfbein. As he points out, even those mill executives who were themselves in favor of modernization of plant and methods found themselves bound to the static pattern of the region by their boards of directors.

Finally, the very pattern of investment in the northern mills stifled many attempts that were made toward modernization. The New England industry was built from the surplus funds of wealthy individuals who were looking for maximization of personal income through ownership of textile stocks. These absentee owners knew nothing of the problems of the textile industry. They exerted constant pressure on boards of directors to translate profits directly into dividends, and they showed little sympathy toward any proposal to divert a part of earnings into plant modernization or expansion—or even toward proposals to obtain outside capital for such ventures by the sale of additional stock in the company. Southern mill managements, on the other hand, had set the pattern of expansion and modernization out of profits and equity capital from the very first; and the practice continued to be typical of the southern industry.

As a consequence, a considerable part of the northern industry found itself, when the pinch came after 1923, with an antiquated plant that was not up to meeting the demands of a mature market. *Senate Document 126* reports that "Obsolescence, therefore, appears to have been an important factor in the trouble of the New England cotton textile industries during the past thirty years and has hastened the transfer to the South." To make matters worse, the possibility of technological obsolescence had apparently been so little counted on by many northern managements that they found themselves with no depreciation reserves that could be called upon. As the treasurer of a New Bedford company explained to H. J. Lahne, "When we were making money and could have put in new equipment, we didn't think it was necessary. Now that we're losing money and need new machinery to keep going, we just haven't got the price."[24]

Thus an important part of the decline of the New England mills can be traced to the inadequate imagery of their managements as to the nature of the world in which they were operating. An absentee

24. Lahne, *op. cit.,* p. 98.

ownership that clung to the right to make major decisions failed to recognize the challenge of southern competition until it was too late to do anything about it. It overestimated its own ability and underestimated that of the new region that was entering the cotton textile market.

Industrial Relations in the Northern Industry.—Northern managements had in general an equally inadequate imagery of the people who manned their mills. Labor was a commodity to be purchased in the cheapest market—if Irish immigrants would work for less than the New England farm girls were beginning to ask, hire them; if the French-Canadians would work for what the Irish had become dissatisfied with, replace the Irish; if south Europeans were willing to work for a wage that had become unattractive to the French-Canadians, then man the mills with them. As each immigrant group became Americanized it tended to move into new industries and occupational groups which paid more and had a higher social standing within their community. The difficulty did not arise out of the fact that this procession of nationalities through the mills represented progressively diminishing quality in the work force, for these people were all potentially good workers. It arose out of managerial attitudes based upon the naïve concept of the commodity theory of labor. Managerial policies and practices, framed in accordance with this idea that the worker was merely a replaceable adjunct of the machine and that the best labor was the cheapest labor, could result in nothing but anxiety and frustration so far as the work force was concerned.[25]

The possibility of working out any degree of understanding between management and labor in the northern industry was further complicated by difficulties in communication, not only verbally but with regard to basic frames of reference. These foreign people who began to enter the New England mills after 1840 oriented their lives against different backgrounds of custom and tradition. Though they were grounded in the Christian ethic, their secondary value systems were not those of their Yankee managers. Misunderstandings arose constantly, resentments accumulated, and distrust mounted to the point that face-to-face contacts between workers and managerial people

25. See Lahne, *op. cit.*, pp. 71-76, for a more detailed description of this ethnic procession through the northern mills and of the generally prevailing managerial attitude toward labor. See Wolfbein, *op. cit.*, 76-79, for a description of the New Bedford work force in the early 1940's.

increased tensions rather than lessened them. As a consequence, work forces of New England mills were in no mood to co-operate with their managements during the 1920's when survival of the enterprises for which they worked depended upon such co-operation; and their managements, finally realizing the great importance of worker attitudes as a factor in production, found themselves unable to change with sufficient rapidity the conditions that had resulted from their own inattention to the human factor for almost a century.

Labor unions have often been blamed for the difficulties that northern textile managements encountered when they attempted to enlist the support of their workers; but union organization was no more a basic cause of the northern trouble than was obsolescence. Just as the latter grew out of failure to appreciate the realities of the industry's economic position, so was union organization an inevitable consequence of labor policies that created a situation in which the worker felt himself to be at the mercy of arbitrary forces. Employee relations have improved greatly in the northern industry in recent years, but like the belated program of modernization, the improvement came too late to be of help to the bulk of the industry.

Community Relations of the Northern Industry.—Only in its very beginning does there seem to have been anything in the Northeast approaching the relationship between the mills and their communities that was and is still typical in the Piedmont. The New England mills were private ventures from the first. They were economic ventures pure and simple, rather than the culmination of a social movement as was the case for the southeastern mills. During their early years their builders were able to point to the fact that they provided opportunities for employment for local people; but after 1840 there was not even this integrative feature.

The New England mills either built their own communities, as they sought out water-power sites away from established centers of population, or they were imposed upon communities already existing. In either case they were established on the periphery of, rather than integrated into, the regional society. There was no sense of "ownership" of the mills except among the very few people who held their stock certificates. To the majority of the people, the mills were interlopers. Their presence was more destructive than constructive; for whatever advantages they might bring in the way of increased payrolls were offset by the problems created by the descent of a horde of immigrant workers upon a folk society unprepared to cope with them. The result was often the destruction of the folk society of the community or its withdrawal into a protective shell of suspicion and distrust that effectively halted its spiritual and moral growth.

Thus the mills could count on little support from the communities in which they were located. It was quite the other way around in too many cases. They were regarded as fair game for excessive taxation, sufficient to lower tax rates respectably for "bona fide" community residents. When unemployment became a problem the mills were regarded as responsible for it. They had brought the now unemployed workers to the community in the first place, and there were further tax increases at a time when the mills could least afford them. *Senate Document 126,* comparing the "Ratio of Taxes Other Than Income Taxes to Gross Sales of Cotton Textile Corporations, 1926-1933," states that in 1926 the average ratio for Massachusetts was better than twice that for the South. Corporations having mills both in the North and South reported to the writer that until into the 1930's they could count on state and local taxes on their northern textile properties amounting to three or four times as much as on their southern branches.

Relief from this burden of taxation came to the Massachusetts mills in the mid-1930's when the state, alarmed over the decline in textile spindleage, forbade local governments to tax the cotton textile industry at all and substituted a substantially lower state tax. But as Wolfbein remarks, "Such a reduction in the tax costs of the mills has without doubt played an important part in keeping them in the state. It has not, however, nullified the effects of the favorable tax differential which the South possessed in the intervening 50 years."[26]

In addition to higher taxes, a somewhat more stringent statutory regulation of labor relations weakened the competitive position of the northern industry. Those regarding child labor were of no importance competitively since there was no employment of children in southern mills after 1920, and their employment (though southern operators did not then so regard it) was an economic liability before that date. Part of the northern burden was the requirement for higher benefits under workmen's compensation laws and later with regard to unemployment benefits. They were justified partly on the basis of higher

26. Wolfbein, *op. cit.,* p. 137.

living costs and partly by the fact that the unemployed and the unemployable in northern communities could seldom look anywhere except to state or local government for assistance. Northern disadvantages in this respect were at least partly offset, however, by the operation of the Piedmont folkways as they related to industrial relations. The southern mill operator might not pay as high workmen's compensation benefits, but, on the other hand, the community expected him to make a job for the employee who had suffered a crippling disability in the mill if there was any reasonable possibility that it could be done.

Perhaps the most restrictive aspect of northern labor legislation, so far as it affected the competitive position of northern firms, had to do with the employment of women in industry. It was Massachusetts' famous "six-to-six" law—thus affecting the most important part of the northern industry—that created the difficulty.[27] Women were forbidden to work in the mills before six in the morning or after six in the evening, which effectively prevented them from being employed on any but the day shift. Approximately 40 per cent of the work force of a typical mill is made up of women, doing work that pays from 5 to 15 per cent less than jobs that are traditionally men's work. Thus for their second and third shifts, the Massachusetts mills had to pay a premium for approximately 40 per cent of their help. This came close to wiping out the savings that were effected by multiple-shift operation. It was, in addition, difficult to get male labor that would accept permanent second or third shift employment. In 1933 the Massachusetts legislature, recognizing the serious nature of the restriction they had placed on their textile plants, suspended the six-to-six law and permitted the employment of women in the mills between six in the morning and ten at night, which enabled them to work on two eight-hour shifts; but, by 1933 Massachusetts had lost better than 5,500,000 of the 11,800,000 spindles it had had in 1924. Once more the modification of circumstances that might have assisted the northern industry in its fight for survival came too late.

Other Factors Contributing to the Decline of the Northern Industry. —Other items contributed to the unsatisfactory competitive position of the northern industry. There was the matter of building costs, for example. Both materials and labor for building cost less in the Pied-

27. *Ibid.*, p. 81.

mont, and, a not unimportant factor, it could be carried on twelve months out of the year. The southern plants required less coal for heating purposes, and their proximity to the coal fields of Alabama and West Virginia meant that they should have got it for two or three dollars less per ton. Actually this has not been the case until recently. Through rigging of freight rates, not only West Virginia coal but Texas cotton could be set down at mill docks in Fall River for less than it could be delivered to mills in Atlanta—this in addition to a differential freight rate on finished textiles that discriminated against southern mills.

The southern mills enjoyed a particular advantage in the matter of electrical power. Until in the 1930's, the private power interests of the Piedmont were developing its power resources faster than the capacity of the region to absorb their output; and so the southern mills enjoyed a buyer's market for electrical power. Not only were southern rates for industrial power lower on the average in the Piedmont than they were in New England, but the Piedmont rate structure itself put the small industrial consumer at less of a disadvantage, compared with the large consumer, than was the case in the North.[28]

Summary of Factors Leading to the Decline of the Northern Industry.—There is some justification for the speculation that had other factors been satisfactory, a substantial portion of the New England industry might have held its own despite the wage differential. Had its productive equipment been kept modern; had its accounting practices been handled in such a way that funds were available for its replacement; had it had community support; had it borne less of the total burden of taxation in the northeast; had its labor relations been satisfactory; had it been less restricted by government direction as to how it was to employ its labor force—had all these been true, the northern industry might have been able to absorb certain high cost factors such as labor, fuel, and power and still survive. This is only speculation: a full-scale economic analysis would be required to prove or disprove it, but the possibility that the seeds of the decline of the New England industry were sown and nurtured in the northeast rather than in the southeast is sufficiently great to warrant the Piedmont industry's taking the total picture to heart as an object lesson.

In almost every thoughtful analysis of what happened, the final

28. Lemert, *op. cit.*, pp. 101-3.

conclusion is that the major factor in explaining the decline of the northern industry is that of labor productivity. The National Planning Association's study *Why Industry Moves South* cites it as the principle cause, for example.[29]   A joint survey made by the National Electric Light Association and the Metropolitan Life Insurance Company in 1927 and cited by Wolfbein found that whether it was with regard to the relocation of a firm, the setting up of a branch, or the setting up of a new local plant, the nature of the labor supply was the matter of most importance in arriving at a decision.[30]   The NPA study also indicates that the various inducements offered by southern communities to northern firms in the way of subsidies, tax concessions, and free buildings have actually had very little to do with the relocation of industry. Most northern firms, coming into a southern town, have preferred to do so with no strings attached.

From the standpoint of our own study, perhaps the most important conclusion to be reached from this brief survey of the competition between the Piedmont and New England is that there were sufficient other factors to insure the eventual success of the Piedmont as to make exploitation of its labor unnecessary from a logical standpoint. Once the battle was joined, there could be little doubt as to the outcome; the Piedmont had every advantage on its side except experience and haulage costs—and the New England mills apparently failed to profit by their advantages even in these respects.

THE PRESENT SITUATION IN THE PIEDMONT

Two trends have been of particular interest in the Piedmont cotton textile industry since the close of World War II—integration and modernization. The Piedmont plants got under way with their program of modernization of facilities as soon as there was steel available for it. As early as 1947, according to the *Census of Manufactures* for that year, the 409 southern establishments making broad woven fabrics expended a total of $68,000,000 for new plant and equipment, an average of better that $165,000 per establishment. In the same year, the 193 northern establishments in the same line of manufacture expended an average of only $56,000 per plant. This was only the begin-

29. Committee of the South, *Report No. 3* (Washington, D. C.: National Planning Association, 1949).
30. Wolfbein, *op. cit.,* p. 79.

ning, for steel was still scarce in 1947. Modernization continued at an
increased rather than a lessened pace; and the economies in manufacture that it facilitated account in good part for the ability of the southern mills to weather the recessions of 1949 and 1951 without large
scale lay-offs or wage cuts. During a series of mill visits during 1951
and 1952 that encompassed better than two-thirds of the cotton-system
spindleage in Georgia and representative samples of that in Alabama
and South Carolina, the writer found that the majority of the plants
visited had either completed or were engaged in major programs of
modernization. In a few cases such programs included an increase in
plant capacity; but generally they were looking toward increased
efficiency of operation through the use of higher speeds, elimination of
intermediate operations, and more completely automatic equipment.
From an industrial relations standpoint it was interesting to note that
whatever else they might include, the modernization programs were
invariably concerned with an improvement in working conditions in
the mill—"ballroom" floors (hardwood floors sanded and shellacked at
frequent intervals to retain the natural wood tone), central air-changing
and air-conditioning, color schemes in the work rooms planned for
their psychological effect, improved illumination, new rest-room facilities, new cafeterias, street-improvement programs, and new school
facilities in mill villages.

The trend toward integration has resulted more from an attempt
to strengthen companies to the point that they can withstand the
rigours of the competitive market, than from any attempt to capture
control of it. A moderately large company operating several establishments has two anchors to the leeward during a period of slow demand
in the market: it can diversify its production among several lines, not
all of which are likely to be equally hard hit at the same time; and it,
of course, has the advantage of somewhat greater financial resources.
This horizontal type of integration has been most common. There has
also been some vertical integration, in which an attempt is made to
process the cotton from the bale to the consumer; but this has proceeded
much more slowly, for it carries the manufacturer into the dangerous
style market where the hard-won gains of efficient operation can be
completely wiped out by a wrong guess as to what color will be "good"
next year. In general, these completely integrated firms have been put

together in a "backward" fashion by converters or selling houses who were already in the style market.

We have already noted one other type of integration that has been widely practiced—that of manufacturing and selling. Before World War II, the United States Census of Business for 1940 reports, only 9.5 per cent of the nation's cotton cloth was sold through manufacturer-owned outlets. In February of 1946 Claudius Murchison reported in the *Daily News Record* that 75 per cent of the post-war product was being sold by the people who made it.

Barkin's analysis of the degree of concentration of ownership in the southern textile industry in 1948, on the basis of which he predicted a trend toward control of production, quite as logically points to the opposite conclusion.[31] There were 42 companies in the Southeast in 1948 who employed more than 3000 workers each. Between them they operated a total of 419 separate establishments (including finishing plants and textiles other than cotton). Yet these 42 companies employed only 58.1 per cent of the southern textile workers and accounted between them for only 50 per cent of the southern spindleage. With 50 per cent of the productive capacity remaining in the hands of a multitude of small producers, all of whom are able with good management to produce as economically as the large companies, there is very little opportunity for production control.

Nor could any of the 42 large companies be called industrial giants by modern standards. Only two of them employed more than 20,000 people. Twenty-nine of them employed less than 8,000 people, and the modal size was the 4,000-4,999 group, with 12 firms falling into this category. These companies are sufficiently strong financially, and sufficiently versatile from a production standpoint, to weather periods of depression and recession in the industry; but no one of them or possible combination of them is likely to influence the market with 50 per cent of the industry's productive capacity in the hands of people who will undersell them at the first attempt to capitalize on oligopolistic market control.

The extent of northern ownership of southern cotton textile spindleage has increased since 1930. The exact degree of northern ownership would require economic research beyond the scope of this essentially

31. Barkin, *op. cit.*

socio-psychological study; but Barkin's analysis of the 1948 situation gives us some hint as to the present state in this respect. Of the 42 companies employing more than 3,000 employees each in the South, 18 were northern owned and 24 were southern owned. Thus northern interests controlled 42.8 per cent of the large southern companies. Since 50 per cent of the southern spindleage remained in the hands of companies employing less than 3,000 people, and since these smaller companies represent a much higher proportion of local ownership, we might be justified in hazarding a guess that in the neighborhood of at least two-thirds of the southern spindleage was still southern owned in 1948.

"Family" ownership of mills is passing out of the picture in the South. In the opinion of several owner-executives with whom the writer has talked, it is not likely to be important after another generation. Not only are stockholdings split among the children in the family, but substantial amounts of stock must be placed on the market to meet inheritance taxes. There has been some experimentation with foundations of the type set up by the Ford family to enable it to retain control of the Ford Motor Company, but this does not appear to be a general practice—few of the family-owned companies are large enough to make it practicable, in any case. In general, it appears that ownership of southern mills is tending toward a pattern of wider distribution of ownership among individuals, at the same time that there is a tendency toward concentration of ownership by corporations.

One further bit of information available from Barkin's study has great significance for industrial relations. The southern mills have remained small, as employing and producing units, even though a number of them may be owned by one company. In 1948, the 42 leading companies had between them 419 mills, including finishing plants. Not including the finishing plants, these mills averaged 28,500 spindles each; and including the finishing plants, they averaged 735 employees each. Thus there has been no change in this important aspect of the pattern of textile production in the Piedmont. The typical textile mill in the region is still a relatively small establishment located in, or adjacent to, a small country town or a small city; and its work force continues to be sufficiently small to permit the possibility of a highly effective organization of its employees under the folkways rather than the massways. The small size of the producing unit does not by any means insure that this will be the case, but it does remove many of the difficulties that might otherwise stand in the way of such informal organization.

PART THREE

THE PATTERN OF THE RELATIONSHIP

CHAPTER V

The Developing Pattern of Industrial Relations

IN THIS CHAPTER we are concerned with how a rural people managed to solve the initial problems attendant upon an almost overnight transition into industry. First we need to know where they came from.

THE SOURCE OF THE WORK FORCE

The mills were built in the Piedmont, and the people who worked in them, with rare exception, came from the Piedmont farms. This is a simple fact, yet ignorance of it has created more misconceptions as to the nature of industrial relations in the industry than all other mistakes combined. "It will be seen that the people came to the mills first from districts immediately surrounding the plant," Mitchell tells us. "Wagons carrying the entire household goods of the new help formed the means of conveyance."[1] The writer has been told by their descendants of families too destitute, in those early days, to afford even a wagon for the move. What remained of their possessions worth saving were packed into a hogshead, through which a pole was thrust, and it was rolled along the road from the farm to the mill village.

The people came to the mills from their worn-out, rented farms. They came from the spectre of five-cent cotton and from fields hungry for expensive fertilizer. They came from tables set with pellagra-breeding fare. They came from a country-side wretched and terrifying in its poverty, in the desolation of its gutted red clay hills. They came poor to the point of desperation, ragged and gaunt, uneducated, uncouth and awkward away from the background of hills and fields; uneasy and suspicious, bewildered and bitter. Privation, anxiety, pain and disillusionment had burned away the facade of personality down to the skeletal framework of elemental vices and virtues.

1. Broadus Mitchell, *Rise of the Cotton Mills in the South* (Baltimore: Johns Hopkins Press, 1921), p. 186.

But they were not "poor white trash" though they were certainly poor white men and women. Recognition of this is vital to an understanding of the pattern of employee relations that developed. They were a people who had been crushed by war and reconstruction, not by the advancing plantation system or by the institution of slavery. They were people who had been left stranded by the partial collapse of a society; they were not outcasts from a flourishing and continuing social structure. They had been impoverished by cotton culture; but it had been cotton they had grown themselves and, to begin with, on their own land. They were not a people bereft of standards and values; they were, on the contrary, a people who had very little left of their heritage except its system of values. They clung to that system fiercely, hoping by means of it to build a bridge from the past into the future—they were searching for a future that would justify their retention of the democratic ideals of the Piedmont frontier; a future that would be meaningful in terms of the past, a future that would not deny all those concepts they had come to hold sacred.

These people who were coming into the mills in 1880 were the men and women and the sons and daughters of the men and women whose determined character had, collectively, supported the resistance of the Confederacy against crushing odds and past belief. They were not people who were likely to accept supinely and without question whatever the future might have in store for them. They did not come to the mills broken in defeat, abjectly surrendering to an unknown fate. They were fighting still—blindly and in bewilderment, but fighting— to maintain their self-respect, to keep an image of themselves in which they could believe and upon which they could depend when they could depend upon nothing else.

This was the labor supply of the Piedmont mills until 1900; a farm people using the mills for an avenue of escape from the land that had failed them and for a bridge into the future. A woman who had been president of a South Carolina mill built during the early years of the Cotton Mill Campaign gave Broadus Mitchell an account of the source of its labor supply:

The section was desperately poor. The village of Greensville would have been called in the foothills. Farming returned hardly anything to the farmers' mouths. There were women and girls—many more women than men, because the war had taken the men—whose lives were empty. The mills opened a vista before them; it was like finding a mine, you know. Most of the mills got local labor . . . after ten or fifteen years the labor of the localities was exhausted, and it was necessary to send to the mountains.[2]

The labor did not come from the plantation area of the Coastal Plain; and despite an impression commonly prevailing, it was not until after 1900 that the mills began sending their "labor agents" into the mountains and the Great Appalachian Valley for workers. "Not until late in the history of the Southern mills . . . did establishments get fresh labor from any distance, and in these cases the stimulus to move came from the mill, not from the people," Mitchell tells us.[3] There were two reasons for the necessity to seek further afield after 1900. In the first place, the mills were beginning to relieve the pressure of population on the land; the rural population was being scaled down somewhat closer to the ability of the land to support it. Even more important, however, was a recovery in the price of cotton. From six cents on the New York market in 1898, the price went almost to thirteen cents in 1903—the highest figure it had reached since 1875. From then until the boll weevil devested the southeastern cotton fields in the 1920's, it would be possible to earn a living on the land; and the mills, still expanding at a rapid rate, found themselves faced with a shortage of local labor.

"If there were not enough people in the immediate vicinity of a mill in the Piedmont, some operatives would be recruited from the higher country a little distance away," says Mitchell.[4] It was always to the "higher country" that the mill turned for additional labor when local sources were insufficient—never to the surplus agricultural population of the lowlands. This has been confirmed time and time again in the writer's own interviews. Only in the mills located in the large cities along the fall line was there likely to be any significant element of Coastal Plain people in the work force, and then this was not so much by preference of the operators as because of the reluctance of the Piedmont people to move to the "city." In these mills, after 1920, the Coastal Plain element would gradually be replaced by upland farmers.

The resulting infusion of mountain people after 1900 into the Piedmont textile work force was to be of considerable significance to the developing pattern of industrial relations. As Mitchell indicates,

2. *Ibid.*, p. 190.   3. *Ibid.*, p. 187.
4. *Ibid.*, p. 189.

these people did not generally seek out the mills. It was they who had to be sought out, to be cajoled into coming into the mills; and they came tentatively, often retaining their mountain landholdings—for, never having been caught into the cotton economy, they had retained title to their land. Some of them, unhappy, returned to their mountains, but not necessarily to stay. As a mill owner in South Carolina told Ben F. Lemert:

> . . . for six months or a year [they] were terribly dissatisfied and finally resigned and went home. Back there, they never saw anyone, their kids could not go to school, had no one to play with and their wives had no one to talk to. The men folks had had the novel experience of hearing coins jingle in their own pockets and it's hard to find even enough to eat back in those mountains. Almost without exception they write back "For God's sake send us money to come back to the mill village." The one trip back weans them away from the mountains and brings them into mill life for good.[5]

For the ten years preceding World War I, the mills suffered from a constant shortage of labor, particularly of trained personnel. The shortage was so great, as a matter of fact, that "labor pirating" became a common practice on the part of some of the less scrupulous operators, despite laws to prevent it which were passed in North and South Carolina and Georgia.[6] In one community, after an irate mill owner had sought out and shot down with an ancient cavalry pistol a neighbor who had lured away some of his most valued employees, the operators met and came to an agreement that open solicitation of one another's help would cease.[7]

After 1920 the boll weevil, particularly in the southern extremity of the Piedmont, again made the mills attractive to the Piedmont farmers; and a new movement from the upland farms began. This was different from the first, however. There was not the same drive of desolate poverty behind it. In many cases it was the attraction of the mills, with their villages modernized out of the profits of World War I, with wage rates considerably above the pre-war level (though down from the wartime peak), and with their better school facilities

5. Ben F. Lemert, *The Cotton Textile Industry of the Southern Appalachian Piedmont* (Chapel Hill: The University of North Carolina Press, 1933), p. 48.

6. See Herbert J. Lahne, *The Cotton Mill Worker* (New York: Farrar and Rinehart, Inc., 1944), p. 76-77.

7. Amusing stories as well have been related to the writer of this practice; of reciprocal raids, for example, that resulted in little more than swapping work forces.

that drew the farmers rather than the desolation and privation of life on the land that drove them. More than one story has been related to the writer by a "thirty-year man" of how "The children were getting of an age where they ought to be getting into high school; and there just wasn't no chance for that as long as we stayed out on the farm. I never had much education myself—my father didn't believe in it, even if there'd been a chance for it—but I figured my kids had a right to it."[8]

Now after 1920 many of the Piedmont folk who came into the mills would, like the mountaineers, retain their farms, living on them while they worked in the mills and taking advantage of the mobility offered by a "T-Model" purchased during the period of war-inflated cotton prices. Many of them, also like the mountaineers, came tentatively or, to begin with, had no thought of remaining permanently. Their employment in the mills was to be a matter only of a year or so, to "tide them over" until the scourge of the weevil had abated and to furnish them with some cash money to pay up their debts. Many of these people who divided their time between the farm and the mill continued to "make a crop," or at least such a crop as the boll weevil would leave for them. Many others began to experiment with beef cattle, chickens, soil-building crops, and other possibilities introduced by the possession of a little cash money and freedom from the depressing cycle of raising cotton to pay the debts incurred by raising cotton.

The mills along the fall line profited particularly from this new movement of farm people during the 1920's. "From a selfish point of view, we profited from the boll weevil," an official of one of these mills told the writer. "Before 1920 we'd had to depend pretty much on floaters, people from the 'shacktown' district here in the city, and sharecroppers from south of us for replacements and additions to our work force. They were a pretty bad lot, on the whole—there wasn't much in the way of human iniquity they couldn't think of, and you couldn't depend on them. After the boll weevil hit the farming country to the north of us, we began to get a different class of people here. They changed the whole complexion of our work force—dependable,

8. See Harriet Herring's *Welfare Work in Mill Villages* (Chapel Hill: University of North Carolina Press, 1928), pp. 32-33.

serious, co-operative, anxious to improve themselves—you couldn't ask for better folks."[9]

Also during the 1920's particular sources of labor for various mills began to be established that still form an important basis of their supply, supplementing purely local sources. From some farming community, often forty or fifty miles away, the head of a family or an elder son would come looking for temporary employment and obtain it, after finding none in mills closer home. Eventually the decision would be made for the entire family to move to the mill. Friends and relatives, discouraged with farming or wanting a change, would hear from them that "the mill's a pretty decent place to work. Beats farming all hollow!" Soon they too would be checking up on the chance of getting a job. Before long it would become an established custom in this rural community for its surplus population to look for work with the Jones Mill before trying anywhere else—there were friends and relatives there already. Not only did their presence help to ease the transition from rural to industrial life, but they had given their stamp of approval to the mill as a satisfactory place to work. The Jones Mill, on the other hand, gave the people from this community preference over everyone except local people—they were good, dependable folks from up that way, and you could not go wrong putting them on the payroll. "If you were to pull the folks from————County out of this mill," a weaver told the writer, referring to a largely rural community some fifty miles from the plant, "I guess they'd have to close the mill down. We just started coming down here from up that way, and we've kept on coming."

An interesting recent variation of this practice is for a group of workers from the rural area to commute to the mill rather than move to the mill community. Riding a total of eighty or a hundred miles each day in a sturdy but somewhat antiquated bus purchased at second-hand, owned either co-operatively or by one of their number and operated on a "share-the-cost" basis, they are able to reap the advantages of industrial employment without renouncing the land.

9. The danger of dealing with stereotyped images is well illustrated by the fact that one of the vice-presidents of the mill where this statement was made to the writer had come to it originally as a dispossessed share-cropper looking for day work.

The Pattern of Adjustment

These people who came to the mills after 1920, who could often, if they wished, continue to live in the country while they worked in town, were actually far better prepared to make a complete break with rural life than were those folk who came into the early mills and who had no choice but to leave the land. Speaking of the period before 1900, Mitchell says, "It is probable that never before or since in economic history has an agricultural population been so suddenly drawn into industry."[10] There was a change of life conditions for these people so sudden, and for which they were so unprepared, that it was almost traumatic in nature. For some of them, it was.

We must remember that though the Piedmont farmers came to the mills from land that had failed them, from a life situation that had betrayed them, they came reluctantly. There were some few of them who came from their worn-out fields broken in defeat, abjectly begging for work only because there were no almshouses to which they might go, but they were not typical. They were, on the whole, a people who had behind them a long history of self-reliance. While they had remained on the land, even when they rented acres they formerly had owned, they were able to maintain a feeling of independence; but coming to the mill meant "hiring out." It meant working for someone else, the surrender of their destiny and the direction of their day-to-day activities into the hands of others.

Establishment of the Co-operative Pattern

Out of the necessity of adjusting to these changed circumstances without sacrificing their self-respect, without surrendering completely the feeling that they were still essentially masters of their own lives, has come the most important characteristic of industrial relations in the southeastern cotton textile industry. The people came to the mills fiercely proud, sensitive to a high degree, alert for the slightest inference that they were "hired hands." It was necessary either that they work in the mills or that they condemn their families to the degrading poverty of their Piedmont farms;[11] but they were able to make the

10. Mitchell, *op. cit.,* p. 173.
11. We should note that "degrading poverty" was not characteristic of all Piedmont farms of the era. It was a time of austerity for all, of pitiful want for many; but as one went toward the foothills, where more of the old pattern of diversified farming remained and there had been less emphasis on cotton, the situation was better. See, for example, Ben Robertson, *Red Hills and Cotton* (New York: Alfred A. Knopf, 1942).

change and maintain an image of themselves that they could continue to live with only by entering into an arrangement whereby it was tacitly understood that they were working *with* the managements of the mills rather than for them.

There could not, in general, be any relationship of domination and submission. There had to be a relationship of co-operation between people who were essentially equals. It was understood that by virtue of varying backgrounds, training, and the operation of chance fate, some people were better prepared for certain positions than others; but this was regarded as a matter of convenience for the mills and a necessary and reasonable division of labor rather than an admission that one man was inherently better than another.

Thus by the very nature of his background, by reason of the pioneer heritage that was his sole remaining legacy of the land, this southern farmer turned industrial worker insisted as a condition of his employment upon the right to co-operate with management. The insistence was implicit. It was not spelled out in any manifesto, nor is it likely that either management or the people were objectively aware of it to begin with. But the relationship could be no mere polite fiction, as those supervisors who unconsciously or deliberately violated its spirit discovered. The status differences that typify the industrial operation were acceptable only for so long as they were played out against a background that marked the essential equality of the participants in other respects.

A mill official recounted to the writer one of his early experiences as a neophyte second hand, not long out of college. Anxious to make a good impression on his overseer, a man whose experience dated back to the opening days of the Cotton Mill Campaign, he was resolved that his section of the weave room should be kept impeccably clean. One of his weavers, an excellent workman and very dependable, was unfortunately not particularly neat in his personal habits. Noticing the floor about the man's loom spattered with tobacoo juice, the young supervisor told him, "Will, you've got to stop spitting all over the floor. If you can't hit the can, stop chewing tobacco." Will silently went for a mop, cleaned up the floor, and ostentatiously moved the tin can that served him for a cuspidor a few inches nearer. The young second hand went on his way, proud of having taken care of the situation so efficiently.

Will did not report for work the next day, nor the next, nor the next. His continued absence worried the second hand, for Will was one of the best weavers he had, and production was suffering. He finally went to the overseer, to find out if he knew what was wrong. "It's not like Will to stay away without letting us know about it," the overseer said. "Did anything seem to be wrong the last day he was here?" The second hand could think of nothing; but conscientously recounting his contacts with Will during the last day he had been at his loom, he mentioned the incident of the floor spattered with tobacco juice.

"There's your trouble," the overseer said. "Young fellow, there's one thing you've got to learn if you're going to get along with these people. You can't tell them they've *got* to do anything. They'll quit, just to show you they don't have to. You should have said, 'Will, I wonder if we ought not try to keep the floor a little neater here in the weave room?' and you wouldn't have had any trouble. You'd have put it up to him for a decision, and he'd have gone along with you on it. But Will's not the kind of a man you can order around. If you want him back you'd better hunt him up and make things right with him."

Fortunately for the beginning industry, the managers of the early mills had sufficient feeling of kinship with their workers to recognize, not only the source of their sensitive pride, but also the importance and the necessity of it. They were able to take the role of their workers, to imagine a reversal of positions. Mitchell speaks of "the mutual respect prevailing between management and workpeople during those first years."

The owners of cotton mills did not look down on their employees. They might and usually did recognize that the operatives were lacking in education, thrift, energy and property, and they applied themselves to alleviate these conditions, but always there was the knowledge that employer and employee were of the same origin, the same blood, and, not remotely, the same instincts. After-war struggles brought an intimacy through propinquity which in earlier years had been impossible. Men who were active in the opening of the cotton mill era in the South resent any suggestion, recognizing in it a slur somehow upon themselves, that the operatives were inferior people.[12]

12. Mitchell, *op. cit.*, p. 188.

Casualties of the Transition

We have said that there were some for whom the experience of moving to the mills was traumatic. There were workers for whom no amount of understanding sympathy could cushion the shock of transition. Torn loose from the familiar pattern of rural existence, they could not adapt themselves to an industrial life, even in a rural setting. They lost faith in themselves, and they sought it vainly. Always at the next mill—down the road, up the valley—they would find an environment where they could feel like whole men again. They became the floaters; the restless, roving men, embittered and cynical. There were as well occasional managements that failed in understanding and supervisors who enjoyed the exercise of arbitrary power. These needlessly swelled the ranks of the floaters with casualties.

There is no data available as to the relative size of this floating population in the early mills. Those older workers who can remember conditions around the turn of the century are inclined to believe that it was not as large as has been popularly supposed. "What you have to remember is that it was nearly always the same people moving," one of them told the writer. "There were some people who just couldn't stay put, it seemed like. No matter how good they had it where they were, they were sure it must be better somewhere else. Anything was an excuse to quit their jobs; and there was always a job waiting for them in some other mill, and a house for them in the mill village. I can't do more than guess, but I shouldn't think there were more than 15 or 20 per cent of the people that were like that, at the very most— but they moved so much, I suppose it must have looked to those who didn't know that everybody who worked in a cotton mill was a kind of gypsy."

J. J. Rhyne made a study of the mobility of 355 North Carolina mill families at a considerably later date (during the 1920s).[13] He found that 20 per cent of the families had never moved. Twenty per cent of them had moved oftener than once a year. The balance had an average length of residence ranging from one to ten years. "Summing up," he concludes, "it may be said that the study leaves the impression

13. J. J. Rhyne, *Some Southern Mill Workers and Their Villages* (Chapel Hill: University of North Carolina Press, 1930), pp. 105-21. See also Herring, *Welfare Work,* p. 22.

that, save for a comparatively few families, the mill families did not have an excessively high rate of mobility." He also concludes, after studying the reasons given for moves, that "the tendency to move is subjective and does not develop entirely from conditions existing in mill villages." Nor did he find any correlation between low wages and high mobility. This is not surprising since one of the factors generally facilitating frequent moves was that the foot-loose individual was a competent workman, and thus not only able to find employment without difficulty but to earn a respectable wage when he worked.

Volatile Nature of the Work Force

Though the mill workers were on the whole more inclined to work out their problems where they found themselves than they were to wander from mill to mill searching for a will-o-the-wisp, they were not by any means, as they were to be represented at a later date by various southern chambers of commerce, "docile" and "tractable." Any impression they may have given in this respect came about because they were dealt with in a sympathetic and understanding fashion. "These people can be *mean* if you don't know how to get along with them," a long-time student of southern labor relations told the writer. "They'll flare up like tinder if you rub them the wrong way." They came into the mills capable of passionate bursts of anger, of stubborn resistance, of deliberate and continuing obstructionism. They exhibited at a very early date their ability to offer not only individual but collective objection to policies and practices with which they were in disagreement. The spontaneous walkout, the "quickie" strike, is an old device of southern workers when they have felt that they were in some way being discriminated against.

Far from being stolid and tractable, they were a volatile work force. Their homogeneous background, with its resulting high degree of interpersonal rapport, meant that group action developed spontaneously, that group decisions were reached by an informal and almost instantaneous process of consensus rather than by logical but protracted discussion. Mill managements discovered at a very early date that it was impossible to deal with the individual worker on an "individual" basis; for though reward, praise, or reproof might be directed toward the individual, the response to it was likely to be from the group. Attitudes of the entire work force had to be taken into account in the seemingly most inconsequential relationship with a single worker.

Yet the mill worker was, and is, as he has been so often described, an individualist. *But his individualism has been exercised against the background of membership in a tightly knit, cohesive social organization.* That the organization has been informal and membership in it implicit rather than explicit has at one and the same time increased its power over him while at the same time it has given him a greater degree of latitude for individual action. He has met the obligations of membership in his society unconsciously; but because he has been aware with the certainty of intuition of the limits for individual action imposed by his social ties, he has moved with a feeling of complete freedom within those limits. He has known without thinking what he can and cannot do; there has been no need for him to proceed with a hesitant step, feeling his way through an area that he hopes is not taboo.

MANAGEMENT AND LABOR

Perhaps the best clue to the nature of early labor-management relations in the textile industry in the Piedmont is offered by the two terms commonly used to identify the members to the relationship. When it was necessary to use a term more specific than "our people"— which, according to the context, might mean every one in the mill from the president on down or only the hourly rated people—a pair of terms that one still hears used frequently was employed. The distinction was made between "operators," meaning management, and "operatives," meaning the work force. Quite commonly the term "hands" was substituted for operatives, but carrying the same connotations. (The latter term has fallen into disrepute, and is seldom heard today.)

Management was the "operator" that planned and directed, and the worker was the "operative," or the "hand," that carried out the function. The formal relationship at the work place, in other words, arose not out of the fact that one man had hired another, but through the fact that they were both involved, through differentiated functions, in the same "operation." Managements and workers alike were "people"; the terms "operator" and "operative" were used merely to indicate that they had certain specialized functions as individuals. There was no implication, in the terms, of a master-servant relationship. They were, as a matter of fact, so impersonal that there was no implication of any kind of a person-to-person relationship. There was a kind of dual relationship existing between managements and their workers. There were the intimate, face-to-face human contacts between "people" regarded as whole personalities; and there were completely impersonal highly objective contacts between operators and operatives undertaking a joint venture.

The *employer-employee* dichotomy commonly employed today in many areas is not impersonal.[14] It refers to a relationship established directly between two individuals, carrying with it a set of rights and obligations that exist apart from any real, functional situation.

Whenever there was an attempt to enforce what amounted to an "employer-employee" relationship there was labor trouble. Though the worker had "hired out," and though he was a "hand," he was not a "hired hand." There was the same almost nebulous but extremely important distinction here that existed in another case: he was "poor" and he was "white," but he was not a "poor white."

Crystallization of the Relationship

This insistence of the Piedmont farmer upon the maintenance of a socio-psychological *milieu* in which he was able to maintain a feeling of independence and the essential elements of self-respect was reinforced by the arrival on the scene, after 1900, of the mountaineer. Speaking of these people, Mr. Baldwin, principal of the Piedmont Industrial School at Charlotte, told Broadus Mitchell:

I am satisfied that they are the finest body of people on earth doing similiar work. Descended from the early English, Scotch and Germans, they have been sleeping, as it were, while the procession of progress has been passing by. Serious, independent, as all hill and mountain people are; sensitive, because of that independence, spirited, for the most part sober, they are a people of untold possibilities, now that they are beginning to arouse themselves from the drowsiness of generations and to grapple earnestly with the duties of the active, work-a-day world.[15]

At a time when we might have expected the pioneer heritage of the Piedmont folk to be in some danger of dilution in the environment of the mills, the strain was fixed and set by the introduction into the

14. It is perhaps significant that use of the term "employee" came into general use only with the development of our great modern mass-production industries. It is a term characteristic of mass rather than of folk relationships.

15. Mitchell, *op. cit.*, n. 22, p. 172.

work force the most concentrated essence of that heritage that could possibly have been found. Says W. J. Cash:

> In effect, it was almost exactly as though so many pioneer backwoodsmen had been miraculously introduced into the scene . . . No other such individualist was left in America—or on the earth . . . The presence of a large body of such men would have had a marked effect on the psychology of the Southern mill worker in any case. But what made the effect more signal was that, never having been subjected to the continual loss of the most able individuals, which had been the case with the common whites elsewhere, this mountain stock averaged unusually high; and mountain men came to leadership out of all proportion to their numbers—in such numbers, indeed, that many Yankee observers were led to report, quite incorrectly, that the majority of all Southern cotton mill workers was of Alpine extraction.[16]

The superiority of the mountain stock by reason of the retention of its most able members, to which Cash refers, arose from the extremely simple structure of its society, in which there was practically no differentiation of status. The highly capable individual remained a common man simply because the society had nothing but "common men." The role of leadership which the mountain men played in many cases was not due so much to their inherent superiority, however (if such superiority existed), as it was to the fact that they brought to the mills in crystalline purity a restatement of the pioneer heritage, the pioneer ideals and value standards. They were able to redefine for the people, in familiar terms, a philosophy that was becoming somewhat blurred around the edges. We remember also that these hill people were likely to retain their mountain farms and to come to the mills only on a tentative basis. Their continued employment was a matter of free choice on their part; and it was a choice they stood ready to revise at the least threat to their feeling of independence. We may recall that the mill operator whom Lemert interviewed spoke of these mountain people as "resigning" their positions, a term emphasizing that the relationship was one into which they entered by choice and that its continuance and termination was as well a matter of their own choice.

Finally, after 1920, the new wave of settlement from the Piedmont farms into the mills clinched the matter. This last group of farm folk were very likely to do as the mountaineer had done—come to the

16. W. T. Cash, *Mind of the South* (New York: Alfred A. Knopf, 1941), p. 214.

mills on a tentative basis, retaining their landholdings. Very often they continued to live on their farms and operate them, in a modified form, in addition to their mill work. There was no question as to their independence of spirit. They felt themselves under no great compulsion to remain in a situation where their self-respect was threatened or to submit to a pattern of managerial domination. Like their predecessors of forty years before, they implicitly insisted upon the right to co-operate with management. They could not have maintained their self-respect under any other conditions.

SUPERVISION IN THE EARLY MILLS

So far in this discussion of worker-management relations, we have been implicitly assuming management to be at the policy-making level. It is a little more difficult to make generalizations with regard to supervisory practices in the early mills. There is, in the first place, little information regarding them. Interest in supervisory practices, to the extent that they are studied, described, and analyzed, is a recent development in the field of industrial relations—as, indeed, is industrial relations itself as a field of inquiry. Such information as the writer possesses has been obtained through interviews with long-service employees in the present mills. Since men and women approaching the age of retirement in 1952 very often began their work in the mills at the age of ten, the memories of people still living and working can carry us back before the turn of the century, to within fifteen years of the beginning of the Cotton Mill Campaign, and they are able to recall stories of an even earlier day related by their parents. One must make allowance for the fact that such memories, perhaps involving oft repeated tales, tend to become stylized and often have as much the character of mythology as of history. Yet, on the other hand, any formalization they may have undergone is likely to be in the direction of throwing into sharper relief the attitudes and feelings that were involved. Any tendency to "make a good story of it," in other words, is likely to preserve and actually outline more clearly the general orientation of interpersonal relationships that existed. When one hears such stories from many different sources, and from mills widely separated geographically, there is also the possibility of cross-checking and of noting the points of agreement among various versions.

Overseers and Second Hands

One's immediate impression, upon reviewing notes covering many such interviews, is that there was nothing that could be identified as a general pattern of supervisory practice. Supervision was a highly personal affair; there were as many different approaches to its problems as there were second hands and overseers. This in itself is, of course, a generalization; and it seems to be one that is rather valid. There does not seem to have been any attempt on the part of any individual management to impose any particular pattern of uniformity with regard to practices upon its line supervisors. "You had the cotton, the machinery and the people—and you were supposed to get out the production," said an overseer (general foreman), recalling for the writer his experiences as a second hand before World War I. "How you did it was pretty much up to you; it was production that management was interested in, and not how you got it."

Exploring the matter a bit further, however, it was discovered that there were certain implicit limits of policy within which this man as a young second hand (shift foreman) was supposed to operate. No one ever told him what they were unless he inadvertently violated one of them—he was supposed to know them as a matter of course—but they were there. There were things he could do and things that he could not do in getting out the production; but he did not think of these guides and restrictions as "policy." "Some things are right and some things are wrong when you're dealing with folks—but if you don't know the difference between right and wrong by the time you're a second hand, no supervisor's handbook is going to teach you." Supervisory policy, in other words, was based upon the ethical and moral code of the folk. The folkways and the mores served in lieu of "personnel policy." The overseer was king of his domain, true enough, but it was a limited monarchy even though he might himself never have occasion to realize it. We are seldom aware of the constraints of the folkways unless we defy them.

There seems to be quite general agreement that supervision in the early mills was stern but just, and, seemingly in contradiction of what we have said so far, inclined to be impersonal in nature. Statements like the following made to the writer by older workers are typical: "They were pretty tough men—they had to be, with some of those drifters we used to get that wouldn't recognize any authority but a pair of fists—but if you did your work you didn't have to fear them." "I remember how the overseer used to come striding down the aisle with his hands joined behind his back under his coat-tails. We'd all bend over our work and we wouldn't look up until we knew he was past. He was a stern man—you wouldn't think of going to him with your problems like people go to the overseer nowadays—but he was fair. I wouldn't say we had any affection for him, but we respected him." "I can't say that there's any difference between supervision now and fifty years ago, when I first came into the mills. Oh, their ways have changed, of course—so have a lot of other things—but as far back as I can remember you never had any trouble if you did your job." "I expect the old-time supervisors were more drivers than they are now; but on the other hand there were some people in the mills back in those days that you had to drive. There was an element that used to move from mill to mill. They were pretty good workmen when they wanted to be, and I guess that's why the mills put up with them; but they didn't have any respect for anybody. But the overseers and second hands were pretty decent to us kids, and I never heard one of them raise his voice in anger to a woman."

The stories one hears of first-line supervision in the early mills leave with one the impression of a group of men who tended to hold themselves aloof from the work force to an extent unknown in the present day mills; who were (and apparently had to be) ready to back up their directions with their fists; who were just and fair, but who would not stand for any "tomfoolery"; and who were parsimonious with praise and with explanations. The people who recall working under them remember most of them, as did the interviewee quoted, with respect though not affection. They seem to feel that many of the practices of early supervision that would be frowned on today were justified by the conditions under which they were administered. "The people now wouldn't stand for the kind of supervision we used to have—but one reason for the change in supervision is because the people themselves have changed. You can talk to people now; you can reason with them—but there were a lot of them in those days that seemed to go around with a chip on their shoulder all the time. It was a word and a blow with them. Old-time supervision wouldn't work now—but the kind we have nowadays wouldn't have got very far then."

In those cases where stories were recounted of early supervisors who were bullies, who delighted in demonstrating their authority, or who were unreasonable or arbitrary, the informant was quick to point out that such people were not typical, and he very often ended his tale with some such phrase as this: ". . . but the superintendent finally got wise to him, and he booted him out of there so fast his coat-tails whistled." Top management is almost invariably absolved of any responsibility for the supervisor's deviant actions. Either it discovers the nature of the deviant activity and metes out swift punishment, or "if Mr.———had known what was going on, he'd have put a stop to it quick enough!"

Top Management and Supervision

This tendency to absolve top management of responsibility for the out-of-line activities of supervisors and to consider the latter as indicative of personality quirks of individuals rather than as representative of company policy is still characteristic of southern textile work forces. It gives us a clue as to the explanation for the seemingly contradictory picture we have presented—a top management that is understanding, that is capable of identifying with the work force, and treats the people as total human personalities rather than as "employees"; and at the same time a supervisory force that is remembered as distant, not encouraging personal relationships, and formal in its actions and attitudes.

It appears that the work force integrated itself into the company through top management rather than through the supervisory force. One runs across a statement something like the following very often in discussions of present-day labor relations: "To the hourly rated worker, his foreman is the company. If the foreman is good, the company is good; if the foreman is bad, the company is bad."[17] This is seldom true in the present-day cotton textile industry in the Piedmont, nor was it true fifty or more years ago.

In the early days of the industry particularly, top management (the president and the superintendent, usually) were the individuals sym-

17. See, for example, Lloyd Reynolds, *Labor Economics and Labor Relations* (1st ed., New York: Prentice-Hall, 1949), p. 45.

bolizing the company to the work force. Labor-management relations were the relationships existing between the people and top management, not between the people and the supervisors. The overseer was usually respected; occasionally he was feared. But he was never "The Company." "The Company" was the president or the mill manager, and to a lesser degree, the superintendent. The overseer, despite his superior status position, was still a man who had "hired out" like everyone else in the work force.[18]

We have mentioned earlier that labor relations in the early industry seemed to exist in two modes; those between "people" and those between "operators" and "operatives." It appears that the operator-operative relationship was almost entirely the task of the supervisory force to administer (though supervisors were not considered as "operators"—the term referred to top management) and that the relationship between work force and management as "people" was the responsibility of the top officers of the company. In a more modern terminology, the overseers and second hands were production people; and while as a matter of practical necessity on-the-spot exercise of the personnel function was delegated to them, they exercised it only under close and continuing supervision from the top. Line supervisors, in a way, stood outside the personnel relationship in the early mills. They were a part of the technological rather than of the human picture in the overall relationship. They had, actually, little time to think of the human factor; their job was to keep the machinery running and manned—no easy task with an untrained work force and a top management usually innocent of technical knowledge.

On the other hand, the plants were small; and a top management genuinely interested in the people was able to keep in close touch with them. Executive duties were not yet as pressing as they would be later; there was time for daily trips through the plant, a moment's conversation during the course of the week with everyone. Says Cash, speaking of "the master of the mill,"

[He] knew these workmen familiarly as Bill and Sam and George and Dick, or as Lil and Sal and Jane and Lucy. More, he knew their pedigrees and their histories. More still, with that innocent love of personal detail native to Southerners, he kept himself posted as to their lives as they were

18. And in the early days particularly, top management was likely to be synonymous with ownership or a respectable interest in the mill. The president was obviously *not* a "hired hand" and thus even more deserving of respect.

lived under his wing; knew their little adventures and scandals and hopes and loves and griefs and joys. Day by day he moved among them full of the small teasing jests and allusions to kinsfolk so dear to the Southern heart, of ready and benign counsel, of sympathetic interest and concern for Granny Meg's rheumatism or the treasured cow that had died—a concern which even in the most hard-bitten wage-shaver was somehow and characteristically real at the core.[19]

There is no mystery as to why this should have been so. It is, in the first place, the way by which one "gets along" in the folk society. The "innocent love of personal detail" is native, not only to Southerners, but to all people everywhere who orient their lives on the basis of their personal knowledge of the people with whom they come in contact. Not only did the "master of the mill' have time for these human contacts; he was quite likely to regard the welfare of his workers as equally important with the product of his mill, a reflection of an important facet of the Cotton Mill Campaign.

The supervisory people, however, were charged with the responsibility of getting out the production that provided jobs; and while the president could take a long-range view and think of the potentialities of the workers as American citizens, the overseer or the second hand was more impressed with the fact that they were untrained, clumsy, sensitive, quick to take offense, and not too well broken to the factory whistle. Thus it was the supervisory people who were prodding the workers for more production, chiding them for their lack of skill, and reminding them of the necessity of regular attendance to their duties; while the men in top management indulged with them in reminiscence of coon hunts under a silver moon on a sparkling fall night, inquired after their children, and spoke of the new South the people of the mills were building. It was top management that reminded the workers that they were after all one people, working together for a common end; it was the supervisory folk who kept them humped over their looms and mindful of the fact that they had hired out.

It was with top management that the working people identified; the overseers and the second hands blended into the background of the chattering looms and the roar of the spinning room. *Top management stood as a buffer between the work force and the supervisory people, a force that could bring an arbitrary and unreasonable super-*

19. Cash, *op. cit.*, p. 212.

vision back into line. A story was told to the writer of a man who has become almost legendary in a section of the Piedmont as a symbol of the management of the early mills. The man who told it began his career under the tutelage of the old man as the career of the latter was ending.

"The Captain's visit out in the mill were a daily ritual. He spent more time in the plant than he did in the office. He never stopped to talk with the supervisory people unless he had a specific reason to do so, and his relationship with them in the mill was distant and formal. He was not on a first-name basis with them in the mill; it was always Mr. So-and-So when he addressed a supervisor and his manner toward them did not invite any familiarity on their part. When the Captain talked with a supervisor, it was strictly business and that was all. He was a different man with the hourly rated people. Many of them had been with the mill as long as he had; and when he stopped to talk with them, it was not a conversation between an employer and an employee—it was two old friends passing the time of day, recalling old times, arguing about politics, making small talk. If he saw a new face, he had to get acquainted; find out who they were, where they came from, whether or not he knew any of their kinfolk, how they were getting along.

"What didn't seem right to me in those days was the way he checked up on the supervisors through the people, especially on the younger men like myself. 'How's young So-and-So getting along,' he'd ask a weaver, for example, referring to some young second hand in the weave room. 'Is he treating you right? Show any signs of getting too big for his britches? Been trying to tell you how to run your loom? Think he'll ever make a second hand?' The Captain was serious when he asked these questions—he expected answers, and he got them. The people didn't have any hesitancy in telling the Captain about it if some young lad with authority he wasn't used to tried throwing his weight around. It kept you on your toes—he'd have you up in his office within the hour if he got a bad report on you.

"As I look back at it now, though, I can see that the Captain was doing us a service. *He held an umbrella over us young second hands.* The people were a lot more patient with us, they'd put up with a lot more from us, and try to teach us and show us how to get things done, when they knew they were protected against our inexperience. They didn't have to take anything from us and they knew it; the Captain would yank us back into line at a word from them—but knowing that, they actually protected us! They'd cover up for us when we made mistakes; they'd make allowances for us—just knowing that the Captain was there ready to help them if the situation got too tough took off the tension. The mill's too big now to handle it in as highly personal a fashion as the Captain did, but we try to maintain his philosophy. If the day ever comes that our people begin to feel that they can't get a square deal in the front office, that's the day you'll see them lining up to sign union cards. They won't have to be 'organized' —they'll *organize!*"

We have here a further clue regarding the respect generally granted the overseer in the older mills, despite the fact that his recognized function was that of taskmaster. It was concerning the performance of young second hands that the Captain made direct inquiry. Capable and proven supervision, not only in his mill but in the bulk of the rest, quite generally could count on a minimum of interference from the office. The fact was that such supervision had achieved capability and proven itself through the agency of a training program that, though informal and for the most part unrealized as such, was rigorous and fundamentally sound.

Held responsible by the Captain and his contemporaries for getting out production, yet kept under constant surveillance by them to be sure that production was not maintained at the expense of the people or in violation of "right" principles of human relations, and working with people who resented any attempt to "drive" them, the second hand who lasted and was promoted eventually to overseer was not merely technically competent. He was forced by the nature of the situation itself to develop qualities of leadership in the best modern sense of the word. The main fault of the system was that it was wasteful. Lack of any planned and positive program, at this early date, for developing the qualities that were implicitly demanded for success as an overseer resulted in an unduly high rate of attrition among the trainees. Yet the system can be credited with turning out a respectable number of men who went on to become leaders in the industry itself.

In-Plant Relationships

"Employee relations" within the early Piedmont mills were merely a translation, into the work place, of the existing folkways and mores. Personnel policy was implicit. It consisted of the ethical code of the region. One did the "right" thing in dealing with other people, and there was no necessity for spelling out what was meant by the "right" thing. One might deviate from it, one might rationalize such deviations; but it was there in the background, a restraining influence. Even so severe a critic of certain aspects of the South as Cash says of those days that the mill owner "rarely used his power beyond the limit traditional on the plantation and was not often too arrogant in its exercise. Men were discharged arbitrarily; but there was perhaps less of that here than has been common elsewhere . . . [there was] the unstudied knowledge that it was easier to cajole these people, to flatter and suggest, than to command and threaten."[20]

But though Cash recognizes that labor-management relations in the earlier mills were cast within the customary and traditional framework of a folk society, he errs, as do so many students of labor relations in the southeastern cotton textile industry, in assuming the folk society to have been that of the plantation South. We have sketched the beginning of the industry and the history of the region and its people in sufficient detail so that the nature of his error should be apparent without its being emphasized; but at the risk of being repetitious, we must remind ourselves that the society of the Piedmont owed little to the Tidewater and the Coastal Plain. It was settled by different people, under different life conditions, and its physiography demanded the development of a different way of life. It was democratic rather than aristocractic. It was the South of Andrew Jackson and Tom and Nancy Lincoln, not of the Cavaliers. Its virtues and its vices were those of the frontier, not of the drawing rooms of Savannah and Charleston. It was not the region of the plantation owner, the Negro, and "poor white trash"; it was the South of the yeoman farmer, the white artisan and the professions.

THE MILL VILLAGE

"The mill village system of the South had its roots in the conditions under which the mills were first built."[21] Thus Lahne explains the

20. *Ibid.*, p. 211.   21. Lahne, *op. cit.*, p. 34.

emergence of the mill village in the Piedmont in *The Cotton Mill Worker*. The system did not, as many people (including some South-erners) are inclined to believe, represent an industrial adaptation of plantation slave quarters or a transplantation of the plantation economy. During the early years of the Cotton Mill Campaign the mills were built along the banks of the rivers that provided water power and a sufficient degree of humidity to enable the cotton fiber to be worked. Later, as steam, electric power, and artificial humidification freed the mills from the necessity of locating in the Piedmont valleys, they were built within, or more usually just outside, the villages and occasional cities of the Piedmont Plain. In neither case was there a labor supply already available and housed, nor were there facilities to house the workers who had to be brought to the mills. "The gathering and retention of a labor supply in this sparsely peopled farm area was an important phase of the development of the mills," Lahne continues. "The establishment of cotton manufacturing meant the erection not only of the mill itself, but of a complete community as well. The mill owner was the only one financially able and willing to provide the necessary facilities for living."[22] In the early days at least, the mill company had probably garnered all the available surplus capital in the vicinity; it was the only agency that *could* afford to build the village.

The village was generally built either before or coincidentally with the mill; it was necessary to provide housing for the laborers who were building it as well as for those who would operate it. In many cases they were the same people. Families of farm folk would appear looking for work almost before ground was broken for the structure. The men of the family might be set to the task of enlarging the village, perhaps even finishing their own quarters, before they were put on the job of constructing the mill itself. As more people appeared from the farms, more houses appeared in the village. By the time the factory building had been finished, the housing for its workers had been completed as well, and the labor complement for the new enterprise was at hand and ready to go to work.

As late as the first decade of the present century, *Senate Document 645* indicates that 87 per cent of the southern textile work force had company housing. A Bureau of Labor survey in 1916 showed 78 per cent of the employees of forty-eight southern mills living in village

22. *Ibid.*, p. 35.

houses.[23]   Quite generally, so long as they were on a one-shift basis, the mills maintained housing facilities sufficient to care for all their people who needed it.   The workers themselves had no resources, there were no existing private accomodations, and no private investor was willing to undertake a large real-estate development, the success or failure of which would hinge upon the fortunes of a single enterprise— nor would he, during an era when 8 per cent was a conservative return on capital, have been content with the low earnings that rentals even twice those charged by the mills would have brought him.   Village housing constituted a real and unquestionable subsidy to the worker.[24]

The earliest mill villages were not laid out with an eye to aesthetic principles.   One basic design generally sufficed for all the houses, and unless extremely difficult terrain prevented it, they were built along a checkerboard pattern of streets.   Trees were sacrificed, and the red clay of front yards was innocent of grass.   Yet even in those early days, to quote Cash once more:

This house they gave the mill worker to live in . . . was nevertheless not only such a house as was entirely acceptable under his historical standard, but a very definite improvement over anything he had ever known.   It was actually a better house than most of those of the yeoman farmers, to say nothing of the huts of tenant and cropper.   For it was by ordinary tight against the rain if not against the wind and usually it had been painted—both rarities in the rural South.[25]

We must remember that by 1880 rural housing in the Piedmont had been subject to twenty years of constant deterioration; and it would not be until after 1900 that money would be available for anything like major repair.

The practice of building identical houses, precisely spaced and oriented, did not prevail after World War I.   Following 1920 the mills called in architects to help them plan their villages and housing units, to help them take advantage of the natural features of the landscape to enhance the appearance of the project.   Though few mills went so far, one company in Georgia imported a landscape gardener from Germany to assist in beautifying its village.   Those mills with older villages did what they could with trees, shrubbery, and lawn seed to relieve the stark monotony of their housing, and they encouraged

23. *Ibid.*
24. See Herring, *Welfare Work,* pp. 235-47.
25. Cash, *op. cit.,* p. 207.

flower gardens and window boxes to lend some semblance of individuality to their identical units.

The profits of the mills during World War I turned loose a flood of renovating and remodeling. Sewer systems were laid in; streets were paved and sidewalks built; plumbing was installed; houses not already so equipped were wired for electricity. Porches were added or remodeled, and various other attempts were made to relieve the appearance of uniformity between one dwelling and another.[26] The villages built after World War I show the results of planning of the sort that seeks to avoid the look of being "planned."

In addition to the dwellings that were provided, the villages from the first provided community pastures and garden plots. Both were much used by the early mill people—probably to an extent greater than on the farms they had come from, where they had planted cotton up to the doorsteps, and the last milch cow had long since been sold to buy fertilizer. There were probably more cases of pellagra that were cured in mill villages than were ever contracted there. It was dietary habits that the people brought with them from the farms that were responsible for such cases as did appear within the boundaries of the villages.[27] And as Lahne notes, ". . . hookworm declined as the operatives became accustomed to the more civilized ways of the mill village."[28]

Contrary to the general impression, the company store was not a common feature of the mill village. Only in cases where it was an economic necessity did it appear, usually in those mills built out in the country and some distance from any settlement. It was a rare feature of mills built within or on the outskirts of an existing community. It is not difficult to see why this should be so, when one takes into account the origin of the early mills. They were founded to rejuvenate an existing society, not to create a new one. The communities that built them hoped to share in their payrolls; and if the mills were immediately to recapture the payrolls, through company-owned retail outlets, one of the prime purposes for their erection would be nullified. Harriet Herring, in her *Welfare Work in Mill Villages,* reports that of 322 textile mills studied in North Carolina, only 63 had ever had com-

26. See Lahne, *op. cit.,* p. 39.
27. See Herring, *Welfare Work,* Chapter VIII ("Health Work in the Mill Village") for examples of mill guidance in dietary matters as well as other aspects of mill-administered health programs in the 1920's.
28. Lahne, *op. cit.,* p. 51.

pany-owned stores, and by 1926 only 35 were left.[29]   Of Georgia mills studied by the writer, less than 10 per cent have ever had company stores; those that had been or were in existence were economically justified by circumstances.

The Mill Village and Labor Mobility

A common explanation for the erection of mill villages has been that the mill owner "wanted to tie the people to the mill, and control their lives." Until well into the 1920's, the mill village system had exactly the opposite effect. Quite generally, so long as the mills were on a one-shift basis, they had adequate housing for close to 80 per cent of their total work force—which meant, since there were always workers who lived in town or on neighboring farms, there were ordinarily vacancies in their villages. This, far from tying the workers to the mills, increased their freedom of movement. One of the factors facilitating the high mobility rate during the early days was the knowledge held by a trained worker that no matter where he went, the odds were in his favor that he would find a house waiting for him in the village. Thus the village, rather than keeping the workers "under the thumb" of management for fear of losing their housing, made it easier for them to escape from a situation that was not to their liking.

This aspect of the mill village system of the early Piedmont mills is never mentioned, and yet its operation has been confirmed time and time again in interviews conducted by the writer. "Folks never worried about quitting their jobs in those days, if they were of a mind to. There was always another waiting at the next mill, and a place to live. Moving wasn't any problem. They could generally load all they owned into a wagon. If they were short of cash when they got to the new job, they could generally get an advance against their first week's pay, so they could stock up with groceries."

The net effect was not only to encourage mobility but also, as a consequence of mobility, to effect rather uniform rates of pay and working conditions throughout the Piedmont industry. The mill that fell behind the procession in either of these respects found itself unable to replace those trained workers who left—for such news spread with the mysterious rapidity characteristic in a folk society that does not as yet rely upon the written word for dissemination of information.

29. Herring, *Welfare Work*, pp. 187 and 192.

We have heard a great deal of the competition between members of the work forces of the early mills for jobs, but the superimposition of the mill village system upon the tendencies toward mobility already present in a significant minority of the work force resulted also in competition between mills for trained workers. As a result there was, in the early mills, rather a nice balance between what the mills could afford to pay and what the workers were willing to accept.

Welfare Work in the Early Mills

Just as the mill village is the physical aspect of the southeastern textile mill that most intrigues those unfamiliar with the industry, so is welfare work the most intriguing aspect of its social climate.[30] Quite generally, the whole pattern of welfare activities in the mills, be they early or present-day, is summarily described by the adjective "paternalistic." Unfortunately the word has been used with so little discrimination that it, like the term "poor white," has come to mean all things to all men.

Welfare work, like the mill village, arose out of necessity. The transition of a rural population into industry on a mass scale was not a matter that could be taken in stride. These farm people had to learn new ways of living and, especially, new ways of living together. They might be able to adapt psychologically; but there still remained the task of social adaptation. As they came into the mills, their ways were those of the land, a land that, having never got far beyond the frontier before 1860, had retrogressed to conditions in some ways even more primitive than the frontier during the days of Reconstruction. They had no notion of the technics of living in close proximity to one another. Personal and social habits that blended into an agricultural background, that possessed even a kind of simple dignity on the farm, were crude and uncouth in the village. Speaking of this, Lahne says, "The newcomers to the mill villages came not only from an impoverished rural background, but from one in which the rudiments of sanitation and progressive existence were almost unknown. . . . In all cases the mill officials had to educate the newcomers to sanitary personal habits, which often proved no easy task against the prejudice of the worker."[31]

30. See *Ibid, passim,* for a full-scale discussion of these activities from the beginning of the industry to 1928.

31. Lahne, *op. cit.,* p. 51.

Nor were the ideas of these people with regard to the training and education of their children any better suited to an industrial society in a semi-urban environment. The exigencies of rural existence had demanded that every member of the family contribute what he could as soon as he could; but more than that, there was a philosophical implication to the typical agricultural point of view toward "book learning." If one was to be a farmer, one learned the art of farming in the fields, not out of books. To be able to do simple sums, to sign one's name, to be able to read the Bible and the almanac—these were all the fruits of formal education that the Piedmont farmer had had need for. He tended to presume, therefore, that if one prepared for life as a farmer by farming, one ought likewise to prepare for life in the mills by working in the mills.

Thus there were a number of things that the mill operator had to do for these people beyond furnishing them with a house. We use the word *for* advisedly. He had to protect them from their own ignorance until such time as they were oriented to the new way of living. These were a people torn out of one context and thrust into another with no preparation for its problems. Paternalism is sometimes described as the attitude of a management that assumes it knows more about what is good for its employees than they themselves know. Only in rare cases is such an assumption warranted in present-day employee relations—but there is every evidence that it was not only warranted but mandatory on moral grounds during the beginning years of the Piedmont textile industry.

Many of the welfare activities of the early mills were resented by the people—those with regard to sanitary practices, those requiring a certain minimum amount of education for their children, and those suggesting changes in dietary practices. There was likely to be a considerable increase in labor turnover, for example, just after the school census had been taken. Fathers who believed that "all this education ain't going to do a thing but put queer ideas into the children's heads" found it convenient to leave one mill and locate at another just after the school census, to insure almost a year of peace from "busybodies" wanting to know why their children were not in school.[32] But one other managerial function—which can hardly be called "welfare," though it is invariably pointed out as a regretable

32. See Rhyne, *op. cit.,* p. 155.

consequence of paternalism—was sought out by the people. This was the habit so many of them had of seeking the advice of the mill owner as to matters of purely personal concern.

We must regard the practice in the light of the conditions that brought it about. There were two important reasons for it. The people were themselves perplexed. They were in a world that was strange to them. They lacked the knowledge of it that would have enabled them to lay out a course of action for themselves. They sought help, not so much because they had lost the power of decision, as because they did not have the information upon which to base self-determined action. But there was more to it than this. They were born and reared under the folkways, and they had not moved out from under them by coming into the mills. In the folk society, one goes to the "old men" for advice, not to books or specialists as one does in the mass society; for the old men, having had the most life experience, are the ones who know the answers. In the folk society of the textile mill, the "old men" (on the basis of pertinent life experience) included the president, the superintendent and the overseers. It was only natural and normal, the thing to do, to seek them out when one had a problem that was too much for one. When an intelligent man has a question, he goes where he thinks he can find the answer; and the people of the mills, though they may have been uncouth and illiterate, were by no means unintelligent.

They were on the other hand practical people who sought the quickest and most effective way of solving their problems; and they did not permit their awe of authority to stand in the way of their use of it. It is another interesting sidelight upon the relationship between the people and the managements that the former, in ascribing "authority" to management, implicitly defined it in terms of a secondary meaning, as that to which one appeals for a decision, rather than in terms of its primary meaning, as that which gives one the right to command.

The formal welfare programs of the mills were rather far removed from individual counsel, advice, or assistance. Even from their beginning their managements worked with the total mill community as a unit. Very little of their activity was directed toward specific individuals. Whether by accident or by intuition, they had hit upon the socio-psychological principle that it is much easier to change the behavior patterns of a group of people than of any one single individual within that group. Many of the activities that came under the heading of welfare were functions that would have been performed by local governments had they been present, or if present, willing and able to undertake them. Just as the mills had built the villages because they had to, they built schools and churches, community halls, and athletic fields. There was no one else to undertake the task.

If the result was occasionally the creation of what appeared to have all the attributes of a feudal manor, it was because the mill and its people existed under conditions that in many important respects resembled those that had created the feudal pattern to begin with. What is important from the point of view of this study is the implicit assumption on the part of mill operators that schools, churches, recreational facilities, health programs, and the like were necessary and important. They thought of the people who worked for them as total personalities whose needs were far from being encompassed by a pay envelope on Saturday. Even more important, the thought never entered their minds that they, as mill operators, were not responsible for the creation of conditions that would permit the satisfaction of these needs.

These welfare activities both illustrate and are explained by the high degree of identification that existed between mill managements and their work forces. They resented a slur on their work force as somehow reflecting on themselves, Mitchell noted. Under such conditions we need not seek far for the animating spirit behind welfare activities. Even the most penurious and profit-conscious operator could not help feeling, in neglecting the people who worked for him, a diminution of his own ego. The obligations of one man to another within the folk society are unlimited; they are not circumscribed by a wage scale.

Even in those cases where an operator, left to his own preferences, might have permitted his employees to fend for themselves, there was that all-powerful control of the folk society, the opinions of others. The judgments of the community of one's friends, neighbors, and associates are weighty factors to consider in outlining any course of action.[33] In line with good bookkeeping practices, the southern textile industry has gone to considerable lengths in the present as well as the past to rationalize its welfare activities in terms of the balance sheet.

33. See Herring, *Welfare Work,* pp. 392-94 for an evaluation of the influence of community and public opinion on mill managements.

Its critics have explained them in terms of a lust for power and control over the lives of the workers. The real explanation for many of them is extremely simple, though not logical in terms of immediate ends. They have been the things one does in an industry in a folk society. They have been folkways in themselves; ways of doing things worked out by the society in order to retain human equity and balance in an industrial situation.[34]

Any attempt to outline a typical pattern of welfare activities would be not only difficult but misleading. Just as managements past and present have denied (quite correctly) the existence of any "average" textile worker, so would they deny, with equal justice, the existence of any "average" mill whose "average" situation called for an "average" set of welfare practices. From his own observation the writer can testify that such programs vary widely from mill to mill at the present time; and from the testimony of those workers who remember the period before World War I, there was the same diversity then.[35] The only generalization that can be made is that there was ordinarily a logical relationship between what was being done and the circumstances under which the practice arose. Large country mills, with their more complex society, generally had a more elaborate program of welfare work than small country mills. Country mills in general had more extensive programs than city mills which might occasionally have no welfare program at all since the needs were being met by civic agencies. Though there were few northern owned mills before 1920, those that there were set up welfare programs very similiar to those that would have been established by a southern management under similiar conditions.

What is important to remember is the implicit assumption on the part of the southern operators that the programs were necessary—that their responsibility to the people who worked in their mills did not cease with the tendering of a cash wage. The Cotton Mill Campaign was a social movement as well as an economic development; and its

34. Many of them, though once stigmatized by the term "paternalism," have come to be regarded as standard personnel practice for any well-managed enterprise anywhere. Despite their modern sound, physical examinations, first-aid clinics, out-patient clinics, unemployment allowances, training departments, employee saving banks, mutual welfare funds, and housing loans were features of the welfare programs of various Piedmont mills before 1930.

35. See also Herring, *Welfare Work*.

leadership as a matter of simple necessity assumed social as well as economic responsibility. Had it not done so, it would never have risen to a position of leadership in the first place. These people were rebuilding a society, and they were "running some cotton mills on the side to get the money to do it with." The people who worked in the mills were a part of the society.

CHILDREN IN THE MILLS

If we have given the impression that these years before 1920 constituted a kind of golden age of employee relations in the Piedmont cotton textile industry, we have erred grievously. These people were trying to carve out new patterns of action, new ways of living, after the old had failed them. They were feeling their way. They made mistakes. They could discover only by a process of trial and error which of their former behavior patterns could be carried over from the land into a quasi-industrial society and which had to be abandoned.

Of all the rural folkways that were brought into the mills, none has received more wide-spread attention than the employment of children.[36] To understand it, we must consider the origins of the mill workers and the work habits they brought with them. On the farm, even today, all are enlisted in the daily round of activities that wring a living from the soil. If all worked on the farm, then why should they not in the mill? Parents who brought their families to the mill saw nothing unnatural in the idea of their children working and expected that an opportunity would be provided for their useful employment. The sins of the mill operators with regard to the hiring of children were as much those of omission as of commission. They were as likely to employ children at the request of their parents as to take the initiative in the process.[37] Had a mill attempted to carry out a policy of hiring only able-bodied adults on an individual basis, it would have got

36. For perhaps the most authoritative discussion of the child labor problem in the early Piedmont mills, the reader is referred to *Report on Condition of Women and Child Wage-earners in the United States,* 61st Congress, 2nd Session, Senate, Document No. 645, 1910-1913 (19 vols.); see especially Vol. VI, Elizabeth Otey's *Child Labor Legislation in Certain Textile States* (Washington, 1910). For a more recent and less detailed account, see Elizabeth H. Davidson, *Child Labor Legislation in the Southern Textile States* (Chapel Hill: University of North Carolina Press, 1939). Lahne's chapter on "Women and Children in the Mill," *op. cit.,* presents an excellent and well-documented short discussion of the problem both North and South.

37. See Lahne, *op. cit.,* pp. 122-23.

few employees. Employment was on a family-unit basis; and the units were likely to include both children and over-age adults. "If you wanted to hire a man and his wife who were really good workers and worth their wages, you usually had to hire a couple of kids, and maybe grandpa and grandma and Aunt Bessie as well," an overseer told the writer in describing hiring practices just after the turn of the century. "If you didn't, they'd go some place that *would* hire the whole family."

We must not assume that the early mills went so far as to discourage child labor, however. In this case they actively supported the continuance of a folkway that without their reinforcement would have passed out of the picture some years sooner. During the decades of rapid expansion of the industry there was a perpetual shortage of readily available labor; and children, because of their nimble fingers, were regarded as particularly well suited for employment in spinning rooms. They were, as a matter of fact, the mainstay of many spinning rooms before 1910.[38] In addition, having three or four wage earners from the same family meant maximum employment of the village; its overhead costs were the same whether it supplied an average of one or an average of three workers per room.

There was another economic aspect to child labor as well. Wage rates in the early southern mills were not sufficiently high for the head of the family to be able to support it by his own labor. There had to be at least one other wage earner, and it was a matter of choice for the family as to whether this should be the wife or one or more of the children. The decision to put the children to work in the mills had its moral aspect as well. "Father figured hard work never hurt anybody; he thought we were better off in the mill than galavanting around getting into mischief. He didn't believe in education—he thought it was all foolishness that the mill would only let us work half a day and made us go to school the other half." There were also the "bucket toters," those fathers who because of real or fancied disabilities let their children support them and confined their own labor to bringing the children their lunch in a dinner bucket at noon. Public opinion frowned upon such practices, however, and the bucket toter disappeared from the picture rather early—unless his disability was real. The roving, restless drifters could be condoned by the society;

38. See *Senate Document 645*, Vol. VI, p. 153.

but unadulterated shiftlessness had no more place in the Piedmont society of the mills than it had had in the pioneer Piedmont.[39]

The economic necessity for more than one wage earner per family was actually increased by the employment of children, though it was not realized at the time. On the whole, their labor was so inefficient that the costs of their employment had to be carried by the balance of the work force. The recollections of long service employees regarding their experiences in the mills as children, even when one makes allowance for the embroidery that has been added to make a good story, support the old bromide that "kids will be kids." They appear to have been much more concerned with what they could get away with than with what they could accomplish.[40] This state of affairs was intensified by the fact that supervision had no real direct control over them; discipline had to be channeled through the head of the family, who would be "spoken to" by the second hand or the overseer. It would not have been right under the folkways for it to have been any other way. If a man wanted to hire his children out, that was his affair; but he rather than they was finally responsible for their actions, and it was his duty, not the duty of outsiders, to administer such corrective measures as might be necessary.

The battle against child labor in the southern mills began almost simultaneously with the initial employment of children. Following the lead of Irene Ashby and such men as the Reverend Edgar Gardner Murphy of Alabama and the Reverend Alexander J. McKelvay of North Carolina, women's clubs, educators, other ministers, and some textile men (after 1903)[41] joined in a demand for legislative regulation of the employment of children in the mills. The issue was unfortunately soon lost in a maze of politics, as local politicians, becoming aware of the growing power of the industrial vote, warned the mill workers that here was an attempt to rob them of their natural rights

39. Attempts to deal with this problem by means of vagrancy laws were unsuccessful, however, Holland Thompson tells in *From the Cotton Field to the Cotton Mill* (New York: The Macmillan Company, 1906), pp. 235-39. See also *Senate Document 645*, Vol. XIX, pp. 655, 692, 788, 836.

40. In defense of their employment of children, managements pointed out that the work was intermittent and that the children spent considerable time playing in the mill and in the yard. The first Labor Bureau investigator to check into the child labor problem in the Piedmont, around the turn of the century, submitted a report that was not accepted by the Bureau and which he later published under the title *The Child That Toileth Not!* See Thompson, *op. cit.*, pp. 226-27.

41. See Lahne, *op. cit.*, p. 119.

over their children—an argument with which many mill workers were inclined to agree. There was in addition the typical antipathy of a folk society toward any form of government regulation. The matter was further complicated by well-meant but unsought aid from the North, and child labor legislation took on a sectional tinge, as southern mill owners portrayed the northern textile interests and labor unions that advocated it as seeking a means of reducing the competitive threat of the Southeast.

North and South Carolina and Alabama passed their first child labor legislation in 1903, and Georgia followed suit in 1906. The bills were of little account, since they contained no provisions for enforcement and were obviously passed to forestall more effective legislation. Alabama remedied this defect in 1907, followed by South Carolina in 1909. In general, the laws prohibited the employment of children under the age of twelve, prohibited night work for adolescents under 18, and limited them to no more than 66 hours of work per week; but the report of an Alabama factory inspector of the period with regard to the laws of his own state could have been applied with equal validity to any of the others: "The laws pertaining to the employment of children in Alabama are conspicuous by their ambiguity, inefficiency, inexplicitness and inadequacy."[42]

One weakness of the laws arose from the necessity of reconciling them with the folkways. Legislation that would not have permitted children to work in the case of a widowed mother or an invalid father would not have been accepted by a society that still regarded the family unit as the principle form of social security; but such exceptions invariably left so many loopholes in the laws that their enforcement, even had there been adequate machinery for it, would have been a problem.

Actually, the problem of child labor in the Piedmont was solved not by legislation but by the developing pattern of the socio-economic picture.[43] The southern mills outgrew child labor. The workers themselves, as they were further removed from their completely rural background, modified their views as to its social and moral desirability.[44] The mills, having experienced under protest the greater efficiency of

42. Quoted by Grace Abbott in *The Child and the State* (2 vol., University of Chicago Press, 1938), I, p. 442.
43. See Lahne, *op. cit.*, p. 124.
44. See Rhyne, *op. cit.*, p. 203-4.

adult labor under the short-lived Federal attempt to control child labor that was declared unconstitutional in 1922,[45] were in no mood to return to the practices of earlier days when compulsion was removed. The rate of expansion of the southern mills had slowed considerably, and there was not the pressure of an ever-present shortage of labor to encourage the employment of inefficient help merely to man the machinery—the advent of the boll weevil also eased the tightness of the labor market. Though wage levels dropped during the 1920s, they were sufficiently higher than they had been before the First World War to lessen the necessity for child labor from the standpoint of family sustenance. New and improved machinery, operating at higher speeds, required more skillful attention than could be depended upon from children. Finally, the long fight that had been started before 1900 by Miss Ashby and the Reverends Murphy and McKelvay had never been abandoned. Slowly it had turned public opinion in the Piedmont against the employment of children in the mills; and the society that forty years earlier had looked upon it with approval now regarded it as morally indefensible. By the time "adequate" legislation had been passed, it was not really necessary. The evil that it was designed to correct had already been corrected, by the healthy processes of social and economic growth.

MILL WORKERS AND THE COMMUNITY

No matter how carefully the transplanted farmer built up the case for himself that he was not a "hired hand," and no matter how tactfully the management of his mill reinforced him in this idea, it was impossible for the bulk of those who came from the land to the mill to avoid taking a blow to their self-respect in the process of transition. Within the environs of the mill and the mill village the worker felt a degree of security and self-assurance; there he was able to justify to himself the importance of his new function, and the fact that he enjoyed a significant status. This feeling was in general reinforced by his fellow workers and by his management. Yet he could not completely rid himself of the suspicion that he had demeaned himself by going to work in the mill, of the idea that industrial employment under a factory system carried a status in the total society lower than he had possessed even as a debt-ridden tenant farmer. He had the

45. See Davidson, *op. cit.*, pp. 250-71.

feeling also that others outside the mill had this same idea—as a matter of fact, his own self-judgement was likely to have come about through his having unconsciously assumed what he thought to be the point of view of those others whose opinions mattered to him—and to preserve his self-respect, he intuitively avoided contacts that might confirm as a fact what he already suspected.

Thus as a group he became clannish. The social isolation of the cotton-mill worker within the overall community that was to become rather marked by the 1920s was not entirely imposed by the community. A good part of it was self-isolation, a defensive measure undertaken by a people who were under the necessity of maintaining an image of their essential worthwhileness, yet who were not themselves sufficiently convinced of it to be able to bear up under critical attack.[46]

And, as long-service workers have pointed out to the writer, some of the isolation that was community-imposed had to be admitted as the fault of the mill workers themselves, largely because of their failure to amend personal habits brought from the land that were not well-regarded by the townspeople. "They didn't have to go downtown with lint in their hair," a member of a Fifty-Year Club pointed out. "It seems like sometimes they were just stiff-necked about such things, like they were telling the people 'If you ain't willing to put up with me the way I come off the shift on Saturday morning, why to the devil with you.' They were poor, but soap and water was cheap, and they could have afforded a nickle comb and a clean pair of overalls. To be honest with you, I don't blame the town people for turning up their noses at some of those folks. They just didn't smell good!"

There was, there is no question, an element of *bravura* in the unkempt appearance of some of the mill folk. There was also the fact that as rural people they were likely to discount the factor of personal appearance to a greater degree than town dwellers. There was also the fact that after a 60 or 66 hour week, the mere physical exertion involved in bathing, combing one's hair, shaving, and changing one's clothes merely to go up town seemed hardly worth the trouble. The ritual ablutions were more likely to be taken after an afternoon of relaxation, in preparation for appearance at church the next day.

And there were, of course, many people in the towns who did feel themselves to be above the mill workers—who did think that these

46. See Rhyne, *op. cit.*, pp. 194-99.

formerly rural folk had lowered themselves by accepting industrial employment. But there does not appear to have been any overt move toward social isolation of the mill people on the part of their southern communities before 1900. Even so a severe critic of the later southern scene as Cash says of the mill worker of this early era that

> We must not picture him as subjected to open snubs and taunts—as intolerably wounded in the ancient pride of his kind, and so as brooding bitterly and continually, as consumed with an ever more implacable resentment. As a matter of fact, his perception of the case was occasional and intuitive, rather than constant and conscious. For the old law of the South still held in those years quite as certainly as ever. If he was more greatly despised, yet, as always, it was mainly behind the arras—and that not so much by way of any hypocrisy or calculation as because the despisers were genuinely reluctant to offend whomever they did not suspect of the will to offend themselves, because their own scorn was itself largely confined to the narrow social sphere, because, when they stood face to face with a man, they were always sharply aware of him, as a member of a class, yes, but first and foremost as a human individuality.[47]

A good part of the conscious discrimination practiced by towns-people against the mill folk in the early days came about as the result of an indiscriminate identification of all textile workers with that group we have referred to previously: the floaters, the people who were unable to make the transition from the land to the mill without a disastrous loss of pride and self-respect. And there were of course some few families of "white trash" that infiltrated the work force—in increasing numbers (though never more than a small minority) when labor became scarce after the price of cotton improved after 1900. These people—the floaters and the simon-pure white trash who came out of the piney woods and the sand hills—were to give the respectable bulk of the mill workers a bad name out of all proportion to their numbers. It is only natural that attention should have been focussed on the fifteen or twenty percent of those people in the work force who, despising themselves despised all men, became quite definitely a bad lot, rather than on the eighty or eighty-five per cent who were honest, decent, and fighting valiantly to maintain their self-respect—particularly since the former seemed to delight in calling attention to themselves, while the latter were unnaturally self-effacing.

47. Cash, *op. cit.*, p. 212-13.

There was finally the physical isolation imposed by the village itself. Socio-psychological tendencies were reinforced by the physical
situation, particularly when the mill village had its own school and
churches.[48] This latter practice, often followed even when neighborhood schools and churches were available, was as often in deference
to the wishes of the mill workers as it was an independent decision on
the part of the mill management. With regard to the workers' desire
to maintain their churches, social and recreational activities apart from
those of the larger community, we are not justified in making a sweeping judgement that it was unwise.[49] Though there is evidence to
support the fact that existing churches sought their membership,
and that in the beginning at least there was an attempt to draw the
mill people into the social and recreational activities of the town, we
must recognize that had the invitation been accepted, the mill workers
would very likely have become meek followers of an already established
leadership. Within their own churches, their own social clubs, and
their own recreational programs, they had an opportunity to develop
their own latent talents, to be leaders as well as followers.

The maintenance of separate schools was another matter. The
segregation of mill children from village children, in those cases where
it would have been possible for them to have attended the same school,
tended to confirm and rigidify a beginning note of class consciousness.[50] It tended to admit as a matter of practice what was denied as
a matter of principle—the existence of a "cotton mill caste." A growing practice, beginning even before the First World War, of bringing
the mill school within the community system whenever it was possible,
was due in part at least to recognition of the socially undesirable consequences of segregating the children of the mill village. As we shall
note later, the present disappearance of anything resembling caste
barriers between the mill village and the balance of the community has

48. This social isolation of the industrial worker that has been widely and correctly
criticized in the case of the Piedmont textile mills is still in existence in large urban
centers of mass production industry and excites little comment. It is accepted as a
necessary evil in an urban mass society, but we feel that it must not and need not be
tolerated in the intimate and personal atmosphere of the Piedmont folk society. We
should note that it is the generally democratic orientation of the Piedmont society that
arouses this feeling, for the folk society is not "naturally" inimical to caste lines. They
may be a part of its mores; see William Graham Sumner, *Folkways* (Boston: Ginn and
Company, 1911), for example.
49. See Herring, *Welfare Work*, p. 397.
50. *Ibid.*

resulted at least in part from the association of village and town children in high school.

The First Phase of Industrial Relations

During this first phase of industrial relations in the Piedmont cotton textile industry, the problems that presented themselves were almost entirely those that arose out of the wholesale transition of people from the land to industry. Despite the inevitable occurrence of tragedies as individuals were unable to make the adjustment, the period is remarkable for the smoothness with which the task was accomplished rather than for its clumsiness. The reason for this lies in the fact that the rise of the mills was, essentially, a social rather than an economic phenomena; and that consequently those who led the movement were those who had been brought into positions of leadership by the very reason of their sensitivity toward and ability to deal with social problems. They were neither sociologists nor psychologists; they were merely men who had the vision to see that the first need of the land was for the rehabilitation of its people.

Personnel relations in the industry were based on the kind of understanding that arises through psychic as well as physical intimacy; and if a manager occasionally said "I know what these people need better than they do themselves," he was probably right. There was a sufficient degree of kinship between operator and operative to permit the former to take the role of the latter with a high degree of accuracy —and there was sufficient informal interchange of information between top management and work forces to enable operatives to understand and see the reasonableness and necessity of managerial decisions that had been formulated against a rich knowledge of worker attitudes. There was no formal code of personnel policy. Problems were worked out in terms of what was "right" and what was "wrong" according to an ethical code that was the common possession of manager and worker—the folkways and mores of a pioneer society based on a Christian morality.

The "personnel function" during those years was the responsibility of top management, delegated under close supervision to overseers. It was a responsibility that was assumed, not as a routine duty, part of one's job, but rather as an avocation. Its discharge was a matter of personal interest; and in at least a few cases there is good reason to believe that the mills were operated in order that the personnel function might be carried out rather than the other way around.[51] The mills were not philanthropic ventures by any means; they were operated to make profits, and by modern standards extremely high profits—but it was expected that the profits would be dedicated to the rebuilding of the region and the rehabilitation of its people. The pioneer concept that private property ought as a matter of course be employed for the public good prevailed, reinforcing and reinforced by the strongly Calvinistic tone of the dominant religious faiths of the Piedmont—the man of wealth was to regard himself as a steward, not as one who possessed in his own right.

Individually, the managers of the early mills were neither saints nor selfless individuals dedicated to the service of society. By the very process of selection that brought them to the top they were men who were well above the average run; but by the same process there was also the possibility that they might be either zealous or ambitious or both, and thus occasionally inclined to justify the means employed in terms of the ends that were sought. Inevitably also, there were scoundrels and blackguards among them, opportunists who had no compunctions about capitalizing on the misery of other men to achieve their own private advancement. There were also those who gloried in their economic power with no recognition of the social responsibilities that accompanied it. But good and bad alike, selfless and selfish alike, they operated under the constraints of the folkways. Community opinion and the human desire for the esteem of their peers held in check those men who might otherwise have taken full advantage of social disorganization for personal aggrandizement.

Supervision was stern, occasionally harsh—but it, like the policies of higher management, was under the necessity of abiding by the folkways; and top level management accepted the task of policing it as one of its natural functions. The result was that though the overseer was primarily concerned with the mill worker in his technical role as an operative, rather than with him in his human role as a person, he was

51. This seems certainly to have been the case with one large mill that delegated responsibility for its welfare activities to a national service organization and footed the bill for them. The welfare program eventually became so extensive that money that should have gone for plant modernization was funneled into it. Unfortunately, top management was so preoccupied with the welfare program that it failed to note that the workers were being driven in the mill to support it, and serious labor problems resulted.

forced as a practical measure to achieve results through leadership
rather than by weight of coercive authority. The minor annoyances
that arose from supervision the worker classified as inevitably a part of
the industrial process. If they became intolerable he was secure in his
trust that top management would deal with their source as it did with
a spinning frame that was out of line, for example—straighten it out
or scrap it.

The transition of so many people at one time from an agricultural
to an industrial way of life meant that there would be carried over
certain of the rural folkways that were unsuitable to the new environment, such as child labor and an extremely casual attitude toward the
necessity for formal education. It meant also that it became management's responsibility to provide not only such practical assistance as
housing, but also to assume a role of leadership in the process of transition from one way of life to another—the "welfare programs" that
have received such wide attention. Such programs were not mandatory
from an economic standpoint. They were illustrative of the unlimited
responsibilities that had to be assumed on occasion under the folkways.

The Piedmont softened and modified the impact of industrial processes upon its industrial workers during this formative period of its
cotton textile industry by the maintenance of a dual set of relationships.
There was the completely impersonal "operator-operative" axis that
arose logically out of the necessities of the industrial "operation." There
was no attempt to humanize this relationship; but it was nevertheless
utilized in a positive fashion to explain the status differences within
the industrial society of the plant. By his understanding of the importance of and relations between these statuses (heightened by the
logical structure of the division of labor in textile manufacture), the
textile worker was able to think of himself as working *with* the
management of the plant in a voluntary co-operative effort. *But this
was possible only because the impersonal relationships were played out
against a fundamental relationship of people with people that was
maintained under the folkways.* The folk were using the factory; the
institution of textile manufacture was a means to an end, and not an
end in itself. Its profits were dedicated to the rebuilding of the Piedmont society, of which its industrial workers were a part; the industrial worker was not regarded as a means toward the creation of
profits as an end in themselves.

CHAPTER VI

Time for Decision

THE INFORMAL, intuitively pursued, and on the whole satisfactory pattern of industrial relations under the folkways that was characteristic of the early period of the Piedmont cotton textile industry has not extended in an unbroken line of descent down to the present day. There had been isolated cases of labor trouble before 1914; but beginning soon after the First World War and gathering momentum all during the 1920s, a situation developed that was to culminate in a wave of strikes between 1929 and 1934.[1] There was every indication during this period that labor relations in the southern industry were turning down the road they had followed in England and New England; that they would eventually be brought under the massways, in other words.

It was during this time of labor unrest, when industrial relations in the industry were at their lowest ebb, that the still persisting stereotype of the southern cotton mills and their workers was formed by the rest of the nation—and by many people in the Southeast as well. A spotlight of national publicity was focussed on cases that were probably least typical of the industry as a whole during those difficult years; and its rays were colored by sensationalism so that only a part of the spectrum was illuminated even in these selected instances.

Yet there was labor trouble in the mills without a doubt. The circumstances that brought about the Elizabethton, the Gastonia and the Marion strikes in 1929 and the Danville strike in 1930 had been creating and continued to create unrest, though it only occasionally broke out in open warfare, among the work forces of many southern mills. The

1. See Herbert J. Lahne, *The Cotton Mill Worker* (New York: Farrar and Reinhart, Inc., 1944), pp. 203-39. The writer will continue to rely heavily on this excellent source. See also Broadus and George Mitchell's *The Industrial Revolution in the South* (Baltimore: The Johns Hopkins Press, 1930) and George Mitchell's *Textile Unionism in the South* (Chapel Hill: University of North Carolina Press, 1931).

general strike in 1934 that forced a number of southern mills to close to avoid the possibility of violence even when their own people were not involved was not entirely the work of the famed "Flying Squadrons" of the A. F. of L. The storm had been gathering for some years. There were many mills that it passed by. For some, it resulted only in mild precipitation—but for others, it culminated in a cloudburst.

Though there was no such reign of terror as sensational reporting in the national press might have led one to believe,[2] there was trouble that was sufficiently wide-spread and serious so that any attempt to discount it as merely random in nature and of no significance, or as merely an unavoidable reflection into the Piedmont of national events, is explaining it away rather than explaining it. It is true that only a minority of the Piedmont mills were affected—but they seemed a significant minority, since the troubles they were experiencing were what students of industrial relations had come to think of as inevitably a part of the pattern of industrialization of a society, the birth pains of a new order.

The difficulties in the Piedmont were heightened by the introduction of a sectional factor. In an industry as highly competitive as textiles, particularly one in which labor costs played so important a role in total production costs, national labor unions had to organize the southern mills in order to protect their organization in the North. It became apparent very early that the southern organizing drives of the A. F. of L.'s United Textile Workers of America (UTWA) were, at least from the standpoint of national policy, as likely to be dictated by the situation in the North as in the South.[3] Northern textile interests, while they were fighting organization in their own plants, were not averse to seeing the south organized ; and southern managements were not too sure that the union drives in their own region, if not subsidized by northern interests, were not at least encouraged by them. One effect of this sectional aspect was to heighten the difficulty of getting any clear picture of what was going on. The actual issues in dispute were clouded in a back-and-forth exchange of imprecations that had little to do with the problems of the southern textile worker.[4]

To complicate matters still further, an international flavor was in-

2. See Broadus and George Mitchell, *op. cit.*, p. 160.
3. Lahne, *op. cit.*, p. 206.
4. See Broadus and George Mitchell, *op. cit.*, pp. 159-60.

troduced by the strike at Gastonia. The last great strikes in the northern industry, before the First World War, had been led by the an-
archistic Industrial Workers of the World (the IWW); and one of
the first great strikes in the South after the war was led by a union
directly and frankly affiliated with the Communist Party.[5] Thus
perhaps the southern mill owners can be excused to a degree at least
for their further suspicion that all labor organizers in the textile industry were either Nihilists or Communists. The ironic fact was that
there was probably no organization in the United States in 1929 that
was more aware of the threat of Communism and that hated it more
bitterly than the American Federation of Labor; but the mill owners
were not aware of the battle that Samuel Gompers and his lieutenants
had been waging, often single-handed, against it ever since 1900.
Communist leadership of the strike at Gastonia added immeasurably to
the indigenous distrust of organized labor already existing in the Piedmont among managements and workers alike.

Labor unions of course retaliated by picturing the southern mill
owner as a conscienceless ogre, provoking labor difficulty by his heart-
less exploitation of the southern textile worker whom the unions sought
only to rescue. But labor unrest in the textile industry during the
period under discussion can be laid neither at the door of mill managements nor of labor leaders. There is a strong tendency, even today,
to explain it in terms of either one or the other; and the tendency was
even more prevalent during the late 1920s and the early 1930s—managements explained their difficulties as the result of an invasion of northern
unions; while the unions pictured themselves as merely responding to
the appeals for help from an oppressed work force.

There were a number of liberal southerners who inclined to the
latter point of view. The attitudes and labor policies of many of the
southern mill managements having labor trouble quite obviously *had*
changed, and the explanation was much simpler to make in terms of
"who" was responsible than to look for "what" was responsible. Broadus
Mitchell, for example, though he decried the sensational reporting of
southern labor troubles in the national press, minced no words himself
when he spoke of the managements of the contemporary mills in the
Virginia Quarterly Review for April of 1927. He had nothing but

5. See Liston Pope, *Millhands and Preachers* (New Haven: Yale University Press,
1942), for a full-scale and detailed accounting of this strike and its background.

praise for the early managements; his account of their work in *The Rise of Cotton Mills in the South* is very sympathetic, and he echoes his earlier sentiments regarding them in 1927:

> These industrial leaders in the South in the opening decades [of the Cotton Mill Campaign] were of a different stripe from most of the cotton manufacturers, mine owners and iron masters who figured in the English Industrial Revolution. The former were gentlemen, the latter were small men who struck it lucky. Only such exceptional individuals as Robert Owen, Richard Arkwright and Samuel Oldknow, who were philanthropists while they were employers, were of the same temper with the first Southerners. In New England the rigors of the outset of factory employment had been softened by such a benevolent proprietor as Francis Lowell. But just as in Old England and New England, gain got the better of generosity, so in the South a second generation of manufacturers chose speedily to hunt with the hounds.
>
> In fact, they are industrialists, business men, capitalists, and congratulate themselves upon supporting these characters. They are not subject to the restraints of their fathers. They do not have an emotional attitude toward their workers. They are not burdened with a sense of *noblesse oblige*. They are not aristocratic, but bourgeoise. They are class-conscious and money-wise.[6]

Mitchell's bitterness, which becomes more apparent as the article progresses, arises out of his feeling that somehow the South has been betrayed, that the great promise of the early days has somehow been stifled by a "money-wise" group who have come to power, and who will soon make of the Piedmont a great industrial slum. He realized what the Piedmont could become if it held to the high ideals of the Cotton Mill Campaign, and he lashed out at those whom he felt were leading it astray. Yet he himself saw that the mill owners were not actually at the root of the change; for later in the article cited he says of "the Southern business man of today [1927]" that "He himself and all the agencies which speak with him are products of a stage of economic evolution."

Mitchell is an idealist—but he is also an economist; and both as an idealist and an economist in 1927 he was impatient with the deliberate processes of social change. He was impatient with the slow and meandering path that a society must necessarily take toward its ultimate goals. He was aware, as an economist, of the powerful forces of "economic evolution" that worked against the fulfillment of the

6. Reprinted in *The Industrial Revolution in the South*, pp. 32-33.

high promises of the early days of the mills. He was not equally aware
of the powerful social forces that might eventually prove to be a corrective factor and set the mills once more upon a modification of their
original path—social forces that included, among other things, his own
attacks upon the deviations of the sons from the ways of their fathers.
Mitchell was not a disinterested bystander, not an objective analyst.
He was himself a part of what was going on in 1927, himself a product
of the Piedmont South, fighting as a reformer for what, as an economist, he could hardly admit as a possibility—the development of an
industrial society that would retain the way of the folk. Mitchell
exemplifies perfectly a trait we have noted as characteristic of Piedmont
thinking, the refusal to recognize those aspects of "reality" that would
stand in the way of the attainment of a goal.

W. J. Cash, though no such scholar as Mitchell, nevertheless comes
closer to what was happening, but like Mitchell, he tends to put the
emphasis upon the *who* rather than upon the *what*. In his *Mind of
the South* he tells us that

In the mills themselves the gulf was growing. Most of the old barons
were dead or dying. . . . In the main, their shoes were now filled by their
sons or successors. Many of these had been trained in the tradition of the
old close personal relationship between master and man, and, particularly
in the smaller mills, sought to continue it; but they . . . had little time really
to cultivate it. Too, the generally greater spread in their education and
background made it more difficult to get close to the worker than it had
been for their fathers.

Still another thing that sometimes cut straight across the tradition was
the Yankee cult of the Great Executive. Seducing the vanity especially of
the young men who had been educated in the Northern business schools,
and their imitators, it led them to surround themselves with flunkies and
mahogany and frosted glass, with the result that the worker who had been
accustomed to walking into the Old Man's office without ceremony could
no longer get to them save at the cost of an effort and a servility which
were foreign to his temper and tradition.

These men of the new generation would by ordinary go on [following
the practices of their fathers]; but they did it, in part perhaps because of
growing calculation, but more . . . because it was something one was supposed to do in the circumstances—habitually and mechanically, but, typically speaking, without the direct interest and zeal which had belonged to the
elder men.

That is to say, the feeling which had lain at the heart of the old notion
of paternalistic duty was fast dwindling, leaving only the empty shell—at

the same time that the notion of paternalistic *privilege* was remaining as strongly entrenched as ever, and even perhaps being expanded.[7]

What Cash is saying is that the content of understanding that must underly the folkways was fast draining out of the relationship between operator and operative, leaving the people in such cases with no effective social organization at all, either folk or mass. He is correct in his analysis, except that he leaves with us the impression that there was what was almost a deliberate turning away of the people in management from the workers. The gulf was there in enough establishments to cause concern; but we are not entitled to assume that it was there as the result of deliberate choice unless we can find no more reasonable explanation.

In this chapter we want to look behind personalities and get some idea of the broad social and economic forces to which managements had to answer—forces which may in their own right have been creating the gulf, manifesting themselves in changing managerial attitudes, policies, and practices, and in changing attitudes on the part of the workers.

Some of the influences were national in origin. They were of an all-pervading nature. No management or work force escaped them completely; they were a part of the climate of the times, influences against which no particular management could erect an effective barrier, influences that were beyond the scope of the region itself so far as protection against them was concerned. Their presence was the price the Piedmont had to pay for its entry into a national market; and all that could be done about them was to learn how to live with them.

Some of the influences were regional. These also were beyond the power of individual managements to combat, but since they had their origin primarily within the regional society, there was the possibility at least that the region itself might be able to deal with them.

That these regional and national influences, having their origins outside any specific mill, should result in labor trouble in some cases and not in others would reasonably depend partly upon their configuration as they impinged upon particular enterprises and partly upon the ability of particular enterprises to contain, isolate, and live with them.

7. Cash, *op. cit.*, p. 270.

This latter ability, in turn, would depend upon certain factors that were largely local, that would have arisen out of the past history and present circumstances of particular organizations. It would be untrue to say that labor troubles would arise in every case because of local circumstances, for there might be instances where national and regional influences would combine in such a way as to render local managements helpless. Certainly local influences would be the final and deciding factor in many instances.

(We must caution that what follows is not intended to be a representative picture of the Piedmont textile industry during the 1920's and early 1930's. We concern ourselves only with disturbing influences and their manifestation in labor trouble. We do *not* concern ourselves with other influences of a stabilizing nature that for the bulk of the industry cancelled out the set we do identify. This chapter is analytical rather than representative. It deals with the infected area rather than with the more extensive one that remained healthy.)

National Influences

The Piedmont, by 1920, was becoming much more closely knit into the national society than it had been previously. Its participation in the national cotton textile market was being supplemented by other ties. The people of the Piedmont were much more aware of what was going on outside their region. Many of its younger men had served in the Armed Forces during World War I. They had trained in military camps outside the Southeast; they had even been to foreign countries. Mass communication media were coming into the Piedmont. Daily newspapers printed in Atlanta, Birmingham, Charlotte, Greenville, Columbia, Augusta, and other large southern cities were finding an increasingly larger number of subscribers in the textile villages. This was partly the result of high wage levels which, during the war years, had permitted such luxuries. It was partly also the result of an increasing level of education that made such media useful. But it was mostly the result of an increasing interest on the part of the textile worker in what was going on outside the mill village.

Industry outside the Piedmont was drawing off its surplus population to midwestern cities like Detroit, Akron, Flint, and Dearborn; and these emigrants kept the people at home in occasional touch with the workaday world outside. There was, finally, toward the latter part of the period, the radio over which the rallying cry for the general strike in 1934 would be sounded by the officers of the United Textile Workers. The Piedmont was in closer touch with the balance of the national society than it had ever been before.

Economic Factors

The textile industry, both North and South, entered the Great Depression in 1921, not in 1929 with the rest of the nation—the brief revival of textile demand and prices in 1921 had proved to be a false dawn. Chief among specific forces having their origin outside the region, that were of consequence to its industrial relations, was the whole economic state of the textile industry itself. This embodied a productive capacity that not only had caught up with but that had outdistanced the national capacity to consume, with consequent surpluses and low prices. It involved a long delayed but finally achieved awakening in the Northeast to the serious nature of the competitive threat of the Piedmont in cotton textiles and the consequent flare-up of sectional feeling; the trek of northern firms to the Southeast; wages cut-backs North and South, with widespread unemployment in the North and considerable "short time" and some unemployment in the South. All of this played out against a background of general prosperity for the nation as a whole.

Wage Cuts and Reduced Hours.—The textile industry had enjoyed high wages during and immediately after World War I. A southeastern male weaver, for example, was earning $29.30 for a full week's work in 1920.[8] This wage was 99 per cent of the national average in the industry for full-time employment. Two years later, the average full-time earnings of southern male weavers had fallen to $17.34, which amounted only to 85 per cent of the national average for such employment in the industry for 1922—and *full time* weekly earnings were no longer a realistic gauge of actual income.[9] Until 1920, wages in the southern industry had climbed slowly but steadily, and the North-South wage differential had been slowly closing. Now for the first time the southern textile worker would contrast present earnings with past earnings that had been considerably higher, and at

8. See Abraham Berglund, George T. Starnes, and Frank T. DeVyver, *Labor in the Industrial South* (University, Va.: The Institute for Research in the Social Sciences, 1930), p. 96.
9. *Ibid.*

the same time he could see his hope for parity with the northern operator apparently fading away just when it finally had seemed within his
grasp.

The southern worker had enjoyed his brief taste of prosperity during the war years just long enough to establish a new standard of living
for himself, but he was unable to maintain this after the wage cut-
back. The Model T that he had financed out of flush pay-checks, for
example, rusted away in the yard because he could not afford the tires
and repairs he needed to keep it on the road. His low wages seemed
particularly vexing to him since for nearly every one else it was a
period of prosperity—his cousin in the auto plant up in Detroit was
writing home of fabulous sums in his pay envelope. But the textile
worker was faced with the problem of paying boom-time prices for
what he bought, out of a depression pay-check that was occasionally
further reduced by short time.

He had not worried too much about the North-South differential
as he had seen it slowly disappearing; but now its re-appearance was
cause for concern. That its revival, plus occasional short work weeks,
at least enabled the southern industry to continue to employ him,
while the northern industry which maintained higher wage levels was
forced to make drastic permanent curtailments in its work force, was
cold comfort to him even when it was brought to his attention.

Demands for Higher Skills.—Economic trends in the cotton textile
industry reflected themselves into the southern picture in a second
fashion. The Piedmont mills were gradually shifting to yarns and
fabrics that made greater demands on the worker for the maintenance
of a quality product.[10] Thus at the same time that his earnings were
dropping, the southern worker was being asked to pay closer attention
to what he was doing and to develop higher technical skills.

Increased Work Loads.—A third manifestation of the economic
situation was directly tied to increasing competition for existing markets and the necessity of cutting production costs. Labor costs per
unit of output can be reduced either by paying less for the same amount
of production or by paying the same amount or a relatively smaller increase for greater production. In the latter case, however, not only are

10. Not always to finer-count yarns and higher-count fabrics. The shift might
actually be to a coarser count but to a fabric demanding higher standards of quality,
such as suitings, cords, draperies, and tapestries.

labor unit costs reduced, but if the greater output can be achieved with no appreciable increase in capital investment or indirect labor, overhead costs per unit of output are lessened as well. The economic exigencies of the situation required drastic measures and so, in addition to wage cuts, the "stretch-out" was introduced into southern mills. That his work load had previously been rather light compared with that of the northern worker was inconsequential;[11] the southern worker compared the number of looms he was now asked to tend with the number he had previously been tending in the past, not with what it was reported others had been doing. And, as we shall note in a moment, his work load was not always increased in the most expeditious fashion or in a manner calculated to gain his co-operation.

The Great Depression.—After 1929, the whole national economy joined textiles in the depression cellar; but it was hardly a case, so far as textiles were concerned, of misery enjoying company. If surpluses in the industry had been hard to move while the nation as a whole had enjoyed high purchasing power, the task seemed impossible now. The people in the mills saw warehouses crammed to bursting with unsold goods. Short time became a chronic condition rather than an occasional circumstance that afforded an opportunity for a fishing trip or a visit to the folks back on the farm. The gloom and despair of an entire nation plunged overnight into a depression the like of which it had never before known, reinforced and intensified the feelings of uncertainty and anxiety that had been accumulating in the textile industry since the opening of the decade.

While the nation as a whole had been prosperous, there had at least been hope for tomorrow for the people in the mills, even if today were lean. They did not doubt too seriously that things would eventually work themselves out. But when every newspaper carried stories of wide-spread unemployment and pictures of the people whom they had depended upon to buy the output of their looms queued up in bread lines, the possibility of the future was hardly something to put much trust in. Emigrant relatives, returning from their boom-time jobs in the now depression-blighted industrial centers of the Midwest, made more mouths to feed when there was less food on the table; and their embittered comments as to the degree of security that a wage

---

11. See Malcolm Kier, *Industries of America—Manufacturing* (New York: Ronald Press, 1938), p. 35.

earner might expect to enjoy in the world of mass production industry did nothing to add to the confidence of those who welcomed them home.

Only where there was the same direct communication and understanding between managements and work forces in the mills during the 1920's and early 1930's that there had been during an earlier day, was it possible for the workers to assume the managerial point of view sufficiently to see the necessity for what was happening with regard to wages, hours, and work loads; but in far too many cases this communication and understanding either was no longer present or was ineffective. For the first time the southern textile worker began to wonder occasionally if he was not being systematically exploited by the people who employed him. For the first time, his faith in the folk society was shaken. For the first time, he occasionally began to think of himself as an "employee."

The Decade of the Efficiency Expert.—The work that Taylor, the Gilbreaths, Gantt, and others of their stature had done in the field of truly scientific management between 1900 and 1920 was of fundamental and lasting importance. Tied in with the work in psychology that had been sparked by William James and was being actively pursued in universities across the country, it investigated the capabilities and possibilities of man as a physiological and psychological mechanism. However, the founders of the work in scientific management seldom forgot that man was a human being as well as a marvellously complex machine that could be "conditioned" and that would "respond" to a stimulus.

Their work came to the attention of others who failed to take into account this implicit assumption of the industrial worker's humanity. These men, many of them opportunists, seized only upon the definition of him as a mechanism. The production of stop watches mounted overnight as efficiency experts lurked behind every pillar, time-studying every conceivable operation. They based their calculations as to how much work a man ought to be able to do upon their estimates of his optimum possibilities as a fuel-consuming mechanism rather than upon his human tendencies and responses. Very often their estimates of his mechanical possibilities were in error since many of them lacked the fundamental scientific background of Taylor and his compeers. They developed complicated incentive systems to stimulate the worker to ever more effort. They cut back the rates when they discovered they had underestimated his capabilities, or when they established standards that were incapable of fulfillment, they blamed the stupidity of the work force or poor or uncooperative supervision for failure to achieve them. Their big mistake was their failure to precede time study with methods analysis, motion study, and work simplification. They expected higher production from the worker but gave him no help in achieving it.[12]

While "efficiency engineering" was originally a northern development, and the mills that came south during the 1920's usually brought its practices with them and were its most ardent proponents, it would inevitably have invaded the Piedmont in any case. With falling prices for their product and increasing costs of operation, southern managements were on the lookout for anything that would increase their competitive position. Their failure to adopt these new methods before the northern mills was not because of their ignorance of them, but rather because of an uneasy distrust of the implied assumptions of "scientific management." Mill managers of the first generation, and many of the second, felt intuitively that in some essential fashion the new ideas of "efficiency" as they were too frequently portrayed denied the humanity of the people who worked for them. The Captain, of whom we spoke in the previous chapter, asserted vehemently and often that there would never be a stop watch in his mill as long as he was the head of it.

There were some of the second generation, however, who were not so reluctant to try out the new ideas; and the others were forced eventually to adopt some means of increasing work loads because the southern work loads *were* low compared with those in the North, and they had to be increased if the southern mills were to survive.

Difficulties, when they arose, were generally not so much over the increase in work loads as because of the methods chosen to increase them.[13] When the cold, business-like technics of the efficiency expert

12. Taylor, for example, was basically a methods study engineer who first devised the most efficient way to do a job and then used an incentive system to enable workers to share in the rewards of increased production; otherwise, he had discovered, they would restrict output despite the improvement in method. Many of the "efficiency experts," however, regarded an incentive system as a lash rather than as a reward. Methods study and time study were not formally combined during the 1920's. Both were practiced, but independently.

13. The fault was not so much with the incentive systems that were used, for many

were employed, there was likely to be trouble. The professional ex-
ponents of efficiency during the 1920's were likely to be impatient with
the human aspect of the worker. They saw no necessity for explaining to him why methods were being changed or an incentive plan
installed. They regarded him as an *employee;* the basic relationship
had been established between himself and management by the act of
employment, and he had no right to question the decisions of management as to how his services were to be utilized during his working
hours. The old assumption of the worker that had sustained his self-
respect and made him a part of the total organization of the plant—the
idea that he was working *with* the mangement of the enterprise in a
joint co-operative venture—was completely ignored. He was expected
merely to respond mechanically to the stimulus of an incentive plan.

Supervisors, in those mills that had "efficiency" trouble, were seldom
better informed as to the reason for the installation of the new
incentive plan or the new methodology than was the hourly rated
worker; and the resulting short answers they were thus likely to give
when questioned about it did not increase the worker's inclination
toward acceptance. Failing to receive a satisfactory explanation from
managerial sources, the worker was certain to seek elsewhere; and very
often the union explanation seemed reasonable to him—this was the
notorious "stretch-out," designed to make him work harder for less
money; and the complicated incentive plans were designed principally
to keep him from knowing how much of his pay he was being robbed
of by the company.

On the basis of interviews with long-service employees, it appears
that experiments with "scientific management" stood next to poor
supervision in importance as an immediate cause of poor labor relations
during the period under discussion. In nearly all cases, the trouble
arose when managements failed to seek the co-operation of their people
in solving the problems that faced them. When this latter course was
followed—and there were many mills in which it was—work loads
were increased and methods changed without serious repercussions.[14]

---

of them were fundamentally sound and are still in use today. Difficulties, when they
arose, could be credited usually either to the ineptitude of the men who installed them
or to dictatorial managements. As a mill official told the writer, "The main trouble
with the Bedaux System was that some of the men who put it in were plain damn'
fools."

14. Yet there were repercussions, though indirect, even in these mills. Smooth

The influence of unadulterated "scientific management" upon some of the mills of the period, however, was tersely described to the writer: "The trouble with some of those folks was, they got efficiency-happy!" The result was unrest on the part of people who resented being treated in an "efficient" fashion.

On important occasions this resentment broke out into open revolt. Broadus and George Mitchell, discussing the origin of the strike in a foreign-owned rayon plant at Elizabethton, Tennessee, tell us that the company "brought in an efficiency engineer who was to teach the people how to dispense with extra motions in their work. Two hundred of them went out, and the next day 5000 were parading. Union organizers flocked in. . . . Another strike against the stop-watch broke out in Greenville, South Carolina."[15]

The ideas of the efficiency expert extended beyond time-studies, wage plans, and methods analysis. The efficient way to do everything was sought, often without sufficient analysis of its long-run consequences. It was this, rather than any sedulous aping of northern practice, that resulted in the adoption on occasion of what Cash called "the Yankee cult of the Great Executive." It was more "efficient," for example, to sit at a desk and study personnel reports and statistics relating to the composition of the work force than it was to go out into the plant and indulge in the time-consuming and highly "inefficient" practice of getting acquainted with the people at first hand. It was "efficient" to save the time of top management people by making them hard to see, by surrounding them with secretaries, frosted glass, and mahogany. The efficiency expert saw the Great Executive seated at his desk, scanning reports, pushing buttons, dictating directives, or presiding at the conference table, as completely isolated as possible from the distracting human element.

The Rise of Absentee Management

In this case, the absentee management was generally northern. The period from 1923 on marked the wholesale trek of northern firms to the South as they sought lower operating costs and a better labor climate. In the majority of cases they employed southern mill man-

---

operation of methods improvement and incentive systems resulted in more production and higher wages, but very often also in a reduction in the size of the work force which aggravated the problem of unemployment.

15. Broadus and George Mitchell, *op. cit.,* pp. 188-89.

agers, or at least left the task of immediate and intermediate supervision
to southerners, and thus gave themselves an opportunity to feel their
way in unfamiliar surroundings. But they did not escape any of the
difficulties that were beginning to plague native southern firms; and
there was introduced into the situation for their work forces the additional element of uncertainty that comes from knowing that the
policy-making function is vested in the hands of outsiders, often not
even on the scene, who are unacquainted with, and perhaps even
contemptuous of, local "ways of doing things."

Thus the work force of such a newly arrived northern company
suffered from more than the usual amount of anxiety. It was alert,
quick to read the worst into every chance move, every experimental
gesture. Though on-the-spot management was often entirely local in
its origin, it did not enjoy complete freedom of action. It was under
constraint even when it was granted autonomy in the task of creating
personnel policy, for its actions were still subject to review by higher
echelons of management. When local management was under the
necessity of administering personnel policy that had been framed
elsewhere, often with little knowledge of the conditions under which
it was to be applied, the situation was even more touchy.

So for an increasingly larger section of the southern work force,
there was the disturbing knowledge that the ultimate control of the
enterprise was vested in an absentee management that had not yet had
time to demonstrate its sincerity, its good will, or its firm decision to
abide by the ethical code that was the foundation of labor relations in
the Piedmont.

Unfortunately also, in a few instances northern managements
demonstrated their apparently deliberate intention to disregard the
whole pattern of implicit understandings that had heretofore governed
southeastern employee relations in general. The disastrous strike at
Gastonia, for example, seems to have been the result of a callous and
contemptuous disregard of regional customs in the industry by an
imported "stretch-out superintendent" who was, reportedly, assigned
the task by his northern management of reducing costs by a half million dollars per year in the mill. The stretch-out itself was ineptly
handled; but Liston Pope, discussing the background of the strike in

Millhands and Preachers, says that

> The deeper causes of strife were not simply economic but cultural in a broader sense. Alien methods of industrial relations had been introduced into an industrial situation which had come to depend, for unity and peace, on paternal relations, and to expect emphasis on community welfare rather than on productive efficiency alone. Emphasis . . . on the latter goal to the detriment of the former led to the importation of workers who were often outcasts from other communities, and largely ignored the problem of creating of these heterogeneous elements a new community. In addition, the older residents of the village were alienated from loyalty to the mill by the unfamiliar tactics of an arbitrary superintendent, and from pride in the community by resentment over the sudden influx of new and cheaper labor. At the end of 1928 the . . . village was an industrial camp, not a community, and its inhabitants resembled, in terms of social organization, a mob more nearly than an organized society.[16]

The sympathies of the Gastonia community as a whole were with the workers, and local clergymen wrote strong letters of protest to the northern owners of the firm with regard to the developing situation. Townspeople were particularly incensed over the company's repeated violations of one of the most powerful of the unwritten customs of the southern industry; it made no attempt to screen the admission of new residents to the village, to appraise their social desirability from the point of view of their future neighbors. It herded "workers who were often outcasts from other communities" into the village like so many cattle into a corral.

Before any steps could be taken to remedy the situation, however, the Communistic National Textile Workers Union moved in on the scene to make capital for themselves out of the existing discontent, and their presence overshadowed the basic cause of the trouble. The N. T. W. U. managed to increase Piedmont management's already existing suspicion of labor unions, however, and the events leading up to the strike tended to increase people's anxiety as to what the future might hold for them if and when their mill was bought out by a northern firm.

The southeastern industry was still largely southern-owned during the late 1920's and the early 1930's; but the discontent arising from misunderstandings and poor handling of labor relations in some of the mills that had recently come under the control of outside interests or

16. Pope, *op. cit.,* p. 232-33.

that had been built by them was infectious. It is perhaps significant that the two major strikes of 1929 at Elizabethton and Gastonia that touched off a whole series of lesser disturbances took place in absentee-owned and managed mills.

Union Activity[17]

Organizational activity was not a basic cause of the unrest of the Piedmont work force during the 1920's and the early 1930's, yet there is no question but that the unions capitalized on the unrest that was already there. In many cases they fanned into open flames what were only the smoldering embers of half-sensed resentment, and they did their best to kindle fires where there were no embers at all. This whole topic of unions and the Piedmont textile industry is sufficiently important and interesting to deserve additional treatment in later chapters; but we must note here that union organizing drives were an important element in keeping the southern textile worker restless and primed for action all during the period under discussion.

Labor unions were nothing new in the Piedmont textile industry. The Knights of Labor, as early as 1886, had more of its trade assemblies in cotton textiles in the Piedmont, proportionate to the extent of the industry, than it had in New England. The A. F. of L. made an appropriation for organizing the southern mills under its International Union of Textile Workers in 1895; and a textile worker from Columbus, Georgia, was president of the union from 1898 to 1900. In 1901 he became secretary-treasurer of the present A. F. of L. union, the United Textile Workers of America, that succeeded the I. U. T. W. in that year. After an unsuccessful strike at Augusta in 1902, union activity in the textile South died down, as the U. T. W. turned to the task of solidifying its position in New England. The latter union renewed its activities in the Piedmont during World War I, and about forty locals were formed; but according to Lahne, "there was no indication of any coherent plan for organizing the South as a whole."[18] He notes also that during this period of prosperity for the mills, when it was possible to increase wage payments without jeopardizing the

17. Unless otherwise credited, this discussion of union activity during the period has been drawn from Lahne, *op. cit.*
18. *Ibid.*, p. 204.

security of the enterprise, "there was no concerted opposition from employers and the union grew in the South as never before."[19]

A strike at Columbus, Georgia, in 1918 was the opening gun in a wave of strikes that swept through the Piedmont in 1919, lessened somewhat in 1920, and collapsed in an unsuccessful effort to prevent the wage cuts of 1921. All the gains the U. T. W. had made in membership in the Southeast during and immediately after the war were wiped out by the end of 1921.

There was practically no union activity in the South between 1921 and 1929. But, Lahne reports,

Starting early in 1929, a powder train of strikes flashed through the astonished South. Many of them were without unionism at all, and were under purely local leadership, whose main concern was the alleviation of the burden of the stretch-out. These were invariably short-lived, small affairs which brought the workers partial success.[20]

The U. T. W. rapidly moved back into the Piedmont, feeling that now, with worker dissatisfaction evidencing itself in spontaneous walkouts, the time had come when it might achieve permanent organization. It took over the informal walkout at Elizabethton, Tennessee, and a few months later moved into Marion, North Carolina, where a company, hoping to recoup a loss of $40,000 suffered through a mistake in the installation of an incentive system, had added twenty minutes to an already long working day. In the meantime, the Communistic National Textile Workers Union had taken over the dispute at Gastonia. The Piedmont Organizing Council, sponsored by the independent American Federation of Textile Workers, had been actively engaged in organizational efforts since late in 1928.

In 1929 the A. F. of L. decided to throw the whole of its strength behind the U. T. W.'s new campaign to organize the Piedmont. The test of strength came in 1930 at Danville, Virginia, where an already existing company union had refused to accept a 10 per cent wage cut. After a strike of four months duration, which started out rather peacefully but which grew more bitter as time went on, it became apparent that the union could not gain its objectives. The U. T. W. claimed a moral victory and ended the strike officially; but it was obvious that it had lost the struggle. ". . . its attempt to gloss over this inescapable

19. *Ibid.*
20. *Ibid.*, p. 216.

fact had lost the respect of the workers as well. This episode closed the union invasion of the South,"[21] says Lahne in summary of his account.

The last upsurge of union activity in the Piedmont during the period came in 1934 as part of the general strike, North and South, arising out of the U. T. W.'s dissatisfaction with the operation of the NRA code for cotton textiles.[22] In the Piedmont, the union organized "Flying Squadrons"—motorcades of organizers and pickets that set out from organized centers and either persuaded or forced the workers in unorganized mills to quit work. In many cases, little persuasion and no pressure was necessary to provoke a walkout; there was "strike fever" in the air. The whole pattern of forces that is the topic of discussion in this chapter, and of which outright organizing activity was only one part, had already operated to create a situation of explosive tension that was touched off by the arrival of the Flying Squadron. There was in addition the fact that for almost two years union organizers had been urging southern workers that "President Roosevelt wants you to join the union," and those who had joined, and had been "payin' their dues to the gov'ment" were beginning to want some action for their money. A present union official who was a leader of one of the Squadrons at that time told the writer, "There was nothing to it. We'd roll up to mill after mill at shift-changing time. All we'd have to do was say to the people going to work, 'Let's close it down, boys!' and out they'd come."

If they did not come out, pickets were thrown around the mill. Picket-line struggles almost inevitably ensued when the workers who were not in sympathy with the strike attempted to go back and forth to work, and for this reason many mills were voluntarily closed to

21. *Ibid.,* p. 224. See also George Mitchell, *op. cit.,* p. 65.
22. While the National Industrial Recovery Act (N.I.R.A.) with its famous Section 7a which gave federal protection to the organization of industrial workers was hailed as a boon by labor, the U.T.W. was very unhappy with the way in which the National Recovery Administration (N.R.A.) under General Johnson set up the Textile Code. They felt that management had been given too free a hand in writing it; and action on their part was precipitated when General Johnson agreed to a management proposal to reduce operations to 30 hours per shift, for 60 or 90 days, at the same hourly wage. The Winant Committee, appointed by President Roosevelt to mediate the 1934 general strike, reported that "the whole system of administering the labor provisions of the code has completely lost the confidence of labor in this industry and is for that reason alone incapable of functioning satisfactorily in the future. (*Report of the Board of Inquiry for the Cotton Textile Industry to the President,* September 17, 1934, pp. 2-3).

avoid the possibility of bloodshed even when their people had refused to strike. Ten thousand National Guards were called out in the South, an informal variety of "martial law" was declared in Georgia, and vigilante committees were organized in the Carolinas. The strike had been called on Labor Day. On September 22 it was terminated by the Executive Board of the U. T. W., on the basis of an expressed hope by President Roosevelt that the strikers would return to work and that the employers would take them back without discrimination. The strike was already beginning to crumble in the South, however, and it is doubtful if any other practical course was open to the union.

Despite the inconclusive settlement, the union, as it had done at Danville, announced as a "great victory" what was actually a strategic retreat. In this case, as at Danville, the workers themselves were aware of the extent of the "victory." Again, Lahne points out, "their resentment rebounded to the detriment of the union and the officials who had led them . . . Greater frankness with the workers would have provided a better basis for future organizational efforts."[23]

The union, in short, capitalized on the existing state of labor unrest in the Piedmont. How much of its activity was due to an earnest desire to improve conditions for the southern workers and how much of it was an attempt to raise southern costs of production sufficiently to keep northern mills in operation is a debatable question which no amount of research is ever likely to answer. The immediate effect of its activities seems to have been more detrimental than otherwise. Its organizational activities achieved nothing for the people who participated in them.[24] The spontaneous, unorganized walkouts had been "short-lived, small affairs that had brought the workers partial success," which was about all the success that could have been hoped for when one considers the economic state of the industry. They had not resulted in serious breaches between operators and operatives; the difficulties had been ironed out and the people had gone back to work.

The union-engineered walkouts were invariably unsuccessful even on a partial basis; but what was much more tragic, they operated in

23. Lahne, *op. cit.*, p. 231.

24. Even where permanent organization was achieved it put the union members out on a limb. If their union disintegrated their managements would discharge them, and they would find it very difficult to get work elsewhere. Under such conditions a local was in no position to bargain advantageously; it might agree to work loads, for example, exceeding those in non-union mills.

a deliberately created emotional atmosphere that drove both managements and workers to extremes of action. Deeds were performed in bitter anger that could not be recalled. Mutual trust and confidence vanished. Managements, stoney-faced in their disillusionment over the actions of the people in whom they had believed, refused to re-employ the strikers. "We lost a lot of good people on account of the strike," a long-service worker soberly told the writer. "I guess you can't blame Mr.———for not taking them back. He trusted them, and it was pretty much of a blow to him when they listened to the union instead of to him. But they were good people, and they had some right on their side too. I tell you this mill suffered for a long time after they left."

REGIONAL INFLUENCES

In addition to the national influences we have just discussed, there were two important influences of a regional nature during the period under discussion that had their effect upon industrial relations in the cotton textile industry. One was socio-economic in nature. The other was socio-psychological.

The "New" Cotton Mill Campaign

During the 1920's, a fresh wave of enthusiasm over mill building arose in the Piedmont. This new campaign was not of the same nature as the first, however. That of the 1880's had been almost entirely a social phenomena. The new excitement had a much stronger economic basis. It was to a degree derivative in nature, a side-effect of more fundamental happenings. Its origin was in the shift of the industry to the Southeast.

Southern communities woke up to the fact, soon after 1920, that the northern textile industry was becoming interested in the Piedmont. It is doubtful if they had a great deal to do with the rate at which subsequent northern investment took place, except as they had already built the mills that had created the economic situation lying at the root of the transfer of interest. But northern money was coming down, and it had to locate somewhere. It was possible to exert some influence over where it was to be invested, even though the original decision to come South was seldom made on the basis of any specific invitation. Chambers of Commerce, Service Clubs, Merchants' Committees, banks, power companies, individuals—agency after agency, official, semi-official and unofficial—sought to direct the new flow of industry to one particular location rather than to another.

It is this second campaign for cotton mills, which was actually competition between various southern communities for the migrant industry of the North, that most people unfamiliar with the history of the southern industry believe to be the first and only campaign. The original campaign did its best to attract northern capital during its first years, but finally gave it up as a hopeless task and directed its activity toward the home front. The second campaign had no need to attract industry South; it was already on its way. Thus its success was foreordained, and it continued and increased in intensity.

The first campaign had been a homespun affair, an extemporaneous movement that had had no touch of professionalism about it but was nevertheless highly integrated on a regional basis. It was one campaign, one all-enveloping social movement, that had the support of all elements in the Piedmont. Its success in one community in no way detracted from, but rather facilitated, its success in another. The second campaign was not integrated. It was actually a multiplicity of individual campaigns, and the success of one lessened the possibilities for success of another. It was, in a way, a Piedmont manifestation of the boom spirit of the 1920's, of the infectious urge to promote and develop that swept the nation during the decade.[25] It appeared as a single campaign only because there was what the sociologist would call "a convergence of individual lines of activity"—a lot of people doing the same thing at the same time, but with no real inter-relation or inter-dependence. It was a mass movement rather than the social movement the original campaign had been. No central organization or leadership developed, but there was nothing homespun about it. Its protagonists used the latest technics of advertising and publicity. The individual campaigns were carefully calculated to appeal to northern manufacturers and were developed along lines that would catch their attention.

They were sales campaigns, and one of the principle items they sold was the labor force of the Piedmont. They stressed the "tractable and docile" nature of the Piedmont worker until one wonders if perhaps their backers did not begin to believe it themselves—though

25. See Cash, *op. cit.*, p. 259.

any of them who had come into any contact at all with the people of
the Piedmont work force knew that tractability and docility were not
among the many and desirable virtues they possessed. They labelled
as "100 per cent Anglo-Saxon" the descendants of Scotch, Irish,
Scotch-Irish, German, and Dutch settlers along with the undeniably
Anglo-Saxon core of the work force. These minor irregularities were
unimportant—what was important was that they *were* part of a sales
talk.

For the first time, influential groups in certain Piedmont communities began to think of labor as a commodity to be sold, something that
could be traded upon and manipulated in a "deal." The prospective
mill worker, in the eyes of those who were promoting the campaigns,
lost more and more the aspect of a human being and took on primarily
statistical significance as a unit of labor. During the original campaign,
the mills had been built for the people. Now, in a sense, the people
were being put on the auction block for the sake of prospective mills.
When a community regards the labor of its citizens as a commodity
to be sold, firms moving into the area are at the very least encouraged
to think of it as a commodity to be bought; and the dangers inherent
in the commodity theory of labor had already made themselves unhappily apparent in the New England mills. This business-like attitude
toward labor that was beginning to develop in some of the Piedmont
communities not only influenced new mills that located in their
neighborhood, but also was bound to have its effect upon the points
of view of managements already located in the communities, if for
no other reason than that it represented a weakening of the coercive
control of community opinion over labor relations in local enterprises.
The community that thinks of its industrial workers as so many units
of labor is not likely to be greatly concerned with how they are faring
as people.

The Gulf Between Town and Village

This businesslike attitude toward the textile worker was to a degree
encouraged by a growing gulf between mill villages and the balance
of the Piedmont society. In turn, of course, the "sale" of Piedmont
labor tended to widen the gap still further. The mill worker and his
family had never stopped in for Sunday dinner with the local banker—
such things are not likely to happen in any society where there is suf-

ficient differentiation of function to require some men to be bankers and others to be mill workers—but on the whole, the Piedmont society of the late 1800's had been one of the most democratic in the nation. Its status differences had still been more largely determined by demonstrated function than by inheritance.

The townspeople of the early days were well aware of the importance of the mill people to their own welfare. They remembered the days of Reconstruction when the poverty of the farm people on their ravaged land had threatened the whole society. They remembered the new life that had been injected into their communities when these people had come off the farms and into the mills. They knew them for independent, proud men and women whom war and the aftermath of war had decimated but had never crushed. They thought of them as people whose history they knew, whose tragedy they respected; and they did not hold them in contempt. They did not deliberately isolate them. They attempted, so far as they were able, to draw them into the life of the community—that they were for the most part unsuccessful can be attributed as much to the stiff-necked pride of the mill workers as to any deficiencies on their own part.

But by now, in the 1920's, the days of Reconstruction were only a faded memory, and stories of the heart-rending poverty of those far-off days were something one listened to in boredom, grandfathers' tales. The mills and the villages were fixtures, and the people within them were something one took for granted. There was talk of the development of a "cotton mill caste"; the people who worked in the mills were somehow inferior. They were "lint-heads," "mill-hands," born to a subordinate status as were the people who viewed them with contempt born to one that was superior. Elements within the Piedmont were beginning to adopt the attitude of the Coastal Plain toward the industrial worker.

Cash had remarked of earlier days that if the mill worker was despised "it was mainly behind the arras"; for "the despisers were genuinely reluctant to offend whomever they did not suspect of the will to offend themselves." In those early days, "when the workman went into town, there was still much the same personal atmosphere that had always existed. As in the old days, there was always some more or less exalted person to invite him into the closet for a drink." But now, in the 1920's

The mill worker might wander the streets all day without ever receiving a nod or smile from anybody, or any recognition of his existence other than a scornful glance from a shop-girl. . . . The business men down town . . . increasingly absorbed in manipulating intangible values . . . inevitably had less and less time to take account of such matters as the personality of a mere workman.[26]

And in the 1920's the contempt was no longer behind the arras. The white collar workers, the growing middle class of the burgeoning Piedmont towns, were particularly likely to display it, confirming the sociological observation that class differences are more keenly felt and more likely to be scrupulously observed as there is less differentiation of function to justify them. The writer was told of an incident that took place during the 1920's. "Ma always hoped that some day she'd be able to afford a pair of pretty shoes. She used to stand in front of the window of the shoe store when we'd be down town of a Saturday afternoon, just looking at the fine shoes with their thin soles and soft leather and fancy stitching that the town women wore. After us kids got out of school and went to work in the mill there was a little extra money once in a while, so one Saturday afternoon she dragged Pa inside the shoe store. She found a pair of real pretty shoes sitting on a counter, just the kind she'd always dreamed of having; and when the clerk finally came to wait on her, she pointed to them and said 'I'd like to try on some like that.' The clerk just looked at her. 'Those shoes aren't for mill hands,' he says. He pointed to a pair of thick-soled, ugly shoes like she'd worn all her life. 'This is what we sell to mill hands,' he told her."

Though the attitude of the shoe clerk was perhaps a bit extreme even for the 1920's, it was indicative of the general sentiment prevailing among those townspeople with whom the mill worker was most likely to come into contact. This has been verified to the writer in interview after interview. The mill worker was made to feel that he was an inferior person and that merchants tolerated his presence in their shops only to take delivery of the money that was theirs by right; if they gave him goods or services in return, it was only as a charitable favor to him. He was taken for granted as a permanent fixture in the economy, a kind of channel through which money from outside the

26. *Ibid.*, p. 268.

region flowed into the tills of the business men and back out to the white-collar workers, and nothing more.

As for social contacts with the townspeople, such few as there were had a negative quality. They no longer merely tended to challenge the mill worker's concept of himself as a respectable, useful, and necessary member of the society; they had every appearance of being deliberately contrived to achieve that effect. In far too many Piedmont towns during the 1920's, the people of the mills felt themselves estranged from the community, unwanted and despised, tolerated for the sake of their pay-checks rather than accepted for their own sakes. And this was at a time when a considerable number of mill workers were actually becoming less "different," less deserving even of the mark of the pariah than had been those of an older generation that had not been so branded.

These younger workers, subscribing to middle-class value standards, many of them with two or more years of high school, had no objection to an open-ended class society based on function. They did not expect to sit down to dinner in the homes of the local elite, to be invited to join the country club—not while they were still mill workers, that is. They would have been the first to defend the right of a man to choose his friends and associates, to select the guests who entered his house. But they resented bitterly the growing implication that they were denied the right of upward mobility, which they had been taught in school was their birthright, merely by the accident of their birth. The attempt, in some communities, to create a caste of mill workers came at a time when a significant number of these people were no longer content merely to assert defensively that they were "just as good as anybody" but were actually bent on proving it.

While it was the white-collar, lower-middle-class element in the towns that was actively engaged in erecting the barrier and emphasizing the separateness of the town and the mill village, community leaders, though not encouraging such efforts, were doing little to discourage them. Their apathy had an important effect on labor relations in certain cases. During earlier days, worker-management relationships had been played out against a framework of expectations on the part of the community in which a mill was located. If top management policed supervisory relations, then community leaders policed management policy in labor relations. But gradually, over the years,

it came to be taken for granted that "the mill takes care of its people."
In case after case this assumption was still sound; the mills were doing
a good job of meeting worker needs. There were cases, however,
where the asumption was no longer valid; and where the upper stratum
in the community was no longer interested in labor relations in the
mill, presuming them to be equitable as a matter of course, the people
in the plant were denied effective recourse to their final court of appeal
—community opinion. This lack of concern for the mill worker either
for good or for bad, as it was developing among leading elements in
many communities, was in its way an even more dangerous tendency
than the outright scorn of the more plebian townspeople. In the latter
case there was at least conflict, which is a social relationship of a kind;
but withdrawal of attention from the affairs of others is implicit denial
of their existence as significant entities in a community.

Rising Educational Level of the Mill People

It is not anomalous to identify the increasing degree of education
possessed by the mill people as a further factor intensifying their discontent during the 1920's. The mills—and the communities—before
World War I and after, had taken education seriously. Perhaps it was
true, as is often charged, that "the superintendent emptied the school
house whenever a rush order came in"; but what was important was
that the children were in the school house to begin with. It would be
rare, after 1920, for a child of a mill worker not to finish grammar
school before coming into the mill; and a good percentage of them
would go to high school.

This latter fact in itself led to friction between town and village
since the mills were not nearly so likely to maintain their own high
schools as they were grammar schools. Town parents were perturbed
over the contamination to which their offspring were being subjected
by thus being forced to associate with children of a lower class; and the
mill children, on the other hand, came home with tales of discrimination and indignities heaped upon them by the children from town.
All of this, of course, increased the feeling of estrangement between
town and village.

But what was really important was that the people who were coming into the mills after 1920 were no longer tied by the bonds of il-
literacy completely within the confines of the local society. They were

aware of a world outside, that "things were different" elsewhere. They were able to be more critical of their own little world at the very time when that world most deserved criticism. They were not inclined to accept it as "the best of all possible worlds" merely because they had no acquaintance with any other. They had, in addition, been subjected to an important process of indoctrination in their school experience. American schools stress the "middle-class virtues"—which bear a marked resemblance to the old pioneer ideals dressed up and re-furbished.

The doffer's son was taught in school that if he worked hard, was honest and dependable, and sought to improve himself, he was as good as the next man and should expect to get ahead in the world. He came into the mill expecting more of it than his father. If it appeared that he was not going to be able to realize his expectations, despite his careful adherence to the formulae for success, there was the possi-bility that he might either grow embittered and cynical—or attempt to do something about it. He was taught, in school, to look at the world through middle-class eyes, to measure it against middle-class standards and to use middle-class value judgements.

There were three courses he could follow when he went to work. He could slough off the teaching he had got in school and fall back into the pattern of thought of the older generation that tended to be less critical and less demanding of the mill environment. He could struggle valiantly to make of the mill environment a world where middle-class values could be realized. Or he could, as occasionally happened, abandon middle-class values and standards as impossible to realize but fail to return to those of the older generation—in which case he was that most dangerous of all men, one who held no standards or values at all. In either of the latter two cases, his activities for a time at least were bound to stir up the mill environment, to cast doubt upon accepted ways of doing things, to "break the cake of custom" in the world of the mill village. Thus the rising educational level of the people in the mills was in itself a ferment within the folk society, a yeast of discontent with things as they were.

LOCAL INFLUENCES

Yet despite national and regional influences that encouraged unrest, dissatisfaction, and discontent within the mills, there were many mill communities that never experienced labor trouble even during the general strike of 1934, mills that even to this day have an unbroken record of labor peace despite the volatile character of the people who work for them. That national and regional factors should have combined to create labor trouble in some instances and not in others was partly, as we have already noted, a result of their combination as they impinged upon particular mills. Partly also it was the result of local developments that prepared fertile soil for the seeds of discontent sown nationally and regionally to fall upon and grow.

These local developments were not entirely local in their origin. That is, we can see the work of national and regional factors in their presence in a particular mill. They were local mainly in the sense that they could have been (and often were) dealt with in a satisfactory fashion on a purely local level. They were influences of a sort that were within the power of local management to change if they would.

The Shift in Responsibility for the Personnel Function

Perhaps the single most important factor of local origin in the widening gulf between managements and workers in the mills was the shift in the responsibility for the personnel function. This in itself resulted from other factors which we shall discuss in detail later; but the fact remained that in a number of cases presidents and general managers and superintendents of mills, who had previously made supervision of personnel work one of their principle activities, were now leaving it completely up to line supervisors who had neither the time, the training, nor, in many cases, the temperament for it. Supervisory people were still being selected on the basis of their technical qualifications; but very often those who were most competent technically were least acquainted with the social skills necessary for dealing with people as human beings. Often possessing a "natural" talent for technological problems, for example, they tended when not checked by top management to be impatient with people who were unable to grasp the technical aspects of an operation as quickly as they did themselves.

Yet we must not blame the deficiencies of supervisors for all the difficulties that arose where the shift took place. They started out from behind scratch. The people had been used to the idea that they could go directly to top management if they wished. They resented the arbitrary imposition of an intermediary between themselves and the

president or general manager in areas other than those connected with
their technical duties. A minor line official's discharge of the personnel
function without any practical possibility of appeal from his decision
was likely to be regarded with a jaundiced eye, no matter how skilled
he might be in that respect. He was not "The Company." He was
just another man who worked for wages, and his assumption of the
personnel function was likely to be regarded by the people as pre-
sumptuous on his part, even though it had been thrust upon him.

Another difficulty arose from the fact that the shift was not actually
a planned and deliberate affair. It was in more cases an almost
unconscious withdrawing of top management from a responsibility
hitherto assumed by them and its necessary but equally unconscious
assumption by line supervision. The overseers had the job to do, but
they were neither supplied the ammunition with which to do it, nor—
an even more serious oversight—were they acquainted by top management with its fundamental importance. This was not surprising since
not even the first generation that administered the function so
splendidly was consciously aware of the importance of what it was
doing along personnel lines. Its performance in that respect was largely
implicit and never objectively defined, and so the second generation
cannot be taken to task too severely for their failure to alert supervision
to the fundamental nature of a function they hardly realized they were
relinquishing completely to them. With no idea either of its nature or
its importance, there was of course no attempt to provide the background necessary for its successful discharge, which was, in the main,
a rather thorough knowledge of the affairs of the company.

Under the old pattern of relationships, informal communication
between the workers and top management had kept the former pretty
well aware of what the company was doing. They were able to understand what was happening today in the light of what they knew the
situation to have been yesterday; and they were able to make predictions as to what they might reasonably expect of tomorrow. The
minor line officials with whom they were now supposed to communi-
cate in those companies where the shift had taken place just did not
have the answers to their questions. They were unable to explain the
whys and the wherefores of low wages, increased work loads, and
tighter quality requirements largely because they were not themselves
too sure of the answers. Too often, to cover up their own ignorance,

they questioned the right of the people to ask for such information—whereas the president, under the older system, would ordinarily have explained patiently and in terms the people could understand the reasons why things were as they were.

But most disturbing of all about the shift was that top management people in these mills no longer stood in judgement over supervisory practices to the degree that they had in the past. In earlier decades, the people were able to appeal from arbitrary supervision to top management; and the line supervisor who would have complained of such a practice or who would have undertaken reprisal against the complainant would have been summarily dismissed. Now, in too many cases, the overseer was effectively the charging officer, the prosecuting attorney, the judge, the jury, and the Court of Appeals. Theoretically it was still possible to go over his head. Practically, it was not a good idea. To make matters worse, unless he happened to be an old-timer he lacked the informal but quite effective training in human relations that had been afforded by scrupulous top management policing of employee relations on the production floor.

Nor was the worker likely any longer in these mills to have any clear idea of just what he was and what he was not supposed to do. Previously there had been only one personnel policy in the mill, implicit though it was—that of the president or general manager. Now there was likely to be a multiplicity of such policies, a different one for every overseer, perhaps. Such a bewildering variety of policy was actually no policy at all. There was no commonly accepted way of doing things to tie the plant into a coherent community of discourse. The worker's image of the meaning of his world became confused.

Against such a background of confusion, the actions of supervision became unpredictable to the people. It seemed to them to be arbitrary and capricious, founded on the supervisor's personal likes and dislikes rather than on any basis of logical necessity, and there was no longer any way of bringing it back into line by appeal to the top. Workers began to feel that they were not only being exploited as employees by top management, but that they had been abandoned as people. They saw themselves as on their own in an environment that was hostile to them.

In talking with workers who remember the 1920's and early

1930's, the writer has discovered that almost invariably they identify poor supervision as the immediate and triggering cause of the labor troubles of the period.[27] It was not poor supervision in a technical sense, but rather in its failure to meet the needs of the people as human beings. It does not appear, actually, to have been as harsh or as stern as the supervision of an earlier period, but the people felt more at its mercy. They could not discount it, knowing that it would be straightened out in a little while by the men at the top. Their experience was that it did not get straightened out. The nature of the period was such that supervision would have been more evident and more of a burden upon the people in any case; for it was line supervision that was charged with carrying out the task of improving methods, increasing work loads, and tightening quality requirements. This activity alone would inevitably have led to friction between supervision and workers; and when the former were left completely responsible for the discharge of the personnel function as well, it is not difficult to understand why they were not always able to accomplish their task to the satisfaction of those whom they directed.

There is no question but that the supervisor of the 1920's discharged the personnel function poorly in many of the cases where there was eventually labor trouble. Even when he did well by ordinary standards, he often had to overcome the non-cooperative attitude of a work force that resented his complete assumption of a responsibility that had previously been ultimately that of top management. The people had been used to going straight to the top with their problems. They had been accustomed to thinking of themselves as working *with* top management; but this new situation seemed designed to put them in their places, to emphasize that they were working *for* the people at the top.

The Changing Attitude of Management

The second factor that was local with particular mills in its manifestation if not completely in its origin was the changing attitude of management, its changing concept of its relations with the people who worked for it. Why had at least a significant minority of the second

27. Thomas Quigley, head of the State Industrial Relations Board in Georgia during this period, told the writer, "Regardless of the pre-disposing causes of labor trouble, most of it that we investigated was triggered by the ineptitude of some minor supervisor."

generation of mill managers shifted the responsibility for personnel
work to the supervisory group (though they might continue to perform certain ritualistic gestures that were the "things one is supposed
to do")? Why had a function that had been an avocation for their
predecessors become to them a routine affair that could be permitted to
go by default to line supervision? Why did they no longer stand in
judgement over their supervisory people, as their fathers had, in matters
touching on human relations? Why had they put themselves, or permitted themselves to be put, out of reach of the men and women in the
work force?

In explaining the changing attitude that provides the answer to
these questions, we must recall first of all the spirit behind the Cotton
Mill Campaign. It had built the mills, and its managers had operated
them as economic enterprises in answer to a social need. They ran
them to make profits, but the profits were dedicated to the rebuilding
of the region, the revitalization of its society. The people who worked
in the mills were a part of the shattered society that the mills, as its
instrument, were attempting to mend. Thus the first generation of
management saw its workers in a dual role. They were of course
mill hands, but they were also an integral part of the whole social
problem of the region that the mills were trying to solve. Their employment was a means to profit, but in an even more important way
profit was a means toward their employment.

The difficulty was that this social role of the mills became, after the
first fervor of the campaign was over, so implicitly accepted that there
seemed to be little point in emphasizing it. It was almost automatic
in its operation. More profits meant more mills, more mills meant
more employment, more employment meant that more people were
being rewoven into the fabric of the society. There was no necessity
to pay attention to it, once the mills were under way. The operation
of the mills as economic enterprises, on the other hand, was by no
means automatic. It required constant attention, explicitly and objectively defined.

The second generation of management in the mills had not been
indoctrinated by the Cotton Mill Campaign. The social role of the
mills, accepted without question by their fathers—so obvious there was
no need to point it out—was not nearly so apparent to them. The sons
were, on the other hand, well aware of the economic aspect of the

mills. They could hardly avoid it, as a matter of fact, for it was constantly brought to their attention that the mills had to show a profit. There was no such deliberate emphasis on the social role of the mills. The first generation assumed that the second was aware of it—if indeed they ever thought about it—but the fathers forgot that the sons had never known the desolate days of Reconstruction, that they had not listened to impassioned appeals from pulpit and press to build the mills for the sake of the land and its people.

It is understandable that in some cases the second generation should have tended to regard the mills primarily as profit-making ventures for the sake of the profits and the people in them primarily as "employees." We have referred to the cotton textile mills of the Piedmont as an institution of its society, and on this basis we should have expected the change of attitude to take place as a phase of institutional development. Everett Cherrington Hughes, in speaking of this phenomenon in a general fashion, tells us that

Eventually everyone forgets the particular purpose for which [the institution] was initiated; indeed, it becomes like other established institutions in that persons asked what its purposes are, will give a variety of general and rationalized answers in terms of accepted sentiments. In the end, loyalty and implicit claims may arise with respect to what was in the beginning conceived as a means to an immediate end.[28]

In the beginning, the profits of the mills were conceived as a means to the immediate end of rehabilitating the society; but by the second generation, it was toward the profits that the "loyalty and implicit claims" began to arise.

There was also, as Cash mentions, a greater spread in the education and background of managements and work forces of the second generation than of the first. It is doubtful, however, if this had as much to do with the increasing lack of mutual understanding, in the sense which Cash intends it, as has often been suggested. For the most part the managements of the mills continued to be southern; and though they might have in some cases gone as far away as Yale or Harvard or the Wharton School of Finance for their education, they were still at home with the folkways of the Piedmont. When they thought of the people in the mills *as* people, they had no difficulty in getting

28. Everett Cherrington Hughes, "Institutions," in *New Outline of the Principles of Sociology*, p. 203.

along with them. The trouble was that some of them entertained a disturbing tendency to think of the operatives as "employees" instead. We must admit that the increasing level of education of the mill managers, when it was in the field of engineering or business (as it usually was) did encourage them to take this latter point of view. It had the effect of centering their attention even more minutely upon the technological or financial problems of the mill, to the exclusion of those that were of human origin.

Abandonment of the personnel responsibility to the supervisory level, where it occurred, was due in great part to this unconscious shift toward defining the work force in terms of "employees" rather than of "people." One's obligations to "people" are innumerable and unspecified. The personnel function involved in their discharge is neither one to be spelled out in terms of rules and regulations, nor one to be lightly abandoned. Management has few obligations to "employees" other than to pay them for services rendered; and the personnel function in this latter case is largely one of seeing that adequate services are rendered for the payment made. What group was better able to do this than the supervisory force? There was actually, from this point of view, no real abandonment of function involved; for the responsibility of exacting a day's work for a day's pay had already belonged to the overseers. It was a part of their traditional administration of the "operator-operative" aspect of employee relations in the old mills.

There were other reasons, and important ones, for the shift of the function. The duties of management were getting increasingly complex. The mills were getting larger, and multi-shift operations were the rule rather than the exception. In some cases the mills were being integrated into chains. It was becoming impossible in many cases for top management to be acquainted with anything more than a token group of the people who were out in the mill.

There was also the economic doldrums into which the industry had sunk, which demanded constant attention from top management to financial, merchandising, and technological factors. The manager of the Piedmont mill of the late 1920's felt himself chained to his desk. If there was any time to spare when he had managed to get his paper work caught up, he used it for a trip to New York to prod the selling agent into a little more activity rather than to go fishing with some old friends from the card room. He thought with envy of the leisurely trips through the mill his predecessor had been able to make, stopping to chat with this one and that one, inquiring after the health of old acquaintances, making of his progress a social event—*but he thought of them as a luxury he could not afford, rather than as something even more basic to the operation of the enterprise than the complicated breakdown of production costs he might be currently toiling over.*

Finally, as we have already noted, there was the "cult of the Great Executive," which was mostly nothing more than a top-level manifestation of the pseudo-scientific emphasis on "efficiency" that plagued the 1920's and was confused with sound scientific management. Where this perversion reached full flower in southern mills, it interposed physical as well as social and psychological barriers between managements and their people. The "efficiency expert" was impartial, at least; for if he advocated treating the workers like automatons, he did his best to create automatons out of their employers. He surrounded them with all the trappings of state suitable to their exalted position, but he kept them so engrossed with the triviata of "efficiency" that he left them little time to behave like human beings during their working hours.

CHAPTER VII

The Decision Is Made

THOSE INFLUENCES that worked to balance out, to checkmate, and to sterilize the forces that were working toward the decimation of the folk organization of the southeastern cotton textile industry during the 1920's were regional in their origin. We can think of them as demonstrating what Odum has called the "power of the folk." They represent those dynamic tendencies of a folk society to retain its structuring and its essential way of life despite adverse circumstances, to envelope those circumstances and turn them to its own account if there is any possibility for it.

We can understand what happened most clearly if we note how, one by one, the disintegrative forces from outside and from within the region were opposed by the integrative tendencies that were native to the region. These latter did not fight unassisted; there were certain economic and technological factors on the side of the folkways as well —though even those would have been different had the industry not been truly regional in its origin in the Piedmont. The plan of presentation we are to follow has one disadvantage. The forces of disintegration operated separately, despite a certain degree of relativity in their origin. They were not opposed by separately marshalled units of the folk culture. This culture opposed them as it had existed and was under the compulsion of existing as a complete and total entity. In recounting the separate patterns of opposition there is bound to be a considerable amount of what seems to be repetition, as the striking force of the folk culture shifts first to one and then another point on the circumference of the zone of battle.

Also, in telling the story, the impression may be created that the forces of disintegration listed in the previous chapter were merely creatures of straw, set up to be demolished in this. Nothing is further from the truth. We presented them as *tendencies,* but they were tendencies sufficiently well-marked in their appearance, sufficiently serious, and sufficiently significant to lead to the conclusion on the part of students of the southern scene, during those days, that they were dominant tendencies, and that, though they affected only a minority of mills or of communities in most cases, they would in the long run be victorious over the length and the breadth of the Piedmont.

The question may be raised as to why these disintegrative tendencies were permitted to appear in the first place, if the Piedmont folk culture was actually vigorous enough finally to defeat them. We must recall that a folk culture acts on an *ad hoc* basis in situations of this sort. Its defenses are not erected in advance and crystallized against a logically predicted assault. They are stimulated into being by the attack itself, taking a shape that no one could quite have foreseen before the advent of the stimulus. They are flexible, unpredictable except in their general outlines, and intuitively adjusted to the exact dimensions of the onslaught—a testimony to the power of improvization that man has developed, individually and collectively, to enable him to exist in the shifting and incalculable world his heightened senses have revealed to him.

Regional Responses to National Influences

There were to begin with certain phenomena of regional origin that operated to soften and mitigate within the Piedmont the distress caused by the economic condition of the textile industry and later by the Great Depression.

Economic Problems

So far as the worker was concerned, the complex economic problems of the industry were summed up in two simple indices: the size of his pay check and the frequency of his pay days.

Wage and Employment Levels.—Wages fell after 1921; and though even at their lowest they would continue to be considerably better than they had been before the war, Piedmont workers were no more inclined to be philosophical about reduced wages rates than workers anywhere —particularly when they were accompanied by increased work loads, short time, and no immediate prospect for their improvement. Yet the regional situation worked to cushion the work force as a whole from the full impact of what might otherwise have resulted in widespread deprivation and want. During the period there would be few workers who would not find it necessary to tighten their belts on occasion, who would not grumble and worry. There would be days when some of them would stare glumly into a future that seemed without hope. Yet only rarely would any of them be pushed to the edge of desperation. Something, in almost every instance, would come through before the last faint and sustaining hope flickered out permanently.

We should note in passing that there was in the Piedmont work force, during the 1920's, an increasingly important component that did not define the situation as one of reduced rates, increased work loads, and short time. For those farmers coming in from areas ravaged by the boll weevil, mill wages facilitated a considerable increase in living standards over what they had been reduced to on the land they had just left. The balance of the Piedmont textile workers remembered the war-inflated wages of the years preceding the 1920's and resented their reduction; but a group that was becoming more and more significant saw little reason to complain and much reason to be thankful that the mills were not only operating but were hiring.

Nor, for the whole work force, did the increase in price levels that marked the whole decade affect the southern worker to the degree that it did urban workers in the North. The regional pattern of the building of the Piedmont mills had kept them in rural areas where both living costs and living standards tended to be lower; whereas the northern worker was exposed without any protection to the boom-time prices of the 1920's. In addition, the southern worker, still living for the most part in company-owned housing with subsidized rental and enjoying either free or nominally priced utilities, plus the use of garden tracts and communal pastures, experienced no increase in already low rental rates or utility costs or (if he wished to take advantage of the privileges extended to him) in the cost of fresh vegetables in season, and milk.

There was in addition, in the matter of the housing itself, a certain psychological advantage accruing to the Piedmont worker that was not enjoyed by his northern counterpart. He was not, during the 1920's, living under conditions of squalor and filth, in industrial slums that in themselves created tensions and animosities. Millions of dollars had been poured into repairing and beautifying his villages during the war years. There were some few that were still squalid and desolate; but by and large he enjoyed paved streets, sidewalks, electricity, water laid into the house, and modern plumbing.[1] The streets were shaded by trees now grown tall, and grass and shrubbery covered the red earth. His house was painted, the roof was sound—and there was fresh air about it and space to move around in. Lemert, concluding a trip through the textile Piedmont in 1930, observed that he "could not find the frightful conditions about which he had read so much before starting out on his journey."[2]

There was nevertheless unemployment in the Piedmont industry during the period as mills found it necessary to go on short time and reduce work forces while they worked out of surpluses that had been too optimistically accumulated and that had tied up their working capital. But the unemployment, unlike that in the North, was sporadic and intermittent in nature. In New England a layoff was likely to be permanent. In the Piedmont the unemployed worker could look forward rather confidently to being back on a pay roll within a month or two at the most.[3] And still close to the land, he had never been as much concerned over occasional unemployment as was the northern operative. Up to a point at least it was a chance for holidays such as he had enjoyed on the farm when the crops had been laid by, an opportunity to go hunting or fishing, to visit relatives, or just to loaf.

The continuing expansion of the Piedmont industry also provided a bulwark against unemployment. Not only did spindleage increase from 15.9 million in 1921 to 19.3 million in 1934, but the bulk of the plants that had been on a single-shift basis turned to two-shift operation. When one mill was shut down, another was hiring, and experienced workers were always in demand. The floating element was still sufficiently large so that the work force of a mill that seemed headed for a session of short time was almost automatically reduced to a size somewhat more in line with its capacity to furnish employment.

The southern mills were not likely to shut down for months at a

1. Herbert J. Lahne, *The Cotton Mill Worker* (New York: Farrar and Reinhart, Inc., 1944), p. 39.

2. Ben F. Lemert, *The Cotton Textile Industry of the Southern Appalachian Piedmont* (Chapel Hill: The University of North Carolina Press, 1933), p. 70.

3. U. S. Department of Commerce, Bureau of the Census, *1930 Census, Unemployment*, Vol. I, p. 96 ff., Vol. II, p. 294-95, 299, 303-4, 308-9.

time, however. Those managers who forgot it discovered that their
communities still operated under the assumption that the creation of
pay rolls was a function fully as important as making profits; it needed
only the closing of the mill doors to let loose such a wave of adverse
community opinion as to make the most profit-conscious operator pause
and reconsider. The operator was himself a part of the community;
when the test came, he was much more likely to respond to the pattern
of the folkways of his own volition than he was to pay heed to the
sophisticated advice of his commission house in the North. He was in
addition usually looking forward with some confidence to an early
resumption of full operation and wanted to keep his work force together.

When full operation was no longer possible, the next move was to
cut the work week for everyone by going on short time—unlike the
northern pattern, which was to close down a section of the mill and
balance permanent layoffs for some with full-time employment for
those remaining.[4] Only after short time was no longer economically
possible would a section of the mill be closed down. The entire mill
closed only as a last and desperate resort. If it were in severe financial
difficulties, and not able to reopen under its own power, the chances
were that it was so deeply in debt to its commission house that the latter
either took it over and started it up for its own protection or found a
northern buyer for it. Only in very rare cases did a southern mill close
and stay closed; it "opened under new management," and the burden
of its financial distress fell much more heavily on its stockholders than
on its work force.

In the matter of layoffs, as well, the customs of the region prevailed.
The mill manager, opposing vigorously the union philosophy of strict
seniority, might assert forcefully that he would lay off whom he
pleased when he pleased; but it usually turned out that those "whom
he pleased" to lay off were those who would be least distressed by unemployment, with due consideration for the "loyalty" rather than the
"seniority" of long-service employees. The head of a family, for
example, if he had been with the mill for any length of time at all,
could expect that he would be one of the last to be taken off the pay
roll. If he were to be laid off for more than a couple of weeks, he
expected the mill to waive rental payments for him during his period

4. See Lahne, *op. cit.*, p. 149-52.

of unemployment and to refrain from billing him for utilities. When he had scraped the bottom of the flour barrel and sliced up the last of the bacon, he expected the mill to carry him on its books if it had a company store, or to assist him in some other way in restocking the larder.

Thus unemployment in the Piedmont was cushioned by the still powerful assumption of the region that the mills were operated to create pay rolls, and that the operator of the mill had certain obligations to the people who worked for him. Cushioned by the continuing expansion of the industry, only in rare cases did it develop to the point of tragedy. It seldom goaded the worker beyond endurance. He was more likely to be grumbling over the inadequacies of his pay envelope than in despair over its complete absence; and even in the latter case, despair was held off by justifiable confidence that he would soon be back on a pay roll. In the meantime, he could get along.

Although it was of no help to him during the 1920's, awakening national consciousness of the problems of wage earners as evidenced in federal legislation finally came to the assistance of the southern textile worker by virtue of his membership in the industrial work-force of the nation.[5] The National Industrial Recovery Act, through the agency of the NRA Cotton Textile Code which it established in 1933, set minimum hourly wages (30 cents in the South and 32.5 cents in the North) and established minimum hours and overtime provisions. Production controls also operated to distribute what demand there was for cotton textiles among a greater number of producers; although in this respect northern workers benefited to a greater degree than those in the South—and perhaps also to some degree at their expense.

The NIRA was declared unconstitutional in 1935, but wage levels did not drop until the recession in 1937. In 1938 the Fair Labor Standards Act again put a floor under wages with its minimum wage provision and operated to spread employment by requiring overtime for more than a forty hour week. As in the case of the NIRA, the new Federal law was not an unmixed blessing for the Piedmont work-force; for while it raised wage levels in many mills, it also forced the abandonment of an informal system of "on-the-job" pensioning that was rather widespread.

"Social Security" in the Folk Society.—In addition to ameliorative

5. See *ibid.,* pp. 157-58 and 164-67.

measures that might be taken by his employer, the Piedmont worker's close tie with the land and the very pattern of the folk society itself helped to cushion the blow of protracted layoff. There were of course garden patches and community pastures that provided a source of food in season when pay envelopes were thin or empty. When these were combined with the ingenuity of the workers, the close-knit texture of their society, and managerial interest in their welfare, some rather interesting expedients were worked out. The writer recalls the case of "cow insurance," for example. In a Georgia plant a number of families had got out of the habit of keeping a cow in the community pasture. When short time finally descended upon the mill, they prevailed upon the president to finance them in the purchase of dairy stock; and for his protection as well as for their own, and on their own initiative, they formed their own informal mutual insurance company to protect against the ever-present possibility that some of their stock might die. Their enterprise operated so well that it outlasted the depression and was not liquidated until in the late 1940's.

Increasingly during the 1920's the mill workers were subsistence farmers as well and had this additional protection against the failure of their cash income. For those who lived in the village, there were invariably kinfolk on the farm; and there was nothing degrading about accepting—or even asking for—a bushel of potatoes or a basket of greens or a side of pork from one's brother or father or cousin or uncle. It was expected that the family would come to one's rescue in times of distress. This dependence was facilitated by the fact that the mills were located in the Piedmont, which, after the coming of the boll weevil, was rapidly returning to the older pattern of diversified farming that enabled rural people to live off the land if need be.

There was also the fact that the veneer of the "business man" that had been adopted by some managements was, after all, rather thin. It might be possible to think of one's work force as made up of "employees" when all was going well, but it was difficult to continue to think of them in that fashion when there was the possibility that they might be in want. They became "people" again even to the most efficiency-conscious southern managements, and their problems once more management's problems. The folk spirit was still strong enough so that difficulties faced by all had the effect of knitting groups more closely together. A management and work force that had been feuding while everything was going well were more likely to close ranks and present a common front to trouble from without than to draw more widely apart.

Skill Requirements and Work Loads

The task of turning out a product held to tighter quality requirements did not prove to be as burdensome for the Piedmont worker as northern operators some years previously had assumed it would be when they had confidently expected his inherent lack of ambition and ability to hold southern production to canvas, duck, and Osnaburgs. The skill potentialities of southern workers had never been realized in the production of cheap fabrics. They were for the most part a people who took pride in what they could do; and working to tighter standards presented itself as a challenge to them rather than as an intolerable burden—for so long as they felt their increased efforts and newly demonstrated abilities to be appreciated by their managements. As it turned out, the matter of a sufficient reserve of technological skill on the part of the work force was never in doubt. The decisive skill turned out to be social, the ability of managements to present their case, and of workers to understand it, in such a way as make a co-operative venture out of the undertaking. In this respect southern enterprises were immeasurably better off than those in the North; for though in some cases they may not have been recently employed, the potentialities for rapport were still there. They needed only to be used.

But southern mill owners and mill managers did not leave the upgrading of worker skills to chance. Adult education was an old story in the Piedmont; and though formerly it had been principally concerned with the three R's, there was no great trick involved in applying the principle to vocational education. The decade of the 1920's saw the rapid development of a program of vocational training in the Piedmont textile mills, both privately and with the assistance of Piedmont state governments, that had no duplicate anywhere.[6]

In addition, the relatively newer equipment of southern mills made quality production less a problem from the technological standpoint. Quality was actually within the control of the worker. He was not

6. See Harriet Herring, *Welfare Work in Mill Villages* (Chapel Hill: The University of North Carolina Press, 1928), pp. 77-84.

subjected to the frustrating experience of having to work with tools
that were not up to the job he had to demand of them.

The matter of increasing work loads was somewhat more difficult;
but here as well the Piedmont had an advantage that was not possessed
by the North. It had a considerable amount of slack that could be
taken up before production requirements became really onerous.
Southern managements had never been inclined to push their workers
—a fact that had had something to do with the North's false sense of
security before World War I. The mills operated at a leisurely pace.
Even in the mid 1920's, Kier noted that working with the same equipment and turning out the same product, northern spinners supervised
about 20 per cent more spindles than their opposite numbers in the
South, and the same was true for weavers.[7] As it turned out, this was
not so much because of any inherent lack of ability on the part of the
southern worker as from a lack of inclination on the part of his
management to drive for greater production as long as present levels
were yielding satisfactory profits.

Here also the generally newer and more completely automatic
equipment in the southern mills was to their advantage. In the North,
the application of the stretch-out meant in far too many cases that
managements were asking an impossibility of their employees; their
antiquated equipment was already being driven at its practical top
speed, and its propensity for frequent breakdowns made supervision
of more spinning frames or looms a frustrating and unreasonable requirement. The Piedmont, unlike the bulk of the Northern industry,
had technological reserves in its equipment as well as physiological
reserves on the part of its people that it had never drawn upon.

The rather casual attitude of southern managements toward absenteeism worked in its favor as well in stepping up production, strange
as it may seem. In the Southeast in 1928, for example, women weavers
worked on an average only 38.1 hours per week though the average
shift was 55.5 hours per week; while in the North, women weavers
worked an average of 42.2 hours per week out of a shift averaging
49.3 hours per week.[8] Between 1926 and 1928, a two year period dur-

7. Malcolm Kier, *Industries of America—Manufacturing* (New York: Ronald Press,
1938), p. 355.

8. See Abraham Berglund, George T. Starnes, and Frank T. DeVyver, *Labor in
the Industrial South* (University, Va.: The Institute for Research in Social Sciences,
1930), p. 85.

ing which work loads were stepped up both North and South, the average actual work week of southern women was reduced by 4.8 hours, while in the North for the same group it was reduced only by 2.9 hours.[9] The southern worker had traditionally worked longer hours than those in the North, but when he felt like taking some time off, he took it—and the management that would have enforced strict attendance to the job day after day would have found itself undermanned in short order. Wisely, it adopted the institution of the "spare hand" to fill in. The result during this period of increasing work loads was that the southern worker who felt tensions building up from the demand for increased attention to the job took a day or two off and released them. He or she returned to the job in a better frame of mind and ready to go. The northern worker, tied to the equipment by rigorous attendance rules, accumulated tensions to the point of explosion.

In a significant number of cases southern managements were not content with relying merely upon the possibilities inherent in taking up the slack in the former somewhat leisurely pace of operation, enlisting the co-operation of their people, and condoning absenteeism. One could expect that faced with—and convinced of—the necessity for greater production per worker, the people in the mills would themselves apply their ingenuity toward streamlining methods and eliminating unnecessary operations. This did happen, and it helped to ease the burden of tending more sides of spinning frames or a greater stand of looms. But we must not forget that in addition to the pseudo-scientific efficiency experts of the era who parodied their work, the solid and legitimate approach to scientific management that had been pioneered by Taylor, the Gilbreaths, Gantt, and others was still going on. Their approach made sense to many mill managers who distrusted the apostles of "efficiency"; and they prefaced increased work loads by careful preparation of machines and material, production planning, more efficient routing, and methods analysis and improvement. Where planned assistance of this sort from their managements supplemented the efforts of workers who had been psychologically prepared for the necessity of the pending increase in their tasks, amazing increases in production were achieved with the expenditure of only a little more worker effort. They were in addition accompanied by

9. *Ibid.*

considerable increases in worker earnings, bringing them well above the regional, and in some cases even above the national, average.

On the other hand, an important factor in alleviating the overall impact of increased work loads was the fact that, as one mill manager explained to the writer, mills learned from the mistakes of their neighbors. In reviewing the history of labor difficulties during the period, it is interesting to note that there was seldom more than one mill in a locality that suffered them to an extended degree, and this one was usually the first to try some new practice. Neighboring mills, observing the tribulations of the innovator, attempted not to duplicate its mistakes; and one lesson they invariably got was that work loads could not be increased arbitrarily. The reason for the increase had to be explained to the people who were being asked to tend more looms or more sides of spinning frames; and then, with the co-operation of the work force, task assignments were increased experimentally and step by step until what seemed to be a reasonable maximum had been reached. Acquainted with the economic necessity for cutting production costs, the people were generally willing to co-operate; but they had to have the feeling that they were participating in a joint project.

It was also greatly to the advantage of labor relations in the southern mills during this period that their people were not of a character to nurse resentments or to hide their dissatisfactions from management for any length of time. If work loads were increased arbitrarily to a figure that seemed unreasonable, and ordinary channels of protest failed to get relief or even the attention of top management, they had no hesitation about staging a walkout. The Mitchells, speaking of this characteristic of the southern worker, remark, "That sort of strike [the spontaneous, unorganized walkout] had happened many times before in the South. Usually it can be hushed up by a talk from the mill owner, who gathers his people about him on the ball field; or else a respected citizen or a newspaper editor will get the facts and smooth out the trouble."[10] We have already noted Lahne's observation that there was a wave of such spontaneous strikes in the late 1920's, bringing the workers "partial success." That is, while their tasks were not cut back to their previous dimensions, a compromise would be worked out that was somewhat more satisfactory to them and

10. Broadus and George Mitchell, *The Industrial Revolution in the South* (Baltimore: The Johns Hopkins Press, 1930), p. 193.

judged to be reasonable under the circumstances they were finally acquainted with.

There was still sufficient rapport between managements and workers in the majority of the southern mills so that the former, if they presented their case to the people, could depend on their co-operation. The southern worker could not be driven to work harder; but given a chance to examine and approve the objectives for increased work loads, and in possession of physiological and technological potentialities for achieving them, he would co-operate voluntarily in setting them up. As the wave of quickie strikes testified, he had no hesitancy about demanding an audience with top management when he felt that he was being ignored in the matter. As his father had done, he still insisted upon his right to co-operate with management even if he had to close the mill down to get it.

The Fate of Scientific Management in the Piedmont

Here again the folkways were too powerful for technics designed to operate in a mass industrial society to overcome. Not all mill managements in the mills during the 1920's were of the second generation; and not all of the second generation were willing to adopt the inhuman definition of the industrial worker required by the 1920 version of "efficiency engineering." The folk wisdom of the region worked to create suspicion of the "expert" along any line—"A fool can put on his coat better than a wise man can do it for him." There was a strong and abiding distrust of anyone who recommended the application of generalized technics to specific situations. It was apparent to anyone who would take the trouble to look that one real situation was very seldom like another; there was, therefore, no good reason to believe that some "system" designed to deal with all situations would be of much value in any one of them.

This does not mean that the Piedmont did not profit by scientific management, for it did. But on the whole, it refused to accept it as part of any package deal. It tore the various packages apart that were presented to it and used such of their components as seemed reasonable under the circumstances. More than that, it used them in its own particular fashion. The efficiency expert claimed in the 1920's that you could not time-study an operation if the workers were aware of it; they would deliberately slow down on the job. The Piedmont discovered that the only way an operation *could* be time-studied, if the results were to mean anything at all, was with the full knowledge and co-operation of the people performing it. (It also began to suspect that it was not very "efficient" to time-study an operation that was inefficient to begin with.) The efficiency expert regarded his rate studies as the final word in rate setting; the Piedmont discovered them to be very convenient first estimates and welcomed them as an advance in this respect, but it checked them against the experience of supervisors and long-service employees before they were adopted.

The efficiency expert gloried in complicated incentive systems. Piedmont managements, not unacquainted by this time with slide rules and work curves on their own account, saw the mathematical and engineering logic in many of them, but they saw a deeper logic as well —that any system so complicated that a man with no more than an eighth grade education could not predict, on the basis of his production, what he would find in his pay envelope on Saturday would cause more trouble than it was worth. Thus though incentive systems were adopted, they were modified in the direction of simplicity.

Fundamentally, the efficiency expert of the 1920's operated on the assumption that if people were not mechanisms, they at least ought to behave like them on the job; he assumed that the human side of their nature must be suppressed as far as possible, since it resulted in nothing but confusion and the confounding of all his carefully prepared charts, diagrams, schedules, and formulae. Piedmont managements, on the other hand, continued for the most part to take the very "inefficient" point of view that the human side of one's workers was something to be enjoyed, that the task of struggling with the human problems of management added color to what would otherwise be a pretty hum-drum sort of job. As the president of a large mill told the writer, "We know that human problems here in the mill cost us money; we try to avoid them, and if they happen, we try to keep them from happening again—but do you know, if we didn't have them, half the zest would be gone out of my job!"

It was perhaps this attitude more than anything else that defeated simon-pure efficiency in the mills. Try as hard as they might, managements could not come to think of human problems as something to be eliminated by wiping out the humanity of their workers. They applauded the objectives of efficiency. Tentatively, they experimented

with its technics, but they refused to pay the final price demanded by
the 1920 version. When it came to a decision, they were committed to
the idea of working with people, with all their faults, their incon-
sistencies, and their refusal to abide by logically derived patterns of
behavior. They saw the human problems created by the industrial
milieu as challenges to be met head on rather than side-stepped by
evasive tactics.

Finally, as in the case of work loads that were tactlessly or improperly assigned, the people in the mills were not reticent about showing their displeasure over tactless use of the paraphernalia of efficiency.
They did not want to be treated "efficiently"; and if a management per-
sisted in doing so, it was likely to have a spontaneous walkout on its
hands. On the other hand, if a program of work simplification, for
example, actually did have some merit, and management took the
trouble to explain the whys and wherefores of it in a way that did not
implicitly define the workers as stupid for not having thought of it
themselves, the co-operation of the people could be counted on. "These
people aren't lazy," the head of a standards department told the writer,
"but they just take naturally to methods improvement. If there's an
easier way to do a job, they're all for it!"

Absentee Ownership Under the Folkways

The power of the folkways against absentee ownership lay in their
persuasive, their essentially universal, nature. The Piedmont absorbed
its absentee-owned firms and made them its own. It was, to be truth-
ful, under the necessity of absorbing them; for the folk society cannot
tolerate the alien in its midst, as can the mass society. It must either
adopt him, cast him out, or stand in constant danger of being destroyed by him. The presence of an unassimilated element is toxic,
for it destroys the intuitively maintained yet marvellously balanced
tensions that give the society its dynamic quality. In a society that is
based on understanding, the stranger must be understood and made to
understand or he cannot be accepted.

The process of absorption was not as formidable as it might appear.
The incoming firm was generally as anxious to earn the good will of
the community as the community was eager that it should be integrated. With a few exceptions that received attention all out of
proportion to their numerical importance, northern firms that bought

or built in the South were almost pathetically anxious to adopt local ways. They had come south because the southern way seemed to be working, and they were sensitive enough to feel that it was based on more than "native white, non-union labor," and low wages. They were not able to spell out objectively the dimensions of this "southern way"—and so as a matter of insurance they were anxious not to deviate in any particular, no matter how insignificant it might seem. They remembered too vividly the ethnic babel, laced with the growing strength of the union, that they had only recently fled.

There were often also, as we shall discuss later, certain groups within the community who were particularly anxious that the integration should take place as rapidly as possible and who did all in their power to facilitate it. Rather than ruin the possibility of good community relations in the future, the company usually took the advice of local people and obtained the services of a Piedmont born-and-bred textile executive to head its local operations. In most cases it carefully maintained a "hands off" attitude with regard to labor relations. Actually, completely local management was not necessary, as was demonstrated in a number of cases. Many textile executives, born and reared in the North, experienced no difficulty in superintending southern operations. The Captain, of whom we spoke previously, was born in New England, educated at Yale, and had never been below the Mason and Dixon Line until he came south as the mill agent for one of the few southern branches of northern companies established in the Piedmont before World War I. A travesty on the southern mill worker equally as false and even more damning than the statement that he is tractable and docile is the one quite frequently quoted that he is "mean" and can be handled only by one of his own kind—presumably even more vicious than he.

The ease with which northern managements fell into the behavior patterns expected of them by southern communities lay, as we have said, in the universal nature of the folkways. They are founded on basic and fundamental traits of human nature; and once one has become acquainted with the particular conditions under which they operate, they seem perfectly natural as ways of doing things. They carry their own logic with them. The orientation of northern managements was further facilitated by their early discovery that the difficulties of "understanding" the southern worker had been grossly misrepresented. They did not have to work at it. All they had to do was relax and be themselves. This Piedmont southerner was no strange creature out of some hill-billy novel, no anachronism from the past, no shambling, brutish, atavistic sadist who interrupted perennial feuds only long enough to join his fellows in a lynching party. He was an American, nothing more, who grounded his judgements in an ethical and moral code that was, perhaps, a little old-fashioned and out of step with the roaring 1920's, but a code that was perfectly familiar. Even his propensity to lapse from it was familiar. "Getting along with him" required nothing more than treating him like a human being, without condescension or undue familiarity—nothing more, actually, than wanting to get acquainted with him for the sake of the acquaintanceship itself rather than for what one could gain from it.

Thus the folk society of the Piedmont swallowed the invader, made him "one of us," by the rather simple process of permitting him to discover that all it involved was being *himself*. He discovered as well that the folkways were not arbitrary in their nature. He learned that they were, within the boundary conditions under which they operated, the simplest and best way to arrive at a solution to a problem involving human relationships that did not, in the solution, violate fundamental concepts of the dignity and brotherhood of man. How well the integration has been accomplished is perhaps best demonstrated by the fact that one can observe no significant degree of correlation between "good" and "bad" labor relations, on the one hand, and local and absentee ownership on the other. That one might expect to find such correlation had the integration not taken place is shown by the fact that, in the past and at present, when one does find labor unrest in the absentee-owned plant, one almost invariably discovers that its employee relations are handled by telephone out of the New York office.

We should perhaps note in passing that it is not absentee ownership but absentee management that creates trouble, and one can find absentee management in the locally-owned as well in the absentee-owned plant. Perhaps one of the most disturbing forms of absentee management occurs at departmental level, when top management insists on complete control over every detail of policy and practice and refuses to delegate any responsibility to on-the-spot supervision.

The Piedmont attitude toward the "invading" mills was also of considerable assistance in the process of absorption. Absentee ownership is ordinarily analyzed from an economic standpoint and portrayed as a means by which profits, legitimately created in one region, are illegitimately drained off to another. Southern communities did not think of their absentee-owned mills in this fashion. They had never, as a matter of fact, been much concerned with the profits of the textile mills except as they had enabled the mills to continue to operate. Mills had always meant employment and pay rolls; they continued to mean employment and pay rolls. If the absentee-owned mill treated its people right, assumed its expected role as a member of the community, and furnished steady employment, it was rather foolish to object to its presence as a matter of economic principle. The Piedmont continued to regard its textile mills as social institutions. The matter of who had legal title to them continued to be of minor importance; they belonged to the region in any case.

The Piedmont and the Unions

This topic is so interesting in its own right that it has been reserved for discussion in the final chapter. For now, we shall merely observe that the battle was far more fundamental than one between unions on the one hand and managements on the other. It was a decisive engagement between the folkways and the massways; a test of strength between two fundamentally differing types of societal organization.

THE REGION PUTS ITS HOUSE IN ORDER

Two self-generated tendencies had appeared in the Piedmont during the 1920's that, if permitted to develop unchecked, could have in themselves wrecked the folk nature of the regional society. The first was the implicit assumption, on the part of certain promotional groups, that the Piedmont work force was something to be sold as a commodity. The second was the development of an increasing social gulf between the mill workers and the balance of the Piedmont people, evidenced by outright scorn on the part of the "white-collar" group in Piedmont mill towns and cities and by a withdrawal of concern for mill workers on the part of their leading citizens.

Disappearance of the Commodity Theory of Labor.—We must recognize to begin with that those people and those agencies who were putting the Piedmont work force on the auction block during the 1920's cannot truly be considered as spokesmen for the total Piedmont society. The original Cotton Mill Campaign had been a true social movement; a co-operative, informally organized movement under a recognized informal leadership. The second cotton mill campaign was a mass movement. There was nothing co-operative about it, no central leadership, formal or informal. It was a convergence of individual lines of activity; a number of people got the same idea at the same time in response to an event that had its origin outside rather than within the region. They acted as individuals, or as individual agencies, rather than as representatives of the region. There were no such men as Henry Grady or D. A. Tompkins, for example, who could be thought of as speaking or acting for the whole Piedmont during the 1920's.

It would have been difficult to have found a community campaigning for northern textile plants during the 1920's that did not have a sizeable and influential group of citizens who were opposed to the idea, who were afraid of the effect that industry might have on their community. Those who backed the campaign were generally quite honestly convinced that it would be possible to integrate an outside firm into the community picture, or they would not have advanced or supported the idea of bringing one in; but they were all aware that securing the industry was only the first step. They were morally obligated to make good on the description of the local labor force they had used as bait, but they were even more under the obligation to make good on their promise to their fellow citizens that the presence of the new textile plant with its northern owners would not be a disrupting influence on community life. Fortunately, both obligations could be discharged simultaneously by getting the new firm to adopt the Piedmont point of view toward labor relations.

They had represented the Piedmont worker as "tractable and docile" when they were actually quite aware that he was not, *except under special conditions*. Their only salvation lay in getting the new firm to adopt those special conditions as speedily as possible, to get them to bring their labor relations under the folkways, in other words. These latter made it quite evident that a textile operative was not a commodity one purchased on the market. He was a human being who had labor for sale; but one bought the labor and not the man. Whatever the original prospectus might have said, when it got located the immigrating firm found itself dealing with whole human beings in its work force, not with units of labor.

There was also the fact that the second campaign was in a sense a regional manifestation of the boom spirit that swept the entire nation during the 1920's. When the national boom subsided, the campaign for mills in the Piedmont took on a more sober tone. Eventually, they leveled off on a local scale to a rather matter-of-fact marshalling of local resources without the accompaniment of any high pressure sales talk; and the developmental function was taken over by state agencies which thought on a regional rather than a local basis—the Agricultural and Industrial Development Board of Georgia, for example.

Thus the commodity theory of labor found no real home in the Piedmont. Its proponents in theory were the first to disclaim it in practice as a matter of common sense protection for themselves. It was never actually representative of regional thinking, despite the publicity given it; and the whole pattern of employee relationships that the immigrating firm found it not only simple but wise to adopt, if it wished to enjoy community respect and support, was diametrically opposed to treating labor as a commodity.

There was, in addition, something very important taking place on the positive side of the picture during the 1920's, a movement that has been little noted yet one that has had a profound influence on the subsequent pattern of labor relations in the Piedmont. We have said that none of the *promoters* of industry during the boom twenties were of the stature of the men of the first generation. But there were, despite Broadus Mitchell's sweeping judgement of them as "class-conscious and money-wise," a group of management people in the industry itself who could measure up to the best of the first generation. Their words were addressed to the industry, and so they attracted little attention even in the region and none nationally. If we think of the Piedmont promoters of the 1920's as men who were willing to surrender to the massways, just so can we think of these others as men who were speaking powerfully with the voice of the folk, pointing the course that had to be taken if the industrialization of the Piedmont was not to turn it into a mass society.[11]

11. In speaking of this effort, Thomas Quigley, who was one of the young "professionals" brought in from the North to help with its administration, told the writer, "The great zestful beginning of this movement came early in the 1920's. It was

There were such men as Victor Montgomery, Ben Gear, Donald Comer, L. W. Clark, the Cones, August Smith, Stuart Cramer, Henry Kendall, the Millikans, the Schoolfields, the Fitzgeralds. All spoke earnestly and in unison on a single theme: *capital's responsibility to the wage earner*. The Southern Industrial Relations Conference at Blue Ridge, North Carolina, was started by these men in 1920. All during the period that the promoters were putting the southern textile worker on the auction block and community leaders were becoming apathetic toward his problems, these men and others who thought like them were crying for recognition of his humanity. They were undertaking the task of defining explicitly, as was necessary if it was to be achieved within the increasingly complex industrial society of the Piedmont, the essential spirit of the folkways; and they were looking for the technics by which it might be manifested in a practical way. This was the period, for example, when mill after mill began training programs looking, not only toward improvement of worker skills, but as well toward the improvement of supervisory leadership. It was the period of the greatest expansion of what was then called "welfare work." In many of its manifestations, it anticipated what would today be recommended as no more than the responsibility of any forward-looking organization toward its employees. And the welfare work was to an important degree under the administration of paid professionals, often trained in northern universities, who lent objectivity to the somewhat more emotional and "feeling" approach of the men who employed them.

It was during this period also that many mill villages were initially built or were improved, landscaped, and beautified in a way that made them superior to large sections of the communities they bordered or neighbored—New Holland, for example, Cramerton, Chicopee, Silverton, Porterdale, Clarkdale, to name but a few. It was during this period that many mills improved their private school systems, both physically and in point of quality of instruction, to the extent that neighboring communities cast envious eyes toward them. It was during this period that athletic and recreational facilities were developed in many mill villages, their use supervised under competent professional

almost a religious revival. The great ownership figures pleaded and exhorted. To be young, as I was, 'in that dawn was very heaven' as Wordsworth would say."

leadership. The children of the mill workers were regarded frequently with envy by their town peers.

Thus, though the "Cotton Mill Campaign" of the 1920's was *not* a social movement, there was one under way during the 1920's, unheralded and largely unnoticed amidst the more spectacular events of the decade; but in its long-run effect it was of immeasurably greater importance to the future of the Piedmont, and it sprang just as surely from the dynamic power of a folk society as had the social movement of the 1880's that seized on industry for the succour of the region.

Re-Integration of the Textile Worker into the Piedmont Society

Paradoxically, one of the principle reasons for the considerable emphasis that was placed upon the "difference" of the textile worker during the 1920's and early 1930's was that he actually was becoming less and less "different." Those who had felt themselves to be better than the mill hand during the early days had nevertheless felt themselves to be under no necessity to draw his or anyone else's attention to the fact that they were *different* from him. Such people were ordinarily more concerned with outward evidence of status than with inward merit; and the whole manner, appearance, habits, and dress of the first generation mill worker had set him apart from the town people.

But now by the mid-twenties, two coincident developments resulted in the mill hand's being explicitly kept in his place, under constant and deliberate reminder that he was an inferior breed. One was that it was becoming increasingly difficult, in many cases, to tell the difference between a mill worker and anyone else. The other was that there was a much larger group of people in the average community who were interested in keeping the distinction clear.

The increasing emphasis on education in the mill village, the night schools for adults, the social activities, the "welfare work," and all the other agencies that the mills had employed for the social rehabilitation of the destitute farm people of the late 1800's, and were employing with renewed vigor and more effectively during the 1920's, were beginning to pay off. An increasing number of bath tubs in village houses suggested that bathing need not be restricted to Saturday night (though they were in a few cases, on reliable report, used to store coal). Living in a neatly-kept village, with flowers in the door-

yard and a house freshly painted, had its psychological effect. Some of
the mill workers spent their high wartime earnings on loudly striped
silk shirts and drinking liquor with a label on it; but there were more
who owned a neat blue serge suit for the first time, some modest
white shirts to wear with it, and a pair of shoes that would take a shine.
Their wives might buy a silk dress suitable for wear to church, some
more frivolous items for less formal occasions, a pair of shoes with high
heels and thin soles, and perhaps even a pair of thin lisle stockings to
be carefully guarded and worn only on momentous occasions.

The new clothes called for somewhat closer attention to one's hair-
dress, to the state of one's nails, to a bath, certainly, before they were
put on and for a somewhat prouder set to one's shoulders. And now,
since there seemed to be some possibility of replacing them when they
wore out, they need not always be saved for Sundays, weddings, and
funerals. They could be worn downtown on a Saturday afternoon.
The work-gnarled hands and the pellagra-sharpened countenance of
the "old-timer" would give him away, of course, but the young fixer
and his wife, window-shopping along Main Street, might be mistaken
for any number of people who had never had lint in their hair. He
would not be taken for a banker or a lawyer or a doctor, of course, but
for a bookkeeper or a clerk or many like people who performed minor
but "respectable" functions in the local society.

It was among this latter group that the most outspoken and vicious
resentment of the mill worker appeared. Some of its members might
themselves have come out of the village, rising from errand boy to
grocery clerk, for example; but in such cases they might be even more
contemptuous of the "lint heads" from the mill who were content to
remain there. In many cases also these people, even in the 1920's, were
likely to have a smaller cash income than the mill hand, their housing
might even be inferior, and this was a further cause for resentment.
The low income but "respectable" group outside the mill was growing.
There was more and more need in the communities for people to fill
various and minor service occupations. Clerks of all kinds, stenogra-
phers, bookkeepers, office girls, and minor tradesmen became necessary;
the pay rolls that the mills were bringing into the mill towns were
finding their way into ever more complex distributive channels, requiring a more complicated economic superstructure.

In the earlier days, the only people from the mills who had made themselves conspicuous in town were the riff-raff. But now, the solid care of the mill community was beginning to venture out of protective hiding, and its representatives had the temerity to behave like the honest, respectable people they were rather than as the previous sample had led the townsfolk to expect. The upper stratum of the social hierarchy in the local community was not particularly disturbed by their advent and their bid for first-class citizenship in the community. Its members were sufficiently well protected by social distance to permit them to be philosophical about it, even in favor of it, if they thought about it at all; but to those people of the new lower-middle class, who had been able previously to cling to the comforting thought that they were at least "better than the mill hands," it was a disturbing revelation. As a matter of protection for their self-esteem, it became necessary to show these upstarts their places.

The power of the folk within the mills proved too strong for those in the towns who would deny them their place in the community. In many instances they received help from an unexpected source though it was indirect and was only incidentally (if at all) intended for their benefit. The early mills had usually been built just outside the corporate limits of their communities, partly because land there was cheaper but also as a kind of community-approved subsidy that enabled them to avoid the higher tax rate of the incorporated area. In those days the mills were desired for their pay rolls; they were not seriously regarded as sources of tax money. As the extent and cost of community services increased after World War I, however, mill town and city governments began to cast envious eyes at extensive and highly developed textile real-estate holdings at their borders that were contributing nothing to corporate coffers. On numerous occasions, they cast covetous glances toward the mills' superior school systems.

In community after community following World War I, movements were begun to extend corporate boundaries to include neighboring mills and to integrate village and town school systems. These movements were generally opposed by the mills, and with good reason. They had already paved their streets, laid in water mains and sewers, improved their schools, built community centers and athletic fields. Inclusion within corporate limits would mean simply that they would now help to pay for these facilities for communities without sharing in their benefits. They knew also that if their school system were integrated with that of the town, they would be expected as a matter of course to subsidize the combined system over and above what they paid in taxes. But despite their reluctance, the mills usually gave in; the old custom of deferring to community opinion was not dead among their managements. In many cases, having surrendered, they went even further, making their recreational facilities available to townspeople and opening their youth programs to town children.

On the other hand, having been legally incorporated into their communities, the mills were in no mood to countenance any open discrimination against mill villagers. They had never ceased to regard their workers as worthy people;[12] it was just that in some cases they had not thought about it recently. The question of discrimination against children in grade school was not likely to come up since they would continue to attend schools located in the village; but the mills seldom had their own high schools. Now there could be no question raised as to the right of village youth to take advantage of community facilities in this respect, particularly if the mill had just added a new field house to the high school plant and was subsidizing teacher salaries. Nor would the mill be likely to look with favor on an attempt to bar mill people from the use of any other public facilities of the community now supported in good part by mill taxes.

It was perhaps the integration of educational facilities that often put town children in village schools as well as village children in town schools that was as important as any other factor in the disappearance of the gulf between town and village. Mills invariably contributed more than their proportionate share of support to community educational systems, and mill children demonstrated their ability to hold up their end as scholars and athletes. In addition, while adolescents are notoriously cliquish, they are likely to base their discrimination on value systems different from those of their elders, values that do not necessarily exclude peers from social strata below their own.[13] While high school teachers subscribed to adult standards and were themselves "white-collar" and middle-class, it was not to their advantage, with their mill-subsidized salaries, to display openly any tendencies they

---

12. See Herring, *Welfare Work*, p. 395.

13. See J. J. Rhyne, *Some Southern Mill Workers and Their Villages* (Chapel Hill: The University of North Carolina Press, 1930), p. 196.

might have to treat students from the mill village as members of an inferior caste.

Another result of the integration, stemming from what might seem a triviality, nevertheless played its role in influencing community attitudes toward young people from mill villages. Southern communities take great pride in their high school athletic teams; and it became rather difficult to continue to be contemptuous of mill people while at the same time the local high school football team, of championship caliber, drew upon the village for better than half its players. The star quarterback is likely to have his pick of partners for the prom, whether he comes from the most fashionable part of town or from the mill village. It is difficult for anything resembling a caste system to stand long under such conditions. The careers of certain village-born young men who used high school as a passport to college, sometimes with the aid of a mill scholarship, sometimes with nothing to support them but their own determination and summer work with the mill, sometimes with an athletic scholarship, tended also to cast doubt upon the fiction of their inferior birth.

Also by this time the effectiveness of the mill village as a segregative device was breaking down in a physical sense. The mills were expanding the size of their work forces but seldom the size of their villages. More and more mill workers were finding residence in the town itself; and though their neighbors might regard the unquestionably respectable Jones who lived next door and worked in the mill as "exceptions," nevertheless they had to admit that there *were* exceptions to the stereotyped image of the mill worker they had previously regarded as all-inclusive. Many of the townspeople also knew many of these new employees of the mills to have been hard-working upstanding farm people a year or so previously; and they found it difficult to believe that they could have changed significantly merely by having taken a job in the mill.

An additional factor had considerable to do with the changing attitude of the townspeople with whom the mill worker was most likely to come into contact. "The strike in 1934 was not good for the mill or for the people," a long-service employee told the writer, "but there was one good thing that came out of it. The people downtown found out how important we were to them. When the pay rolls from the mill stopped, the merchants had to lay off most of their help. There just wasn't any money in the town. The clerks used to treat us like dirt before the strike—like they were doing us a favor to take our money— but it was sure different afterward. It was 'Mr. Smith, what can I do for you' and 'Mr Smith, I'll be glad to help you' and 'You come back now, Mr. Smith.' I was never called 'Mr.' so many times in my life as I was when I went down town to spend that first pay check after the strike. It never did go back to what it was like before." This was not merely a local phenomenon. The general strike had the effect of reminding many textile towns that their whole economy was geared around the textile worker and his pay check; and that they did not enjoy his custom as a matter of right.

While the mill people themselves noted the change, after the strike was over, in the attitudes of the white-collar people with whom they customarily came into contact, there was a change of attitude in another quarter in these communities that, though less noticeable, was even more important. Community leaders who for quite some time might have been taking labor relations in the mills for granted, content to let mill managements assume total responsibility for them, began to pay attention once more. They had no desire for the community to suffer another strike, nor did they desire to attract union organizers to the vicinity if they were not already there. In many cases it became evident after the fact that managerial deficiencies in personnel policies had led to, or at least had contributed to, what had happened. Evidently what went on in the mills was a matter of concern to the community, and evidently also one dared not assume as a matter of course that a mill management would "treat its people right." Community leaders re-assumed as one of their responsibilities informal but nevertheless effective policing of personnel policies as those policies made themselves evident in practice in neighboring mills. They brought the mill workers back under the protection of the folkways.

We cannot overlook, as a factor in closing the gap, the power of self-criticism that the Piedmont had always displayed. There were many in the Southeast who were alert to the dangers inherent in the creation of a permanent caste of cotton-mill workers and who minced no words in their critical attacks upon what was happening. Mill communities bristled under the lash of their acrid words and pointed out, with some justice, that the picture was being painted blacker than it actually was; nevertheless they looked about them uneasily, not too sure despite their insistent denials that there might not be some truth in the criticisms. There was no great wave of reform; but there was increasing sensitivity to the possibility of improvement as the result of the constant prodding of the voice of conscience of the Piedmont. The Piedmont South has never been a region to follow directly the suggestions for reform that are made by its critics. As in the case of all folk societies, its first response to critical attack is likely to be a highly emotional defense of the *status quo* simply because it has accepted that *status quo* largely on the basis of faith rather than reasoned logic. But by the same token, it is extremely sensitive to criticism; and while it may refuse to accept the well-meant advice of outsiders as a matter of pride, there is nothing more certain but that it will, in its own way, attempt to remove the basis for further criticism from that quarter.

The social isolation of the textile worker during the 1920's, now that we can look at it in retrospect, was only one phase of a developing situation, an understandable reaction on the part of a society that had to make certain adjustments to readmit him to full membership now that he himself felt ready for it. There were some people who had to move over to make ready for him, and they resented it. Once he had joined them, they discovered that he was not such a bad fellow after all. What was happening was another act in the drama of the resurgence of the common man. There continued to be social distinctions in the mill communities as there always had been, as there was in the most democratic of contemporary communities elsewhere in the nation, as there inevitably will be in any society sufficiently complex to call for differences in function and status among its membership. But the tendency to make a caste of mill workers was defeated; and the possibility of mobility from one class to another, as one deserved the benefit of such mobility, was admitted.

MANAGEMENT TAKES INVENTORY

In discussing local influences that led to labor unrest in the Piedmont during the period, we noted that while poor supervision was the triggering cause of much of it, this latter was actually only one manifestation of changing practices and attitudes on the part of top management. What seemed at the time to be a significant minority of mills were drifting into a business-like and impersonal attitude toward employee relations that resulted, among other things, in shifting the personnel function to a supervisory group unprepared to handle it. This minority was regarded as significant by contemporary students of the scene principally because it seemed only reasonable to suppose, on the basis of past experience with mass production industries in other regions, that an increasing impersonality in industrial relationships was foreordained, an inescapable conclusion to the industrial process.

Yet somehow when the test came, the "significance" of this minority seemed to dwindle. When they were finally roused to action by the turn events were taking, it appeared that the power to dominate the future still lay with the less spectacular majority, mills in which a first generation management, or a second generation that carried out the spirit as well as the letter of the old relationship, set the pattern of labor relations. They were the mills that called the turn when the chips were down and the choice had to be made.

There was no possibility of escaping the necessity for making the choice. The question had been put in terms that could not be evaded by the union campaigns of 1929 and 1930, and it was reiterated in the fall of 1934. The mills had to make a decision, and there were three choices open to them.

1. They could capitulate to union organization.

2. They could fight the union as the main threat to the serenity of their relationships with their employees, assuming that once it was defeated their troubles were over.

3. They could fight the union as a preliminary skirmish while they attempted to seek out and engage the main body of the enemy—those conditions that had caused their people to turn to the union for relief in the first place.

Southern managements were no more inclined to capitulate to the union without a struggle than were other managements anywhere. The whole idea of collective bargaining offers a challenge to management's basic philosophy, which has been well summarized by Lloyd Reynolds in his *Labor Economics and Labor Relations:*

Trade-unionism challenges the cardinal points in management's philosophy. It interposes between the employer and employee the trade-union, an organization which many managements believe is more interested in its own growth and power than in the economic welfare of either workers or the company. It refuses to accept survival and profitability as the sole aim of business management. It interferes with management's effort to achieve lowest money cost of production, and with the freedom of maneuver which most managers consider essential to successful performance of their functions. At point after point the union says "You can't do that," or "You must consult us before doing anything." Many management people see in this a deliberate policy of union encroachment on management functions. They ask themselves where the process will end, and whether they may not be forced eventually to abdicate control of the plant.[14]

By reason of the very fact that they performed the management function, southern executives must have been expected to oppose the unionization of their plants. But their major opposition, and the measure of its intensity, arose from a deeper and more fundamental source than the objections that Reynolds identifies above as arising out of the nature of the management function itself.

These men and their subordinates in the managerial hierarchy of the Piedmont textile industry were still of the folk society. Some of them had drifted insensibly into ways of behaving that were more characteristic of the mass society, but when the crisis came they were still of the folk. They had never, actually, departed from the implicit assumption that their relationships with their people ought to be based on mutual understanding, but some of them had presumed an adequacy of understanding that no longer existed. They had never, actually, ceased to identify themselves with the people in the mills, but some of them had identified with an image that through unconscious over-simplification had become invalid. There had in these cases been an imperceptible drifting apart; and the widening gulf was never called to their attention until finally the union had come in to ask the people to stand up and be counted.

These managements, when they became aware of the gulf, did not want it there. They could have built a bridge across it with the union, as managements under the massways had found it wise to do, and it might have been the most expedient way of settling the matter after some preliminary haggling over the price. But this could not be the answer under the folkways. The existence of the gulf, though managements did not admit it openly, was a reproach. They could not help but feel, though they might not even confess the fact to themselves, that somewhere along the line they had failed. Somehow, in some way,

14. Lloyd Reynolds, *Labor Economics and Labor Relations* (1st ed., New York: Prentice-Hall, 1949), p. 159.

they had not met up to a responsibility that had been laid upon them as a part of their heritage.

We must remind ourselves that man sees himself in the mirror of others. His judgements of himself reflect to a high degree what he thinks the judgments of those others to be whose respect he cherishes and whose good will he values. In the Piedmont textile industry of the 1920's and the early 1930's, even during the hey-day of efficiency, there were two groups of men to whom one listened in sober attention, intuitively sensing that they spoke with the voice of the region. One group was made up of still remaining figures of the first generation, many of them managers of modest country mills that were lost in the forest of spindles now covering the Piedmont, others like the Captain (whose mill never lost a day of work all during the turbulent period), were the heads of larger enterprises who had stubbornly refused to listen to the siren voice of "efficiency." These men had a simple philosophy: *If you treat your people right, you won't have trouble with them.* In the other group, some of them first generation also, were those leaders in the industry who were actively reminding managements of their responsibility to the wage earner.

Unconsciously measuring their own present situations against the stark and uncompromising simplicity of the value standards of the elders and the measured judgements of the apostles of corporate responsibility, the managements of those mills whose work forces had turned against them could not help but feel that though they had the support of these men in their struggle with the union, there was nevertheless an element of disapproval in the air. Because the criticisms were for the most part unvoiced, they were all the more powerful. They functioned as a kind of "voice of conscience" that would not be quieted. There was also the suspicion that though the leaders of their communities supported them, here also the support was perhaps more the result of an identification of the union as a common enemy than an indication of unqualified approval of the personnel relationships that had preceded the strike.

Thus to have accepted the union as a settlement to labor difficulties would have seemed in a sense tantamount to an admission that a management had failed in the "right" treatment of its people to the point that the breach was irreparable. It would seem a confession that there was nothing left except to deal with them through an intermediary, that management had broken faith to the extent that its people would no longer trust it to do the right thing except at the point of a loaded weapon.

This was not, of course, the explanation that was offered to the public. One could hardly expect managements to offer in public confession what was in their own minds perhaps no more than a vague and disquieting whisper that refused to be quelled. The union was fought with every resource that was available. Those in the work force whom it was suspected had become deeply tainted with its philosophy were thrust out along with it. (And also, after the strike was over, there was frequently a "house-cleaning" conducted by top management, or ownership, if need be, that removed from the scene those management people who by their insensitivity, obduracy, or stupidity were felt to have precipitated the trouble in the first place.) The union was branded an enemy and its adherents traitorous. It could not be otherwise, for if the gap was to be closed, the first task was to remove the foreign matter that had found its way in and cleanse the edges of infection. The folk society, we have said, cannot tolerate the presence of an unassimilated element. It must either absorb it, thrust it out, or accept with resignation the probability of its own eventual destruction.

The Piedmont was able to assimilate the northern firm and to make the branch plant a part of the local society. It was not able to do this with the northern union; for collective bargaining, in the guise in which it was presented, was the antithesis of everything the folk society stood for. It would replace the folkways with rules and regulations, consensus with a contract. It would substitute conformity for understanding, rigidity for adaptability. It was a calculated rather than a spontaneous relationship, anonymous rather than personal. It dismissed the importance of attitudes and stressed the importance of acts. It would list specified rights and duties, contingent upon specified circumstances, rather than unspecified and mutual obligations, categorically binding. To surrender to the union meant that one must abandon the whole philosophy of the folk society and embrace that of the massways. Northern managements might come to advocate "learning to live with the union"; but those of the Piedmont could not. They saw the advent of the union as far more than the possibility of managerial inconvenience or even as a threat to the survival of the firm.

They saw it as a fundamental threat to the very social structure that had brought the mills into being.

The stand that managements took against the union was reinforced by their communities and by a good part of the people who worked for them. These two groups, as a matter of fact, on occasion waged the battle with an excess of zeal that was more embarrassing to management than it was helpful. We must remember, if we are to understand what went on, that joining ranks with the union could not, from the point of view of the folk society of the Piedmont, be a matter of personal choice to be exercised on one's own volition. It was desertion to the enemy. It is not without reason that the union organizer even today is described in the textile Piedmont as a "foreigner" though he may have been born and bred in the region. In these calmer days he is no longer branded a traitor in explanation when the matter of his birthplace is raised; but he is regarded as an expatriate. He has renounced the society of his birth and naturalized himself into another.

But though the fight against unionism had a life-or-death aspect to it, yet Piedmont managements could not regard it as the main event. It was only a preliminary action, the cleansing of a wound that needed still to be sutured and dressed. The elimination of the union from the scene had not closed the gap between people and management. It had, rather, widened it. To rest now would be only to invite the organizers to return, and the next time the union might not be repulsed. It could have been this time, had the people really wanted it, a fact of which managements were uncomfortably aware. The main task still lay ahead. The elimination of the misunderstandings, the distrust and the suspicion, the unrest and the dissatisfaction that had provided the soil in which the union had taken temporary root was the serious problem. The defeat of the union as an accomplishment in itself offered only temporary respite. It was a kind of delaying action that provided an opportunity to prepare and launch the main attack against the real enemy.

In achieving this saving delay, Piedmont textile managements had profited by a major mistake in strategy on the part of the U. T. W. and the A. F. of L. Union attempts to organize the South in full-strength drives in 1929-30 and again in 1933-34, largely based on the northern situation, were premature. The folk society of the Piedmont cotton textile industry had not yet become atomized to the point that the massways were necessary to achieve social order and the union a necessary intermediary between managements and work forces that were hopelessly estranged. Had the full-strength drive on the South been deferred, it is quite possible that its textile industry could have drifted insensibly into a condition in which the division between managements and the work force would have become so acute that the latter would have found it necessary to organize itself for its own protection. As it was, the attempt to organize from the outside before organization was felt to be necessary had the effect of alerting managements to the dangers toward which they were heading. It gave them an opportunity to strengthen the society from within to the point that it was resistant to threats from outside.

This task of strengthening from within, of cementing the bonds between labor and management to the point that they were invulnerable to attack from without, was not easy. It was not merely a matter of returning to the ways of the fathers, for the inescapable fact was that the mills were not the mills of the fathers. The maintenance of the close personal relationship between top management and the people had become a physical impossibility in many of the larger mills. The company that in the old days had consisted of perhaps three or four hundred people in a single mill, all on one shift, might now have six thousand people divided between six mills and three shifts. The president of such an organization could not have acquired the personal knowledge of his employees necessary to operate under the old intuitive system that had worked so well for the first generation had he devoted every moment of his time to the job. That was why the personnel function had gone by default to supervisors in so many cases. They were the only people who were still close enough to the work force to handle it in a completely informal fashion.

Yet leaving the personnel function completely in the hands of these people could not be the answer. The dangers inherent in such a policy had already been amply and quite expensively demonstrated. It could very easily result in a crazy-quilt pattern of personnel policies within the same organization, one department set against another in an operation that required a maximum of co-operation between all departments for economical operation. There was every possibility of complete bewilderment on the part of the worker as he saw orders issued today unknowingly countermanded by a higher echelon of management tomorrow and the complete and unpredictable reversals of policy as each new supervisor took over.

Attempting, or merely continuing to duplicate, the *practices* of the first generation without taking into consideration that the situation under which those practices were applied had changed, meant actually violating the *principles* of the first generation. It was the spirit that had led to the practices rather than the practices themselves that were important. Going through certain gestures in a perfunctory fashion because they were what one's predecessor had done was worse than useless. What was required was going back to the basic principles of the old days, making them once more effective through policies and practices that were in line with modern conditions.

It was here that the still basically folk nature of the industrial society of the mills made its full power for regeneration felt. The principles were still there. They had never been lost. There had merely been an assumption as to their implementation in many cases that was not justified by the facts. They were no different from what they had always been: the ethical code of the region, founded on the premises of the Christian religion; the dignity of the human spirit and the brotherhood of man. It was the common possession of this ethical code by managements and work forces alike, and their common agreement that problems involving one man's relationship with another had to be settled in terms of it, that made it possible to close the gaps that had appeared. There was a common area of agreement in terms of which differences could be worked out, the possibility for a meeting of the minds in any particular situation as to what was "right" and what was "wrong" according to concepts of justice, dignity, and decency, that were universally accepted without questioning.

What had been lacking in the bulk of the mills that had experienced labor trouble had not been agreement between managements and people as to the nature of the fundamental principles upon which industrial relations ought to be based. *It had been communication that had degenerated, not the moral and ethical aspects of the situation.* The informal but rich and continuing interchange of information that had taken place as the managers of the old mills had made their daily rounds had meant that any particular problem tended to look the same to management and to the people. Each had not only relatively complete factual information about what was going on but an appreciation of the point of view of the other. Each was able to assume the role of the other, to see a problem as the other saw it. There was not "my" point of view and "your" point of view, but essentially "our" point of view, and under such conditions, given a common scale of values against which to measure whatever was being assessed, there was very little disagreement as to what was the right and what was the wrong thing to do under any given circumstance.

As for one reason or another managements and people had grown further and further apart in various mills, there had been not only less and less sharing of the factual aspects of problems, but even more regrettably, less and less ability to take one another's point of view. Thus what might seem right to management might seem wrong to the people even though still judged against the same standards. Communication had been the basis of the personnel function under the old system. It was the restoration of communication that was essential in those mills in which managements had lost touch with the people, communication of facts and, even more important, attitudes, intentions, objectives, and points of view.

The story of the strengthening of bonds between managements and work forces in the mills since the early 1930's has been largely the story of restoration of this communication where it has been lost and safe-guarding of it in those cases where it had never disappeared. Just how it was accomplished in any particular instance was a function of the particular circumstances of the instance; that it was in nearly every case accomplished as successfully as it was resulted in great measure from the fact that each management operated within the realistic dimensions of its own situation. In every case of which the writer has knowledge, its restoration seems to have rested upon explicit recognition of three basic premises:

1. The importance of the personnel function.

2. That though it might be shared, final responsibility for it rested with top management.

3. That it had to be based on continuous, two-way communication.

That the first part of this three-fold requirement was achieved almost automatically was due partly to the premature attempt of the U. T. W. to organize the Piedmont and partly to the fact that the function had not been buried beneath generations of insensitive disregard for the human aspects of the industrial situation. There were, as a matter of fact, numerous contemporary examples of it in full flower. The operation of the industry under the folkways had made the personal nexus imperative; at the first real intimation that it might disappear, managements awoke to what it had meant to them. It had been so universally present to begin with that it had been taken for granted; but the threat of its removal, and the maintenance of labor relations upon an impersonal basis, was a prospect the industry could not face with equanimity. Fortunately, it was granted the opportunity of missing the water before the well ran dry through the agency of a stoppage that proved to be temporary rather than permanent.

Recognition of the second part of the three-fold requirement followed upon the first. If a function was so important that, improperly discharged, it could threaten the life of an enterprise, it was not a function that top management could turn its back upon. As a practical matter it was necessary to share it, as indeed, it had been implicitly shared by the first generation. But as an equally practical matter the overall nature of its operation on a shared basis had to be kept under scrutiny, as it had been by the first generation. Furthermore, it had to be shared deliberately and not by default, with due emphasis upon its importance and with its essential policies outlined; it had proven too important for its development to be left to the chance whims and caprices of the supervisory force.

As for the third part of the basic requirement, that communication be recognized as the very heart of the personnel function, here again was a case of a phenomenon defining its nature by its absence. Those managements that had found themselves in difficulties with their people during the period were in nearly every case taken by surprise. They had had no idea of the developing state of unrest, of the fact that they were misunderstood and guilty of misunderstanding. They awoke to the unpleasant realization that they had not been aware of what had been going on in their own companies, that they had been operating for quite some time on the basis of inadequate and invalid assumptions as to the feelings and attitudes of the people who were working for them. In nearly every case they had been conducting their affairs with the best of good will toward the people in the work force, and they had been prone to assume that there was equally good will toward them.

It came as somewhat of a shock for managements to discover that they were neither credited with good will nor the recipient of it. They had always assumed that good will and loyalty had to be earned; but they had tended also to assume that if a particular course of action were followed with good intentions it could be expected as a natural consequence to beget a reciprocal attitude equally good. They discovered now that this had been true in the past only because there was agreement to begin with as to the essential rightness of the action and the wisdom of the intentions.

Good will and loyalty, in other words, could not be earned merely by doing what managements thought to be "right." The actions had to be judged as "right" by the people as well if the desired results were to be obtained. There was only one way by which the two definitions as to what was right could be aligned, and that was by communicating, by bringing together points of view that were becoming increasingly divergent, by seeing that both parties were looking at essentially the same set of facts. Only when one was in sufficiently close touch with the people to be certain that there was essential agreement as to what *was* the right thing, could one be sure that following the advice of the first generation of management, "If you treat your people right, you won't have trouble," would get the desired results.

But merely to recognize the importance of the personnel function, to realize that responsibility for it could be delegated only under continuing supervision, to understand that it was for the most part a matter of effective communication was far from being sufficient to reintegrate estranged managements and work forces into single and effectively functioning social units. Demonstrably, the matter could no longer be left to pursue its development in an informal fashion for that was what had caused much of the trouble in the first place. The increasing complexity of organization for production meant that what had formerly been left to follow its own meandering path must now be deliberately planned for, that relationships which in older days and simpler organizations could safely be left implicit must now be explicitly spelled out, and that exchanges of information which could once be accomplished by informal conversation and through informal channels must now be supplemented, though not replaced, by formal means.

What happened, between 1934 and the beginning of World War I, was a demonstration of the power of a folk society to respond to changed life conditions. Just as in 1880 the Piedmont found that the pattern for its salvation had already been outlined some decades previously by men with particular sensitivity to the destiny of the region, so now the industry it had developed found the answer to its labor problems already at hand, worked out by men who had seen even before 1920 that if the principles fundamental to equitable industrial relations were to be maintained in a changing world, it could be done only through new policies realized in new practices. Following the lead of these pioneers of the 1920's, the mills began rather generally to develop explicit and objective technics not only to solve their problems but to create the kind of climate that would keep them from developing. They used practices developed by legitimate scientific management for ordering industrial relations under the massways, but they used them in the spirit of the folk. They picked and chose among them, applying those that seemed reasonable under specific circumstances, casting aside those that appeared to have no merit when considered against the needs of a particular organization and the situation it faced; they avoided the use of "package deals."

We cannot overlook an assist from the massways arising from quite another source. The days were past when it was feasible for the superintendent to "keep his personnel files under his hat"; yet many mills were loath to apply the impersonal technics of bookkeeping to the task of keeping track of their people, and this was not entirely because of whatever additional cost might be involved. The implication carried by such practices that they were dealing with units of labor rather than with human beings was genuinely repugnant to many managers of mills. But federal legislation during the 1930's made it increasingly necessary for individual records to be kept on the people in the work force, for Social Security, for withholding taxes, for substantiating that a worker actually was discharged for inefficiency and repeated absence from work rather than for union activity. Even the smallest mill soon found itself with something that corresponded to a personnel department, with more or less elaborate records on each of its workers.

It was not long before the people in management, from second hands on up, were finding it convenient to consult these records to refresh their memories; and eventually, in many mills, the personnel section was moved out of the treasurer's office, dignified with departmental status, and charged by top management with the responsibility of compiling all sorts of information about the people in the work force. Some of the most elaborate personnel *dossiers* the writer has ever seen are in the active files of Piedmont textile mills, which is not surprising. For in a society in which social action is based principally on the knowledge which its members have of one another as *persons,* a personnel folder must approach the dimensions of a case history before it becomes really useful.

What managements did was to recognize the realities of their particular situations and make them workable. In the matter of supervision and the personnel function at the work place, the heart of any industrial relationship, it was apparent that managerial resumption of the responsibility for policing it did not alter the fact that the burden of responsibility for exercise of the function, as it rested on overseers particularly, was considerably greater than it had been in the old mills. The only reasonable solution was to make an explicit delegation of responsiblity—which would, as a by-product, increase the dignity of the supervisory role—and do whatever else could be done to facilitate the supervisor's discharge of an increased load of responsibility that only he was in a position to handle effectively.

1. In the first place, since the sharing was now deliberate and explicit, the respective areas of responsibility could be traced out, and the supervisor could be told what was expected of him.

2. The supervisor could be given practical guidance in personnel matters by definition of policy at the top level. Not only would this make his task easier, but it would restore uniformity to a situation that had, during the 1920's, become increasingly confused.

3. Future supervisors could be chosen with the idea in mind that personnel work would be an important part of their duties. Technical competence, though still important, should no longer be the sole criteria. Their ability to "get along with folks," the extent of their patience, their ability to teach and to explain should be taken into consideration as well.

4. Present and future supervisors could be trained for the discharge of the function, alerted to its importance and given some practical advice as to how it might most effectively be accomplished.

5. Higher management could stand ready with advice and assistance when it was needed.

6. Since the personnel function was largely a matter of communication, it was not only advisable but imperative that the supervisor be taken much more closely into management than he had been in the past, made acquainted with the company's problems, and informed as to its plans. If he was to act as an intermediary between the people and top management, he had to be an informed intermediary, both for the sake of his morale and that of the people. He could not help the people to understand what was going on when he did not know himself.

7. He could, when necessary, be given assistants who could carry out certain of his routine technical responsibilities, thus giving him more time for working with the people themselves.

8. He could as well be relieved of the routine aspects of the personnel function, recruitment, record-keeping, and other similar jobs. These activities could be more efficiently performed in a central office in any case.

9. Through more careful selection, more adequate training, he could be given more capable people to work with.

10. And finally, someone could be specially delegated to assist him in every way possible with his share of the personnel function: to study the people and their problems, to keep him in touch with new ideas and what other people had been doing about problems that were similiar to his; in other words, to make expert advice and assistance available to him.

In short, top management's share of the personnel function under this approach was not so much to perform it as to make it easier for the supervisor to perform it and to insure that it was being properly performed.

But top management did not play a completely behind-the-scenes role. In those cases where it had retired behind glass and mahogany it came out into the open again to resume two important functions that the first generation had carried out as an avocation. First, it had to get to know the people if it had permitted itself to drift away from them. The personnel office, with its new files and its personnel records, its statistical breakdowns and its reports (all technics borrowed to good advantage from the massways), was able to present an overall picture that had been lacking for too long, but this cold, impersonal, mathematical picture did not mean much until one went out into the mill and met the living flesh and blood behind the manila file folders in the office. One could not know all of them, as the first generation often had been able to do, but one could get acquainted with a representative sample and give that sample an opportunity to get acquainted with top management. The relatively small size of even the largest production units in textiles, when compared with those of other modern industries, and the homogeneous nature of the southern work force both worked to furnish top management of a plant with a rich, adequate, and valid image of their work force even when they could not call every man in the plant by name. The personal bond between top management and the people was re-established where it had been permitted to lapse, not as "something one was expected to do," but out of sincere interest in the people and what they thought and felt.

The second function that was re-assumed by management in those cases where it had been permitted to go by default was one that had been the corner stone of the folk relationship under the first generation and was equally important to those that succeeded. Top management re-asserted itself as the Court of Appeals in cases of real or fancied injustices and grievances. It stood once more in judgement over the exercise of the personnel function by subordinates. It might be necessary, in a large organization, to set up something that looked like a grievance procedure and attempt to get more or less conformance with it; but one did not tell anyone that he could not bring his problems directly to the top if he wished. If the folk organization were to continue to exist in spirit in the mills, the confidence of the people in the integrity of top management had to be won; there had to be the feeling that "you can get a square deal from the Old Man." This could not be done by evading the responsibility of deciding what was right and what was wrong in specific cases. Again, the function was not re-assumed as "something one is expected to do." When a management took back ultimate responsibility for the personnel function in the mill, the manner in which it was being discharged at lower levels became a matter of personal interest. Recent experience had demonstrated the fallacy of assuming that things were the way one hoped that they were; and if there was misunderstanding, or supervisors were unknowingly or deliberately violating personnel policy, or if the policies themselves were impractical or unfair, it was as important to top management to know about it as it was to the people involved to get it settled.

Management made itself accessible to the people. The "open door policy" is generally decried as hypocritical and unworkable; and in most cases outside the Piedmont with which the writer is familiar, it is. It did not work in those mills in the Piedmont, during the period of unrest, where the people were made to feel like employees. But the Piedmont work force had lost none of its independence of spirit. Its men and women still thought of themselves as the "people" of the Piedmont cotton textile industry rather than as its employees. They still perferred to co-operate with management, to work *with* it rather than *for* it. They still continued to think of themselves as differing from the men at the top only in terms of differentiated functions, rather than as in any way intrinsically inferior to them. Under such conditions, the "open door policy" has different significance. The worker thinks of himself as bringing to the attention of a man whose status enables him to do something about it, notice of a condition of mutual interest that he feels must be corrected for the good of the enterprise as well as for his own personal satisfaction.

These changes, innovations, and reassumptions that we have been discussing were most evident in the minority of mills that for one reason or another had experienced worker unrest. This does not mean, however, that all the mills did not profit by what was going on. Those mills that had never departed from the spirit of the original Cotton Mill Campaign were alerted, if they were not already aware of it, to the importance of what they had always been doing. They were awakened to the value of what they possessed before they let it slip away from them. Not only were the relationships they had always enjoyed personally satisfying, but they were now recognized as industrially important. Other mills were spending time and money to recapture them. The mills that had never lost the trust and confidence of their people or adequate communication with them took steps to insure the retention of what they had. Though in small, single-unit mills the personnel function was still, and would continue to be for the most part, discharged as much by top management as by the supervisory force, the importance of sharing the function with the latter was realized; somewhat more care was taken with regard to their selection, and steps were taken to train them in the essentials of personnel work.

Not only were training programs set up by the majority of the mills to improve supervisory practices, but there was much wider adoption of employee training to enable hourly rated people within the mill to step into vacancies calling for higher skills or into supervisory jobs. The mills were consequently less dependent than they had been upon the floating population of textile workers to fill jobs calling for some degree of skill. This had its advantages, particularly during a period when labor unrest was in the air, since these workers were often rovers in the first place because of socio-psychological maladjustments that made them potential sources of infection. Additional advantages became apparent as employee training was broadened both in scope and adoption. The people were not subjected to the frustrating experience of seeing men from outside continually come into the plant and take the best jobs. Promotion from within on the basis of objectively measured performance in a training program was much less vulnerable to charges of favoritism. Because the training was deliberate and supervised, the workers were better qualified technically. Perhaps most important of all, homogeneity of the work force was maintained; whereas the continual importation of supervisors and skilled people from outside tended to break up the feeling of community within the group that was so important for the operation of the folkways.

CHAPTER VIII

The Present Pattern

THE CRUCIAL TEST of the programs undertaken by managements of the Piedmont mills to revitalize and strengthen their relations with their work forces came during the period following World War I. Heavy demands for production during the war years had been met with the full co-operation of the people in the mills. This was not in itself a reliable indication of good personnel relationships, however, for estrangements can be temporarily forgotten in the face of a common danger. What is significant is that the problems of readjustment to a peacetime economy did not bring about wide-spread labor unrest as they had in the Piedmont during a similiar period from 1919 through 1921, nor as they did for other major national industries from 1946 through 1949. A high level of rapport existing generally between southeastern cotton textile work forces and their managements enabled the latter to take full advantage of the release of pent-up wartime consumer demand and strengthen themselves technologically and financially against the lean years experience had taught them to expect. Their expectations were unhappily justified after 1949; but though the disappearance of overtime (rather than pay cuts) reduced worker take-home pay, worker morale remained high in the Piedmont. It is to this latter circumstance that managements attribute their ability to maintain or to increase the pay scales of the prosperous years and to hold to a work week seldom averaging appreciably under forty hours. The potentialities of newly-modernized plants could not have been sufficiently realized for this to have been done without the highest degree of worker co-operation.

The bonds between managements and their people have remained firmly cemented through a period first of socio-psychological, and then of economic, adjustment since 1945. The C. I. O.'s "Operation Dixie" was not able to enlist any appreciable addition to union membership in the Piedmont; yet we recall that following World War I there had been a large increase in union strength among the region's textile labor force. The ease of penetration of a union into an industry is in direct proportion to the degree of unrest and dissatisfaction existing among its workers. The following statement, made to the writer by an official of the C. I. O. in 1951, is perhaps as significant a measure as any of the general pattern of relationship between managements and workers in the Piedmont's cotton textile industry since World War II. "There is not likely to be another large-scale organizational drive in textiles for quite a while. We can't get anywhere, and we may as well face it. We'll continue to keep our organizers in the field, and we'll pick up a plant now and then; but our strategy in the forseeable future is to organize around textiles." At the time of the interview there were twelve organized textile plants in Georgia. By the spring of 1954 the number of collective bargaining contracts existing in the state's textile industry had dropped to eight, covering only 5,000 of its 109,000 workers.

A further indication of the union's judgement that the Piedmont does not at present offer a fertile soil for union organization was the removal of the regional offices of the Textile Workers' Union of America (C. I. O.) from Atlanta to Charlotte. Their function now appears to be service of existing locals, concentrated in the northern end of the Piedmont, rather than direction of organization in the almost completely non-union southern end of the region.

Since the southeastern textile workers have rather clearly rejected an alternative for them, we can assume that the present pattern of industrial relations in the Piedmont industry is on the whole satisfactory to the people who man its plants. In this chapter we shall attempt to outline the nature of that relationship, based on the writer's own acquaintance with the industry gained through visits to companies in Georgia, South Carolina, and Alabama employing a total of 50,600 people. These visits have been supplemented by a comprehensive inventory of the characteristics of the work forces and nature of the personnel principles, policies, and practices of 23 representative companies in Georgia employing a total of 29,900 people in a total of 34 establishments. (Unless otherwise indicated, quantitative data that follow are with regard to the Georgian industry only, and no claim is made as to their representativeness for the entire Piedmont. On the other hand, there is no reason for believing that they are not reasonably suggestive of conditions in the balance of the Piedmont. Spot checks by the writer indicate this to be true for South Carolina and Alabama.)

THE PARTIES TO THE RELATIONSHIP

In this section we meet the people who man and manage Georgia's 3,272,000 cotton system spindles and who, during the year ending July, 1952, accounted for 15.3 per cent of the nation's total active spindle hours of operation.[1] Of the state's total textile work force of 109,700 (in 1953) we are particularly concerned with the 71,600 who operate its broad-woven-fabric mills and the 18,000 who work in its yarn and thread mills.[2] In 1952, these two groups were employed in a total of 145 establishments divided among 99 companies and scattered through 84 villages, towns, and cities.[3] Only 10 of the establishments, located in as many towns, were in the state's Coastal Plain; the balance were located in its upland area.[4] According to *Davison's Textile Blue Book* for 1953, 54 per cent of the establishments in which these two groups worked were the only production unit of a locally owned company. Twenty-one per cent of them were part of locally owned and managed chains, and 25 per cent were part of chains of which the majority stock interest was held outside the Piedmont.[5] Seventy-three per cent of the establishments in which they worked operated less than 30,000 spindles; 50 per cent of them were in towns of less than 5,000 population; only 19 per cent were in cities of more than 50,000 population.[6]

With due regard for the dangers inherent in such a practice, we can paint the following picture of the "typical" Georgian broad-woven-cotton textile mill in which the larger of these two groups worked in 1952. It was a locally owned and managed establishment employing

1. Department of Commerce, Bureau of the Census, *Annual Report for 1952, Cotton Production and Distribution.*

2. Georgia Department of Labor, *Georgia Employment and Earnings by Industry, 1952-1953,* p. 10.

3. Compiled from data in *Davidson's Textile Blue Book: 1952* (Ridgewood, N. J.: Davidson Publishing Company, 1953), pp. 230-49.

4. *Ibid.*   5. *Ibid.*

6. *Ibid.*

in the neighborhood of 700 people divided between three shifts. During the year it gave them sufficient employment to enable them to average 38.8 hours each per week for an average weekly wage of $46.95.[7] It was located on the outskirts of a small town in the rural Piedmont and had a mill village in which a considerable sum of money had been invested since the war, but the village was able to house no more than 40 per cent of the workers. It had a recently modernized plant which produced a standard product "in the gray" for a highly competitive market which had, ever since 1949, required a high degree of managerial astuteness if the plant was to show a profit.

Stable employment with relatively little short time had been enjoyed by its work force ever since the war, but on several occasions the company's warehouse had been crammed with unsold goods produced for stock. During the war years the company had paid itself out of debt to its commission house and acquired independent working capital. More recently it had set up its own selling agency and was thus relatively independent of all outside influences but the market itself. Its management was resigned to a continuing "normal" market for its product and felt that only by ever-increasing technical efficiency and the continued co-operation of its people would the firm be able to hold its head above water.

The Work Force

The picture we have just portrayed of a "typical" Georgian textile mill is likely to be true in its essential details for the bulk of plants in Georgia, not only in 1952, but as this is written two years later. It would be meaningless to attempt to set up a similiar sketch of a "typical" textile worker; but we can with some justice and realism outline the overall dimensions of a group of 1,000 textile workers drawn from a number of mills in the central Piedmont in the summer of 1952 to, let us say, a political rally and barbecue.[8]

7. Georgia Department of Labor, *op. cit.,* p. 10.
8. Unless otherwise credited, statistical data following with regard to the Georgian textile work force has been compiled from analysis of data furnished by 23 textile companies operating in Georgia. Fourteen of the companies had less than 30,000 spindles; 4 had between 30,000 and 60,000 in operation; 3 were in the 60,000 to 90,000 category; 2 operated over 90,000 spindles. Only 2 of the companies—of 75,000 and 40,000 spindles respectively—were "city" mills. Of the balance, 10 were located in communities of less than 5,000 population, 6 in communities of between

Of this group, 600 would have been men and 400 women. One hundred twenty would have been less than 25 years old, and 420 less than 35; 330 would have passed their 35th birthday but not their 45th, and 160 would have been 45 or better but less than 55. Of those over 55, 70 would have been less than 65, and 20 past that age.

Of the 1,000, 580 would have had some work in high school, and 220 of these would have received a high school diploma. The remaining 420 would have had educations varying between third grade and grammar school. The level of education would have decreased with age; scarcely 10 per cent of the group over 55 would have finished high school, as compared with better than 35 per cent for the group under 25, and better than 30 per cent for all those under 35. We would have noted a rather interesting phenomena: for the total group under 45, the ratio of men to women high school graduates would have increased steadily as age decreased until for the group under 25 the men were in the lead, with 38 per cent of their number high school graduates compared with only 33 per cent for the women. We might with some justice have concluded this to mean an increasing awareness of the practical value of formal education. Only 30 out of the group of 1,000 would have had any formal education beyond high school, and all of these below the age of 45; none of them would have had a college degree.

Of the total group, 880 would have been born and would have spent their lives within 25 miles of the mill where they were presently

---

5,000 and 10,000 people, 3 in communities between 10,000 and 15,000 population, and one each in communities, respectively, of the 15,000 to 25,000 and 25,000 to 50,000 class.

The relationship between the size of the mills and the size of their communities for the sample is given by the tabulation below:

SIZE OF COMMUNITIES

Size of mills (spindles)	Under 5,000	5,000- 10,000	10,000- 15,000	15,000- 25,000	25,000- 50,000	Over 50,000	Total
Under 30,000	7	4	1	1	1	—	14
30,000-60,000	1	1	1	—	—	1	4
60,000-90,000	—	1	1	—	—	1	3
Over 90,000	2	—	—	—	—	—	2
Total	10	6	3	1	1	2	23

Of the 23 mills, only the 2 largest, both located in communities of less than 5,000 people, had created their own communities. The balance were within or adjacent to communities that were in existence at the time the mills were built. Other data with regard to the nature of the mills will appear in the body of the discussion as it is pertinent.

employed, suggesting a relatively low rate of mobility. Of the rest, 70 would have been born in the state, and 20 in some other part of the South; only 30 would have come from outside the South. Possibly 8 of the latter were born in a foreign country. Of the 880 who were reared in the immediate vicinity of the mill, 380 would have come from farms, 280 would have spent their childhood in the village of the mill where they are now working, 120 would have come from small towns neighboring the mill, and 100 would have come from a neighboring city.

In this group, 400 would have been living in mill villages; but of these, 160 would have bought their village house from the company. Of the balance, 180 would either have owned their own homes or lived in a family-owned home in the town where their mill was located. Those living in rented homes outside the village in the mill town or city would number 290. Of the 1,000, 130 would have lived on farms, 90 of which were owned by themselves or their families. Altogether, counting those who lived in the village, in town, and on farms, 430 would have been property owners or living on family-owned property; 60 of them would have commuted 10 miles or more to work each day. Of the total group, 520 would have worked for their present employer for at least 5 years, and 300 out of the 520 would have been with their company for at least 10 years.

Looking for somewhat more detailed information about these people, and particularly seeking evidence as to the presence of trends with regard to their overall characteristics, we might have consulted the accession records for the past five years (1947-52) of a representative sample of the companies for which they worked. We would have discovered that eighteen of their companies (two of them "city" mills and the balance located in rural Georgia), employing a total of 23,951 people in 1952, had added a total of 26,234 names to their pay rolls during the preceeding five years. Since their work forces had remained relatively stable in size during this period, this latter figure would have approximated their turnover. Expressing it on a percentage basis in terms of average *monthly* turnover, we would have discovered it to be 1.82 per cent, a remarkably low figure since the national average for all industry during the same years was better than twice as high. Calculating it separately for the country mills, we would have found it amounting only to 1.35 per cent.

With regard to the origin of their replacements, we would have noted some significant trends. While 42 per cent of the people working in the mills in 1952 came from farms, only 22 per cent of the recent additions to the work force would have been of rural origin. Comparing the accessions of the sixteen country mills with those of the two city mills, we would have noted that the latter obtained a significantly larger percentage of their replacements from their own locality, a much smaller percentage from farms, and a considerably larger percentage from other mill towns than did the county mills. They would also have ranged further afield for replacements, drawing significantly larger percentages of new employees from farms and mill towns more than twenty-five miles away than did the country mills.

Checking the occupations of the fathers of the accessions, we would have discovered that the city mills drew their new employees almost exclusively from people whose family background was rural or in textiles while the family backgrounds of 24 per cent of the people added to the pay rolls of country mills would have been neither rural nor textile, a phenomenon attesting to the increasing "respectability" of textile employment in the rural Piedmont. Of the second and third generation textile workers who did come into the country mills between 1947 and 1952, 72 per cent would have been going on the pay roll of a company already employing their father; but this would have been true for only 43 per cent of the same group who came into the city mills. We would have concluded that there seemed little danger of the creation of a permanent "cotton mill caste," however, for only 31 per cent of the accessions to the country mills and 45 per cent of the accessions to the city mills would have been second or third generation textile workers.

Forty-five per cent of the people who came into the country mills during the five-year period would have had no previous industrial experience; this would have been true only for 14 per cent of the city accessions. Fifty-five per cent of the country additions would have had better than a grammar school education, as contrasted with 24 per cent of the people added to the work forces of the two city mills in our sample.

Though a cotton textile mill does not have an elaborate superstructure of white collar workers, a number of salaried, nonsupervisory employees are required to keep its affairs in order. A survey of 18 mills in 1952 indicated that they employed an average of 24 people each in this capacity. Only 4 per cent of these people had not gone beyond grammar school, and there were only 4 per cent who had started high school but had not finished. Ninety-two per cent were high school graduates, 16 per cent had had some work in college, and 12 per cent were college graduates.

Very briefly, this has been a picture of the work force of the Georgian broad-woven fabric and yarn and thread mills as it existed in 1952. It has, on the whole, been a portrayal of a work force largely located in small towns and small cities, a work force which was rural and small town in its origin. It was slightly younger on the whole than the national average, with 75 per cent under 45 as compared with 69 per cent under 45 for the nation as a whole in 1940.[9] It was not quite as well educated as the national average for "operatives and kindred workers," with an estimated median of 7.4 years in school as compared with a national figure of 8.5,[10] but this is not quite a fair picture of relative levels of attainment since the greater share of the elementary schools in Georgia were on a seven-year basis until 1952. Taking this into consideration, we can say that the average Georgian textile worker has gone as far past an elementary education as has the average factory operative nationally; in both cases, the median was about half a year past the requirements for graduation from elementary school.

These people were, in addition, a group who were working in establishments with which, for the most part, they had had a degree of familiarity all their lives, among people whose origin was to a large degree common with their own, and in establishments for the most part small enough to permit them, not only to know a good share of the balance of the work force, but also to know and be known by the management group. The sketch we have drawn of the workers has been based on information supplied for 1952; but there is no reason to believe that it is not still representative in 1954. Any changes that may occur will be in the direction of increasing age and educational levels, with a somewhat smaller proportion of people fresh

9. Department of Commerce, Bureau of the Census, *Sixteenth Census of the United States: Population;* Vol. III, *The Labor Force* (Washington, D. C.: United States Government Printing Office, 1943), p. 19.

10. *Sixteenth Census of the United States, Comparative Occupational Statistics, 1870-1940* (1943), p. 181.

from the farms and an increasing number of people whose back-grounds, previous to their employment in the mills, has been neither rural nor textile. There appears to be no tendency toward the creation of a caste of cotton mill workers. On the contrary, the writer's re-search experience has indicated that the mills, particularly in rural areas, are likely to be used, on a generation by generation basis, as stepping stones to occupations in which Piedmont people can use their abilities to even greater advantage. This will become even more evident as the industrialization of the Piedmont continues to increase and diversify.

The People in Management

Now we meet the on-the-spot management of the Georgian broad-woven fabric and yarn and thread mills, those people who are responsi-ble for the supervision, co-ordination, and integration of their opera-tions.

The Supervisors.—Twenty mills reported to the writer in 1952 that they required the services of a total of 397, or an average of 20, second hands or shift foremen each to supervise their operations. More of these men, proportionately, had high school educations than the hourly-rated people (28 per cent as compared with 22 per cent); but more of them had gone no further than grammar school (50 per cent as com-pared with 41 per cent). The explanation for this latter deviation is the higher overall age of the second hands. Thirty-nine per cent of them were over 45, whereas this was true of only 25 per cent of the hourly-rated people. Of the 32 second hands who were reported as less than 30, however, 72 per cent had finished high school as compared with 33 per cent of the male workers in the same age group.

The second hands appear to have moved about more than the hourly-rated people. Only 59 per cent of them were local, as compared with 88 per cent for the work force. Eighty-eight per cent were born within the state, however, and less than 1 per cent were born outside the Southeast.

The Overseers.—The same 20 companies reported that they needed a total of 181, or an average of 9, overseers or general foremen each to co-ordinate the activities of the first line of supervision and assume on-the-spot responsibility for performance of the supervisory function. Better than half of all the overseers in the sample and better than 65 per cent of those under 50 had finished high school. Of the group, 17 per cent under 50 and 31 per cent of those under 40 were college graduates. Of 7 overseers reported as under 30, all were college graduates. Despite their much higher educational level, the overseer group was considerably older than the first-line supervisors. Fifty-five per cent had passed 45, as compared with 39 per cent for the second hands. There is apparently a definite correlation between educational level and success in supervisory work in the Piedmont cotton textile industry.

The overseers are less likely to be from the locality than either the shift foremen or the people in the work force. Only 48 per cent were of local origin; 79 per cent were from Georgia, and 93 per cent from the Southeast. The balance of 7 per cent came to the Piedmont from textile mills in the Northeast.

The Mill's Officials.—The term "official" is not used in its legal sense as meaning an officer of the corporation, but rather to identify those men having a rank equivalent to superintendent or better who take a hand in shaping the policies of their companies. Twenty-three companies reported that they needed the services of a total of 156, or an average of 6 or 7 officials each to manage their affairs. Actually the companies reporting ranged from a small branch plant having only a general manager and superintendent in the "official" category to a large multi-unit company that counted 27 men with the rank of superintendent or better. While there is no definite pattern of organization, a "typical" locally-owned company is likely to have a president, a vice-president also acting as general manager, a secretary, treasurer, and two or three superintendents. The "typical" branch plant will follow the same pattern, except that the president and vice-president will be replaced by a vice-president (of the national company) and a general manager respectively; and the secretary and treasurer are likely to have the term "assistant" affixed to their titles.

Only one of the 23 companies supplying information as to their officials did not have a personnel department, yet only 5 of them listed their personnel director as an official. This was not because personnel activities were considered so unimportant that the man responsible for them ranked below a superintendent. It was the other way around— the function was considered so vital that it was usually a part of the official duties of the president, vice-president, or general manager. The "personnel man" in the small or even medium-sized organization is usually responsible only for the more routine aspects of the function, the bookkeeping aspects of it, so to speak. A line official at the policy-making level is relieved, if need be, of certain of his other more routine duties to give him time for it. Only in a large, multiunit company is the individual who is called the "personnel director" or by some similiar title likely to be regarded as an official of the company. In those cases in which he must necessarily assume the bulk of the responsibility because it has become too burdensome for a line official to take on as a part-time activity, the importance of his function is often recognized by making him a vice-president himself. In many cases, as a matter of fact, he will have been a line official to start with whose other activities have finally been completely crowded out by the personnel function.

Twenty of the 23 companies supplying information as to their managerial structure went on to give the age distributions, educational levels, and certain other data regarding 133 of the 140 officials heading their firms. Fifty-eight per cent of them were college graduates, and 17 per cent had had post-graduate work—usually a graduate degree in management, business administration, or engineering added to a bachelor's program in textile or mechanical engineering. The undergraduate degrees were nearly all in engineering taken at southern technical schools.

The age levels in the sample were interesting since they gave an idea of the degree of continuity with the past afforded through the linkage of the officials themselves. If we assume that these men entered the industry in their initial capacity around the age of 22, better than 9 per cent of them, the "over 60" group, started on their careers before the first rumblings of World War I. Those in the 50 to 60 year age group, over 22 per cent of the sample, started in the mills between 1914 and 1924. Over 38 per cent of the sample, comprising the 40 to 50 year age group, entered the industry between 1924 and 1934; and 28 per cent, as represented by those between 30 and 40, came in between 1934 and 1944. Three per cent, those under 30, began their careers after 1944. Thus 31 per cent of top management in the sample, though it cannot be called of the first generation itself, received its indoctrination in the mills under the first generation; and this was, for the most part, during years of prosperity and labor peace. The balance of the management group, however, that 69 per cent of them under 50, had known only three years when there had been anything like real prosperity in the industry, that brief and idyllic interlude following World War II. For them, the professional career had been a constant battle with production costs and a matter of maintaining objectively and deliberately the delicate balance of labor relations. These are the men who remarked to the writer in the spring of 1952, while the market was in a depressed state, "Well, the industry's finally back to normal!"

Thirty-nine per cent of the officials in the twenty mills were from the localities in which the mills were located, and 78 per cent of them were native Georgians; 86 were from the Southeast; and the balance of 14 per cent were from the Northeast. These latter were most numerous in the 50 to 60 year group, constituting 31 per cent of its total of 29 members.

In our sample of officials, 39 per cent of the men entered the textile industry initially as hourly-rated workers, and 30 per cent of them as non-supervisory salaried employees. The initial nontraining status for 12 per cent was supervisory, and for 8 per cent it was administrative; 5 per cent began their careers in textiles as staff officials, and 6 per cent at an executive level. The majority of the men in these last four categories, however, had in all probability "worked through the mill" in a training capacity before assuming an initially responsible position. The Piedmont textile industry is a firm believer in the value of experience as a nonsupervisory employee, on a sink-or-swim basis, preferably out in the mill, as preparation for more important work. Working through the mill to become acquainted with its people and its operations is regarded as the most important phase of the would-be official's education; and it is a course that a number of people, including sons of owner-managers, have failed.

Here is one clue to the quality of the rapport existing between top management and labor in the Piedmont textile industry. A high percentage of its officials know from their own experience how it feels to be the low man on the totem pole, to receive orders but never to give them. Even though their educational background and training may potentially qualify them for more exalted positions, it must in general be supplemented by practical experience with production problems and first-hand acquaintance with production workers before they are considered to be qualified for responsible appointments. "Taking the role of the worker" in its most realistic sense is an experience that not even the son of the owner-manager is likely to escape if he aspires to exercise real control over the property that, inheritance taxes and other heirs permitting, he may some day control in a legal sense. With this background it is possible to predict with considerable accuracy the probable response of the work force to any particular policy, especially since those who have demonstrated themselves to be insensitive to worker feelings and attitudes during the course of working through the mill are either placed in positions where their inability to establish rapport will not be potentially dangerous or are advised to turn to more congenial lines of endeavor.

Perhaps the most interesting data of all concerning the officials is that which was supplied with regard to the occupations of the grandfathers of 94 and the fathers of 110 of the officials of the 20 companies supplying detailed information concerning this group.

> The fathers of 6 and the grandfathers of 6 were semi- or unskilled laborers.
>
> The fathers of 13 and the grandfathers of 7 were skilled workers or foremen.
>
> The fathers of 12 and the grandfathers of 26 were small farmers.
>
> The fathers of 19 and the grandfathers of 9 were small merchants or "white collar."
>
> The fathers of 11 and the grandfathers of 11 were professional men.
>
> The fathers of 4 and the grandfathers of 13 were plantation owners.
>
> The fathers of 12 and the grandfathers of 7 were minor executives.
>
> The fathers of 10 and the grandfathers of 2 were major executives (non-owners).
>
> The fathers of 23 and the grandfathers of 13 were owner-executives.

Fifteen men were the third generation and 33 were the second generation of major textile executives. The other 77 men whose fathers are represented above, however, had no such background that might have been expected to give them a head start in the industry, and the fathers of 50 of them, in the first 4 categories listed above, could hardly have been expected to be able to give them more than their blessing as a start in life. There is quite possibly some correlation between this figure of 50 and the 51 executives who were reported to have started in the industry at the hourly-rated level. This cross-check unfortunately was not possible on the basis of the information requested and returned.

The mill executives, on the basis of this sample at least, do not appear to be descendants in any great number of the "planter aristocracy"; nor does there seem to be any tendency to develop a "managerial caste." On the contrary, the mills have acted as engines of democracy for 50 of the executives, enabling them to rise from backgrounds that a sociologist would classify as lower-middle class or under. While 23 out of the 110 executives for whom this information was furnished were sons of owner-executives, in only 11 of the 20 reporting mills was top management closely identified with ownership. In the remaining 9 the road to promotion was open all the way to the top. As we noted in an earlier section of the study, the splitting of ownership by inheritance and its decimation by inheritance taxes is rapidly reducing the number of owner-managed mills in the Piedmont and placing greater emphasis upon career management.

Principles, Policies, and Practices

Having met the people, now we can turn to an attempt to outline the more objective aspects of the action structure by which they orient their relationships with one another at the work place.

The Principles

Principles are the ultimate criteria by which one orients a line of action, whether it be in the physical sciences, theoretical economics, or human relations. They are the basic assumptions that are the ground against which everything else is measured, the things we must take for granted because there is nothing more fundamental in terms of which to prove them. In human relations, these principles are ethical in nature. They are the standards by which we determine what is right and wrong in our relations with other people. In western civilization they are embodied in the Christian religion. Christ, quite wisely, made man himself the measure of them. In the Sermon on the Mount, He said, "Therefore all things whatsoever ye would that men should do unto you, do ye even so unto them." If you wish to be understood, then try to understand. If you would be treated fairly, treat others fairly. If you wish to live in peace, extend the hand of friendship. He did not spell out rules and regulations, for He knew that as the world changed so would the rules and regulations need to change. He based his advice, meant for all men in all times, upon the one mortal attribute

He could count on persisting—human nature itself. He had sufficient faith in mankind to believe that in all ages and climes, man could be counted upon in the long run to know what was best for himself.

We must remember, however, that Christ himself forsaw that the Golden Rule would operate as it should only in a world of brotherhood, of sympathetic understanding. He had no illusions as to the treatment his disciples would receive when they went out into a hostile and unbelieving world to practice the Rule and preach the Gospel. "In the world ye shall have tribulation," He told them.

In a world lacking in understanding, the Golden Rule operates very imperfectly. One cannot even be sure that others *wish* to be treated as one would wish himself to be dealt with. There is the possibility that others will misinterpret one's actions and one's intentions. Others are not likely to agree as to what is right and what is wrong in any given situation. Thus, when the managements of textile mills in the Piedmont announce quite seriously that the only personnel principle they find necessary is the Golden Rule, those outside the region are likely to regard the statement with some cynicism. It does not work for them, and they are rather dubious that any principle so vague and so subjective can work anywhere.

Nevertheless it does operate, and rather well, as the basic and one of the few explicitly outlined personnel principles in the industry. If it is supplemented, it is with other principles equally vague. "We believe in giving everybody a fair deal." "It is our desire to deal fairly with our people at all times." The Golden Rule and its derivative principles work in the Piedmont because of the homogeneity of the people who apply them. This is not a homogeniety of racial strain, but of value standards and ideals, the common possession of a code of ethics tested under pioneer conditions in a new world and refined to give meaning, structure, and direction to everyday patterns of living in a powerful and dynamic folk society.

The Golden Rule simply says that one will see one's own actions toward others reflected in the nature of their actions toward one. The folk society of the Piedmont holds up a mirror relatively free from the flaws of interpersonal misunderstanding. One can examine one's own conscience with reasonable certainty that it will display an answer that most people will agree with. We remember also that one's "conscience," or one's "generalized other," "super-ego," or whatever one wishes to call it, is a composite image of the generalized attitudes of the society in which one lives. The more homogeneous the society, the more reliable is one's own conscience as a guide to action that will be considered commendable by others.

This study can do little more than refer to the Sermon on the Mount as embodying the personnel principles of the industry. The people in the industry are no more "christian-like" than those anywhere else. If they go to church a bit oftener on the whole than people elsewhere, it is partly because church is a social as well as a religious experience for them. There are as many sinners in the Piedmont textile industry as in any other, and because of the intimate nature of its society, perhaps even more of them can be pointed out. But the Golden Rule actually works in the industry as the basis of personnel relationships, simply because there is a sufficient feeling of kinship to make it work. It will operate in a society where the social bond is understanding; it will not operate with any degree of success when the social bond is conformity.

The Policies

No matter how ethically correct they may be, principles are valueless in themselves. They are of little worth even as statements of intention since there is nothing else that one could "reasonably" say. They not only are, but they *must* be, platitudes; they must be so unquestionably right that no one can disagree with them. Therefore, when a management announces its principle of "fair treatment," the cynical are likely to remark, "What else could they say? Who would announce their intention to take advantage of their employees?" and regard the announcement as mere window dressing. Principles remain meaningless until they are translated into action, and *policies are the guides by which the practices are established that implement the principles.* Once the sincerity of one's avowal as to the nature of one's principles has been demonstrated through practices that carry them out, the principles become valuable in themselves, for now they are regarded as reliable statements of one's intentions for the future; but the typical human being is likely to take the attitude that "talk is cheap" when he sees no real effort being made to live up to noble sentiments impressively announced.

Policies, unlike principles, are not platitudinous. They always represent a choice between alternative courses of action, all of which may be ethically correct and for each of which something favorable may perhaps be said under given conditions. "Fairness" as an announced principle, for example, must apply to promotions as well as to other aspects of the personnel relationship. Various policies can be adopted to achieve fairness in promotions. Under some circumstances, the policy of promotion on the basis of seniority may be best when a skilled craft is involved, for example, in which there is a high correlation between seniority and capability. Strict seniority is unlikely to be a fair policy for promotion for the machine tender, however, because there is no necessary correlation in this case between the number of years one has spent on the job and one's qualifications for advancement. In the Piedmont textile industry the policy of "individual bargaining" seems to work well in the great majority of cases to achieve the principle of fairness in labor relations; yet in many industries in other regions the policy of "collective bargaining" seems not only desirable but necessary if the same objective is to be achieved.

Policies are guides to action. They commit management to a definite way of doing things, to a choice among possible alternatives, that still permits some latitude for action in "practical" performance. One might compare a policy to a transmission line leading from a hydro-electric generating plant. Its location has definitely committed the plant to the service of one area rather than another, but many alternative uses for the delivered power still remain.

Policies are definite statements of future intentions in terms of real actions; but like principles, they remain meaningless until the actions have been carried out in practices. In personnel relations they are important only because they permit the principles of fairness, equity, and justice to be realized in actual situations. The principles are unchanging—we want to be fair under all conditions, for example—but the conditions do change. Therefore, if we want to adapt unyielding principles to a fluid world, we can do it only through policies that can be modified when necessary. Policies must have a certain amount of stability about them if they are to be of any use as guides for action, but they cannot be permitted to become rigid. Above all, they cannot be regarded as sacred. Worship of policies is a kind of idolatry that obscures and denies the inviolate principles they are intended to effectuate.

The Piedmont industry's attitude toward policy is responsible to a high degree for the success of its labor relations. In the smaller mills and in many of those of medium size, policies are implicit and unwritten. There are no elaborate supervisor's handbooks to which additional leaves are added each week, no continuing codification of policy. There is, however, a "customary way of doing things" with which everyone is familiar. Because this "customary way" (which is actually nothing more than policy in its implicit form) is not written down, it is subject to imperceptible change. On superficial acquaintance one forms the impression that present policies date without exception from ancient days until one begins to trace their origins and discovers them often to be in the immediate past.

It seems to be, merely, that policies take on the patina of antiquity with considerable rapidity. The writer questioned people at all levels about this phenomenon. Few of them had ever thought about it. When it was called to their attention, they were aware that changes had taken place in the policies of the mill. After reflection, most of them were in agreement that the reason they had little conscious realization of these modifications was that they occurred a little at a time and that, while one noticed them when they were made, they always seemed so reasonable departures from previous policy as to be nothing to get excited about or even remember. Even so major a departure from tradition as the sale of the village to the work force appears to be taken in daily stride. While there may be considerable excitement about it for a month or so, within a couple of years the casual visitor would presume that the people had always owned their houses in the mill village.

But if policy in many smaller mills is permitted to remain implicit, to grow and change as it will, the decision to allow it to do so is in most cases deliberate. Southern mill managements are not unaware of the modern attitude as to the necessity of objectively derived, explicit, and written policy for good personnel relations. Their failure to share it is calculated. "We don't have any written body of policy for the plant," the general manager of the Georgia branch of a national organization told the writer. "We don't want it written. When you write policy down, you freeze it. It gets out of step with what's going on. You get so you try to change things to fit your policy, without thinking whether it's right or wrong. It gets in the way of your doing the right thing. We have policies, of course. Everybody knows what they are—but we want to use policy, not be a slave to it. Our policies seem to change almost by themselves as they need to—and everybody seems to know about it when they change. We don't find ourselves in the position of trying to deal with a situation in the present in terms of some policy that was set up ten years ago and out of date five years later, and still on the books."

Another executive told the writer, "You can't possibly develop a written body of policy that's extensive enough and yet detailed enough to deal with the situations you meet. Either you have to be constantly making exceptions to your policy, or else you stick to the policy and make a lot of decisions that actually aren't fair. We have a few simple rules and regulations about tardiness and absences and vacations and drunkenness on the job and things like that; but for the most part, we stick to the Golden Rule as our personnel policy—and with the exception of that one, we haven't got a rule or regulation we can't break if it stands in the way of doing the right thing."

The large mill, particularly if it is in the midst of an expansion program and drawing in new personnel from outside the locality, usually finds it cannot get along without written policy. It cannot rely, as can the smaller mill with its short lines of communication and its tightly knit, locally originated work force, upon everyone being familiar with "the way we do things around here." It must commit policy to writing as a communicative device if for no other reason. One large company visited by the writer had only recently completed the task of objectifying and codifying its policy in order to insure uniformity of action throughout its recently expanded plant. The manner in which it had gone about the task was unique, however. The work was not done by top management alone, or even mainly by top management. During a series of weekly supervisory meetings presided over by officers of the company, the body of policy that had served the company implicitly was dug out, analyzed, and codified. The process lasted almost two years, which is not an undue length of time for the task when we realize that what was taking place was a kind of psycho-analysis; much of the policy in any organization of this sort will be so completely internalized that one is aware of its presence only when a specific situation calls for its application. To dig it out objectively, under artificial stimulation, is a tremendous undertaking.

When the writing was finally completed, the supervisors who had helped to bring the body of policy into the open were told that actually they had only begun. In the future they were to consider it their responsibility to bring to the attention of top management any objectively defined policy that they found in practice to be inequitable, inadequate, invalid, or unrealistic; they were to ask for definitions of policy for situations where it was needed and not in existence. Their arduous work in the policy conferences had resulted only in putting together a first approximation that would have to be continually revised and rewritten as long as the mill was in operation. Policy was to be used; if it was not usable, it was either to be scrapped or made usable.

To one who is familiar with the prestige of "policy" in industry under the massways, the Piedmont attitude toward it is alarmingly casual. One gets the impression at first that every problem is settled on an *ad hoc* basis, that there is either no consistent body of policy at all, or that it is used only when it is convenient. Piedmont managements have been accused of refusing to crystallize policy objectively in order to avoid making commitments to their work forces that might hinder advantageous reversals of practice at a later date. The writer's own research did not indicate this to be the case, however. Interviews with hourly-rated people disclosed that there was likely to be the most confidence on the part of the workers as to what management might be expected to do in any particular case in those mills where the least emphasis was placed on policy.

The casual attitude toward policy is explained by this fact: *problems are settled in terms of principles.* When an existent policy or an existent custom does not achieve a settlement in line with principles, it is the policy that must give. Actually, the implicit body of policy is more powerful by reason of its very flexibility; it "gives" without breaking. It remains in force and is accepted and respected by the work force, simply because the latter knows that it will be amended when necessary to obtain justice in a particular instance. The situation is, nevertheless, bewildering to one who is not familiar with the folk society and who has been indoctrinated with the sacred nature of written rules and regulations under the massways.

Personnel Practices of the Industry

Policy, whether written or oral, whether explicit or implicit, is still no more than a statement of intentions and a guide for action. The test of it must come through the practices by which it displays itself in actual situations. One may have decided, for example, that it will be the policy of the company to promote on the basis of merit. The practical question still remains: how is one to determine the relative merits of those individuals who are candidates for promotion? One may adopt various "practices" calculated to bring about the desired result. A merit rating system may be used. Training programs may be instituted and the candidate's progress in this formal preparation for more highly-skilled work be used as an objective criteria as to his fitness for promotion. A certain weight may be given to seniority even though the basic policy is promotion on merit. The policy must be put into practice. The effectiveness of the practice is not measured in the Piedmont cotton textile industry, however, by how well it carries out the policy. It is judged against the principle that the policy was designed to implement.

Generalizations as to the actual nature of the personnel policies and practices of the industry are likely to be misleading since in nearly every case they will be functions of the particular circumstances facing a particular mill. Some general idea as to their nature may be gained from the following discussion of certain of the more important dimensions of the personnel function in a number of present-day mills in the Georgian Piedmont.

The Personnel Office.—The role of the personnel office in discharging the personnel function will of course vary with the size and structure of the organization. Twenty mills returned information to the writer as to the functions for which their personnel offices had primary responsibility and those for which they were expected to serve in an advisory capacity. Analysis of this information disclosed that on the basis of the sample (which covered 25 per cent of the employees of broad-woven fabric and yarn and thread mills in Georgia), personnel offices in the Georgian Piedmont textile industry are in general held responsible only for the more routine aspects of the personnel function. All of the companies reporting expected their personnel departments to assume primary responsibility for the recruitment of new employees, for the selection of candidates for employment, and for the maintenance of employee records. Only half of them, however, were expected to assume responsibility for personnel counselling or for educational programs. Only seven were held responsible for supervising recreational programs. Only six were expected to take charge of the village or of youth activities. Only five personnel offices were held responsible for employee training, for the handling of grievances, for social activities, or for community programs. Only four played any part in the discipline of employees. Only three were expected to play a primary role in the preparation of supervisory manuals or to interest themselves in cultural programs.

Yet, with the exception of the last two items, all of the above activities were indicated as constituting a part of the personnel function in the mills reporting. *But in any case involving subjective relationships with employees,* top management was much more likely to retain responsibility for the activity than to delegate it to a personnel office. The latter, in the Georgian textile industry, is regarded for the most part as an agency for keeping records and for relieving line management of the responsibility for routine and objective phases of the personnel function, but there is little delegation of the highly significant subjective aspects of the function. Top management retains them as a primary responsibility and is much more likely to administer them through the line hierarchy than through a staff department.

The backgrounds of the personnel directors for the companies supplying information varied considerably from plant to plant. In two cases, the superintendent also acted as head of the personnel department. Of the remainder, five had been line supervisors, four had been clerical workers from some department other than personnel, three had been high school teachers, two had been clerical workers in the personnel office, one had been a minister, one had done veterans' counselling, one had been a YMCA secretary, and one had been an army officer. Explaining this great diversity, a top official of a mill told the writer, "There has been no uniformity at all about the process of their selection, except that for some reason or other the management of a particular mill has felt that the person chosen would be able to handle the personnel problems with which the company was faced." We have already noted that these men are very unlikely to be regarded as officials of the company. In those large organizations in which the personnel director does hold this status, he is generally a top line official, often a superintendent, who has been transferred into the position. In these cases the personnel department will also have primary responsibility for virtually the whole of the personnel function.

Recruitment.—Except in the case of large mills that find it necessary to expand their work forces suddenly, recruitment does not present a problem. For 23 companies reporting in 1952, better than 80 per cent of their vacancies could ordinarily be filled from applications already on file. Of 19,668 people recruited by 16 companies between 1947 and 1952, only 8.2 per cent were obtained as the result of a deliberate program of recruitment carried on by the companies employing them. The advice of a friend already employed decided 35.4 per cent to apply for a job. Fifty-two per cent applied because they were looking for a job and had heard that the mill was a good place to work. Less than 1 per cent were employed through the State Employment Agency. Among other reasons, one frequently given in the case of certain mills by the head of a family was the superior reputation that the mill's school system (or the community's mill-subsidized school system) enjoyed. In all cases, the mills reporting stated that they depended upon their present employees to serve as their major agency for recruiting new help.

The Selection Process.—Examination of detailed selection procedures of twenty-two mills discloses that in this case the managements of the cotton textile Piedmont display the reluctance we have previously noted to rely in an across-the-board fashion upon scientific procedures. Once again we see a line drawn between the objective and the subjective aspects of the process. Pre-employment interviews, detailed application forms, and employment histories are standard practice, and references are required and checked. All except the smallest mills require complete physical examinations. Particular attention is paid to eyesight, and when defects are found it is standard practice in an increasing number of mills to provide the new employee with a prescription, at no cost, which will correct his difficulty. In some cases arrangements are made for him to have the prescription filled at a reduced rate. A growing number of mills are also concerning themselves with correcting, at little or no cost to the employee, foot troubles which might cause excessive fatigue on the job. The larger mills are beginning to use physical dexterity tests, eye-hand co-ordination tests, and similiar devices calculated to measure innate physical characteristics.

But there is wide-spread suspicion of paper-and-pencil tests that measure such attributes as intelligence and personality. This does not mean that there is no interest in these characteristics of the applicant. The writer was told time and time again, "The best way to solve personnel problems is to keep them from happening; and you start the job by picking the right kind of people to go on your payroll in the first place." Once the objective phases of it have been got out of the way, the process of "picking the right kind of people" seems uniformly to be handled in a very informal manner. Great reliance is placed upon personal interviews. Recommendations of people already working for the company are given great weight. Family connections and where the applicant was born and reared are important, often in combination. A good part of the employment interview, as a matter of fact, may be devoted to establishing just "who" the applicant is in terms of his kinfolk and in terms of people whom he and the interviewer know in common.

Some of the mills, especially those which are southern branches of national organizations, have experimented with paper-and-pencil tests recommended for placement purposes. The local attitude toward them is in general one of tolerant amusement. Far from being perturbed over the lack of correlation between predicted performance and actual performance generally discovered, they find it mildy gratifying, as substantiating their suspicion of such devices.

"We're driving Doc——crazy," a personnel director told the writer with obvious satisfaction, referring to the psychologist who headed the testing program for the national organization of which the Georgian mill was a branch. "He wanted us to give these intelligence tests, aptitude tests, and personality tests to everyone we took on, so we've been doing it for several years now. We've finally got enough of them to enable us to run correlations between test scores and performance—and we can't find any! On the basis of our experience, the tests just can't be relied on. They have no predictive value for us.

"I've thought about it quite a lot, and I think there are two things that are wrong with them. In the first place, our people are too much alike in too many respects; there isn't enough variation between the best and the worst for the tests to pick out significant differences between them. In the second place, I don't think they measure enough characteristics to do any good. People have a way of making up in one direction what they lack in another, but the tests just measure the obvious factors, and not those you might call compensating. Doc showed us the dope on the tests in the plants up North, and there was pretty good correlation—but there was also a much greater range, both in test scores and performance, than down here. We keep on giving the tests; but we don't pay any attention to the scores people make on them when we're deciding who to hire and who not to."

Depending upon the source of the labor supply of a particular mill, its turnover rate, and other factors, from 10 per cent to 80 per cent of the applicants will be weeded out in the selection procedure. The median figure is 50 per cent. As a general policy the mills feel that careful selection is a positive step in the direction of good labor relations. Preference is always given to local residents first at all levels of employment.

Employee Records.—Unlike the old mills in which the president, the manager, or the superintendent kept all personnel records in his "memory file," the modern personnel office of a Georgian textile mill is likely to keep an elaborate dossier on each employee in the mill. In addition, one very important function of the department is to analyze the information contained in the records which are kept up to date with regard to such items as absenteeism, turnover, and training and submit regular reports based on it to top management. The latter is particularly interested in data regarding the source of, and causes for, separations.

Employee Training.—Twenty-two companies supplied the writer with information concerning their training programs. Of these, only three reported that they provided no training for new hourly-rated employees. Of the balance, six relied on informal "on-the-job" training; new employees were assigned as helpers or trainees to experienced workers, but there was no formal direction or supervision of their progress. Thirteen companies used formal on-the-job training. New employees were assigned to experienced people who had been selected for their ability as instructors and who had themselves been given formal training in the techniques of job instruction. The progress of the new employees through a formally outlined program of instruction was checked and reported on at regular intervals. The instructors were given extra compensation for their additional duties. One company in this latter group also used a "vestibule" training program in one department in which special equipment and instructors, not in the production line, were used for training purposes.

Seven of the nineteen mills trained all new employees on the day shift. The balance assigned trainees to whichever shift had vacancies. Ten mills had no probationary period; new employees went on the pay roll immediately. The balance placed new employees on probation for a period averaging six weeks. Only three mills put their new employees on regular piece rates immediately; the balance were paid a guaranteed wage during the training period, usually $87\frac{1}{2}$ cents per hour (in 1952). Eight mills required no progress reports on new trainees. The balance of eleven required progress reports to be submitted, usually at two week intervals, during the training period. In no case was the new employee assigned permanently to the day shift after completing the training period.

Training for Higher Skills.—Eleven mills out of twenty-three reporting offered in-plant courses to enable present employees to advance to higher skilled work. Most frequently they were designed to prepare loom fixers (loom repairmen) and fixers (spinning frame repairmen); but courses were also offered in weaving and spinning and in preparation for supervisory work. Instruction of a more general nature but having vocational importance was offered to supplement the technical instruction; courses in shop mathematics were especially popular. Thirteen mills of the twenty-three reporting encouraged their employees to enroll for correspondence courses and their successful completion of them was entered in their personnel record. Four of these mills refunded the cost of the course to the student upon his successful completion of it.

Training for Supervisors.—Fourteen companies of twenty-three reporting gave detailed information as to the nature of their training programs for supervisors. One company indicated that it had supervisory training but did not describe its nature. The balance of eight offered no formal training for supervisors. Seven of the fourteen companies supplying information stated that their supervisory training programs were open both to present supervisors and to those who were candidates for supervisory positions; in this case, however, non-supervisors were permitted to take the courses only with the permission of the company. Nine companies were continuing to use a modified form of the Training Within Industry courses developed during World War II. The balance used courses they had either developed themselves or that were offered in conjunction with the Georgia State Board of Vocational Guidance. Ten companies supplemented their training programs (usually offered as need arose) with periodic meetings of supervisors at which problems of current interest were discussed. These meetings were ordinarily presided over by the superintendent and held at regular intervals of two or four weeks.

Eleven companies maintained a job rotation program ("working through the mill") that lasted from eighteen to twenty-four months. In two companies the program was available only to college graduates initially employed as managerial candidates; but the balance indicated that job rotation training was available to young men in the ranks who showed promise of being managerial material. This represents a reversal of a tendency that was beginning to appear during the late 1920's and early 1930's when some mills began to feel that a college degree ought to be prerequisite even for a supervisory position. The president of a mill visited by the writer told of his experience in attempting to fit himself for advancement. With not even a high school diploma behind him, no one paid any attention to his pleas to be permitted to work through the mill; they would not even permit him to transfer from one department to another. He finally solved the problem for himself by quitting his job at one mill as soon as he felt himself to be fairly well acquainted with the work he was doing and asking for a job at the next mill along a different line. It took a different mill for each different process in textile manufacture, but he finally attained his objective. The majority of the present-day mills feel that capable people in the ranks should not only be encouraged but should be assisted to go as far as they can. The general feeling is that it is bad to "slam the door in a man's face" in matters of promotion. If the opportunity is there for them, those who fail to go up the ladder will generally rationalize their failure and be content with the level they have achieved; but when the opportunity is arbitrarily denied them, even the most incompetent are likely to feel that they could have done much better for themselves had "the company only given them a chance."

Younger high school graduates in the work force, in those mills where they were offered promotional opportunities equal with college graduates, faced up to their situation realistically. They indicated their awareness that their lack of a college degree was to their disadvantage, but they felt, on the other hand, that they possessed advantages in their better knowledge of the people in the mills and of the practical aspects of textile manufacture. They realized that the odds were against their ever achieving a top position, but they felt that even so they had a better chance in the textile industry than in any other.

Grievances.—None of the mills supplying the writer with information concerning their personnel practices used a formal grievance procedure. Twelve of the twenty-three, however, indicated that they attempted to encourage adherence to the "chain of command" with regard to grievances. That is, an employee might approach whomever he wished to present his case, but it would be suggested that if he had not already done so he go back to his immediate superior and follow up the line to see if he could not get satisfaction at a lower level. In six cases, employees were encouraged to come to the personnel office initially with their grievances; but in three cases the personnel office did not figure in the grievance procedure at all. In the majority of cases it was a step between the superintendent and the general manager or president. It is the writer's experience that in those cases where a worker comes first to the personnel officer with his difficulty, the latter has no power to settle it but has shown himself to possess a talent for reconciling divergent points of view. His usual procedure is to bring the parties to the grievance together and play the role of conciliator or mediator.

In most cases employees tended to go first to the overseer with their grievances, thus by-passing the first line of supervision. The majority of workers with whom the writer talked were of the opinion that "you can count on getting a square deal from the overseer." Since the 1930's an ability to deal with human problems has been an important qualification for his selection. His role has changed completely from what it was in the older mills. The workers still tend to regard the second hand as fulfilling primarily a technical role in the mill, and they depend upon the overseer to exercise a coercive influence over him if he shows a tendency to slight the human aspects of industrial employment. The writer found little indication that second hands resented being thus by-passed. They expected the people to go directly to the overseer with their problems. They regarded dealing with grievance situations as one of his principle functions and felt that his failure to exercise it would put an undue burden on the first line of supervision.

"A lot of their troubles are things we can't do anything about anyway. When they are, when the complaint involves something we've said or done, or haven't said or done, the overseer calls us in and gets it straightened out while the man is still there. Usually it's just a misunderstanding on one side or the other; but it seems like the overseer keeps us calmed down while we're gtting it straightnd out. We'd much rather have the people go straight to the overseer with their grievances—here in this mill, at any rate—and then get called in on the ones where we can do some good." A second hand explained his feeling in this manner to the writer.

Numerous interviews with overseers bear out the evidence of the information reported to the writer regarding his role in the sample group of mills. They felt, in general, that better than 50 per cent of their time was devoted to helping people "get their troubles straightened out." Overseers as a group impressed the writer as being men selected with an eye to their ability to deal calmly and dispassionately, and yet sympathetically, with problems involving human relations. They had the air of men who would not be surprised by any vagary of human nature but who would as a matter of fact regard it as an interesting problem to trace down and work out. The overseer is almost invariably one of the "council of elders" in the folk organization of the mill. In many cases his implicit *previous* election to this role by the people is an important qualification for his formal advancement to general supervision.

For the twenty-three companies reporting, 80 per cent of their grievances were settled at or below the second line of supervision. Fourteen per cent went to the superintendent, and 3 per cent each were settled finally either by the personnel office or by top management. Management in the industry is aware that maintaining open lines of communication for the swift and equitable settlement of grievances is the most important requirement for harmonious labor relations. If the informal grievance procedures do not work, the almost inevitable alternative will be formal grievance procedures policed by a union organization. In the long run, the success of any non-union grievance procedure rests upon two factors: first, the absence of fear on the part of the worker that he will suffer supervisory reprisal if he voices his displeasure over a real or fancied violation of his rights, especially if he goes over the head of his supervisor; and second, vigilant and impartial policing of the grievance procedure by top management itself.

Along this latter line, management must be constantly on guard, particularly in the larger mills, that in trying to attain a necessary degree of systematization in the grievance procedure it does not formalize it to the extent that the work force feels itself confined to "channels." In this latter case, the workers are likely to feel themselves to be at the mercy of line supervision with no realistic right of appeal to the top. If top management does not want a union policing the grievance chain, it must exercise the function itself.

The Mill Village.—The Piedmont textile worker who lives in a mill village is well housed. His villages will range from rather depressing arrays of identical houses built along geometrically laid out streets to fine examples of advanced suburban planning. In almost every case, however, his housing will be as good as the mill can reasonably make it. As they did during and after World War I, the mills have used a considerable proportion of their profits in recent years to renovate and bring their villages up to date. Rentals have not increased proportionately. They range from as low as 35 cents per room per week to as high as $1.25 per room per week. In this latter case, a six-room house will cost $30.00 per month, which is less than half what a comparable dwelling in the vicinity would cost.

The villages are not as crowded as they once were. It is no longer possible to house more than 40 per cent of the workers in the average village, so there seems to be no point in making those people uncomfortable who do live there. As a superintendent told the writer, "These people won't stand for crowding nowadays. We used to require that each house in the village furnish as many workers as it had rooms—now we average less than two workers per house." For the twenty-one companies reporting which had villages, the occupancy rate was less than one person per room per house, and the mills averaged only 1.5 workers per house.

All the housing reported in the inventory had electric lighting, running water, modern plumbing, and bathrooms. In general, water was furnished free, but the occupant paid for electricity, usually at a rate lower than that prevailing in the community. If gas was available in the community, it was ordinarily piped into the village. Garden plots were uniformly available, and community pastures were still common. In the writer's experience, however, the garden plots and pastures are not made use of as frequently as in the past. No attempt was observed by the writer to "regiment" the villagers with regard to the planting of shrubbery and flowers. If any tendency was present, it was to encourage tenants to express their own ideas in such matters and add variety to the appearance of the village. A few mills maintained crews of men to tend the village lawns; but this was regarded as a service to the employees and not interference with their private tastes.

Seven of the twenty-one mills reporting which had villages had (in 1952) recently sold all or a part of them to their employees. Since that time one additional village out of the group has been sold to the writer's knowledge and others may have been. The sale of the mill village is a definite trend, one which illustrates excellently the impotence of tradition to continue in force a practice that is no longer reasonable. The village is no longer either an economic or a social necessity. With the average mill able to house less than 40 per cent of its employees, assignment of housing has become a major problem. "More grievances arise over the assignment of housing than anything else," the writer was told time and time again. Since the low rent constitutes a definite subsidy, it must be regarded as an increase in pay for the family assigned a village house and handled accordingly. Newcomers to the village must be carefully screened as to their desirability from the standpoint of their neighbors. Its maintenance is a constant problem. Consequently many mills are cutting the Gordian knot by selling their villages to their employees.

More villages would doubtless be sold if the problems surrounding their sale were not as complicated as they are. The matter of who is to have precedence of purchase is of course important since they are invariably sold at a price considerably below the going market for comparable dwellings in the community. Financing must be arranged by the mill so that no reliable employee eligible to purchase a house will be denied the opportunity because he is short the down-payment at the time the village is put up for sale. Usually the mill accepts a second mortgage which he pays off on a monthly basis. Very often the community is unincorporated, and the question of who will look after the streets, the sewerage system, and village government has to be settled. As excellent discussion of these many problems is presented by Harriet Herring in her *Passing of the Mill Village,* a detailed and recent study of this trend from Virginia to Alabama.[11]

It will be many years before the last mill village is sold, however. Not all managements are impressed with the desirability of the move, particularly when there is no incorporated community to take over the formalities of community government. In those rare cases where a mill is organized, the union is quite often in opposition to its sale although the workers in unorganized mills are in general enthusiastic over the opportunity of becoming property owners. In a few cases, villages have been enlarged within the past few years. In more cases, however, mills have assisted their people to build their own homes, advancing them the necessary down-payment when they do not possess it. Complete villages are no longer being built. New mills erected within the past few years have found them unnecessary.

The Company Store.—Out of twenty-three mills reporting, sixteen have never had a company store. Only two are operating a company store at the present time. One operated a store until 1947 but now leases it to a private operator. The other three own store buildings but have never operated them themselves. They have always leased them to private operators. The myth of the poor mill hand perpetually in debt to the company store seems not to be well-founded in Georgia, at least, if we can rely upon a sample of better than 20 per cent of the industry in the state. We have already noted that on the basis of a much larger sample, Harriet Herring found the same to be true for North Carolina a number of years ago.

Recreational and Social Facilities.—Three of the twenty-three mills reporting were located in communities of sufficient size so that there was no necessity for the mill to provide facilities of this nature for their employees. Between them, the remaining twenty companies possessed the following facilities: 33 ball diamonds, 26 Scout huts, 14 adult club houses, 11 basketball courts, 10 tennis courts, 9 outdoor swimming pools, 8 auditoriums, 7 gymnasiums, 6 football fields, 6 club houses for youth organizations, 5 motion picture theatres, 4 indoor swimming pools, 2 private lakes developed for fishing, swimming, and

11. Harriet Herring, *Passing of the Mill Village* (Chapel Hill: The University of North Carolina Press, 1952).

boating, 2 bowling alleys, and 1 golf course. The average value of these facilities, for 10 companies that supplied this information, was $107,800.00 per company. The maximum value reported was $440,000.00. Like the mill village and the company store, these installations appeared because there was a need for them. They testify to the assumption of the managements who built them that employees were people and needed more than a cash wage. Since their villages have become firmly integrated into the community structure in recent years, many mills have ceased to expand their physical facilities for recreational activities on a private basis and now contribute to community projects, with the expectation that their employees will benefit from them as citizens of the community rather than as employees of the mill.

The majority of the mill-supervised recreational activity of today is directed toward the children of the employees rather than toward the employees themselves. The organized athletic programs for children in the larger mills visited by the writer are completely abreast of the times in such activities. The "midget" football, baseball, and basketball teams, for example, are designed to achieve the highest degree of individual participation, rather than to win championships. They are not only carefully organized to gain balanced strength among them and at the same time give everyone a chance to play, but they are deliberately not representative of anything except themselves. Representative rivalry is reserved for adult and high school teams though even in the case of mill-sponsored adult teams there is a growing move to support what might be called "intra-mill" rather than "inter-mill" athletic programs. The recreational director of one large company that under an earlier policy had turned out a series of league champions told the writer, "You show me a mill with a championship team, and I'll show you a mill where everybody stands on the sidelines and watches the stars play. We don't want that here. We want everybody in on it, even the dubs."

In addition to their athletic programs, the mills are firm believers in supporting various national organizations for young people. If it has nothing else, the smallest mill is likely to have at least one scout hut. Boy Scout, Girl Scout, and Campfire troops are sponsored. YMCA and YWCA organizations are supported by the larger mills if community resources are not available. Various church-affiliated youth organizations among the young people have the use of mill-owned facilities. One mill has sponsored a state-wide swimming meet for the past several years and has supplied a respectable number of the entries. Another mill has actively supported an annual horse show that brings young people from all over the state into their small community. Pageants and carnivals in which young people participate actively are common.

Beyond making the facilities available, few mills today take the initiative in organizing recreational or social activity among the adults. If the mill is large enough to support a recreational director, he may give advice and assistance during the formation of the project; but the membership is expected to make a going proposition of it. In those cases with which the writer is acquainted, the imaginations of the people seem to be sufficiently fertile to keep him busy even if thus restricted. The writer visited one large mill just after a group of women had decided to organize a bird-watching club. Its recreational director was looking forward rather unhappily to the prospect of arising at 4:00 A.M. for the next two Sunday mornings to help them get the organization under way. In discussing his role in the mill community, he told the writer, "I regard myself as a catalyst in community activities. I help to crystallize them, and then I withdraw. After that they must succeed or fail on their own."

Newer mills, built without villages and drawing their work forces from already established communities for many miles around, do practically nothing in the way of recreational or social work. "We're all cotton mill people, and so after we had the mill built and under way we thought we ought at least to have a soft ball team," the personnel director told the writer. "It never went over. We're using the ball diamond for a parking lot. We tried a few other things with the same lack of success, and then we stopped. We discovered we didn't have to provide recreational or social opportunities for our people. They have them in their own communities. If they want to play soft ball, they play with a community group, not a mill group. If they want a Christmas program, they have that in their community. The older mills *were* the community. They brought the people into them, into the villages, and they had to provide them with an opportunity to live satisfying lives. But we don't have to. The people who work for us are already citizens of established communities within a radius of twenty miles of the mill; and we don't bear the same relationship to them that we would if we'd pulled them all into a mill village."

Cultural Activities.—These, like organized social and athletic programs, are likely to be inversely proportional in scope and extent to existing community facilities, and directly proportional to the size of the mill. The most important of them are generally undertaken through the village school system or through the community schools which the children attend since, again like the social and athletic programs, they are principally for the children of the workers rather than for the workers themselves. They may range from nothing more complicated than straight subsidization of the community school system in order that it may strengthen the standard curriculum, to elaborate supplementation of the curriculum over and above the three R's in those areas that provide for personality development rather than merely the acquisition of information. In this latter case, classes in dancing, music, art, and drama particularly are likely to be added. The most interesting developments along this line were observed in the privately supported school systems of large country mills or where the school systems of small communities were subsidized by large mills on their peripheries. Artwork particularly was outstanding, oriented along expressive rather than representational lines.

While mill-supported cultural programs of the sort just described obviously cannot be underwritten except by the larger mills and are not typical of the entire industry in Georgia, they are the rule rather than the exception when they can be afforded. Their presence gives rise to some rather interesting speculations. Far from insuring the presence in their community of a new generation of workers with minds that have been stunted and confined, whose limited vision will make them contented with little and "tractable" when they come into the mills, the larger mills seem deliberately to be encouraging exactly the opposite development and the smaller companies to be following their example to the limit of their resources. Imagination is encouraged rather than stultified; and a set of secondary values are being instilled in young people that will make them discontented with what we have come to regard as the typical life of an industrial worker. Their fathers, largely because of higher educational levels, demanded more of the mills than the generation that preceded them.

In a significant number of cases the coming generation will be still more critical.

The writer discovered that mill executives were aware of this aspect of their sponsorship of cultural programs. "In a way," one of them heading a mill with an elaborate program of this sort told the writer, "we've grabbed a bear by the tail with all these things we're doing for the young people. We're teaching them to appreciate a way of life that we've got to help make it possible for them to continue to enjoy if we want them to stay on here in the community and work for us. These young people that are being taught in our grade and high school to express themselves in modern art forms, in music, in drama, in dancing, aren't going to be content with the humdrum existence of their parents. We're going to have to do more than just supply them with jobs. We're going to have to help them build a community life that's rich and satisfying, or they're going to look for it somewhere else."

COMMUNITY RELATIONS

The present-day relationship of the mills and their communities is the culmination of the long line of development that we have traced throughout this study. The mill workers are full-fledged members of the community; the mills are an integral part of community life; their managements are community citizens rather than merely sojourners.

The Community and the Work Force

As nearly as the writer was able to discover by questioning both in the mills and in their communities, the tendency to think of cotton-mill workers as a caste has passed out of the picture. Certainly, they are still regarded individually as members of one class or another, the society of textile towns is no more egalitarian than American society anywhere, but the fact that a particular individual or family is employed in the mill is now only one of a number of items implicitly considered in assigning class status; and even in this case cognizance is taken of the level of skill of the work performed. During the 1920's, the descriptive phrases used in describing mill workers, "no account," "poor white trash," and "shiftless," indicated that they were ascribed what the sociologist would describe as "lower-lower class" status.[12]

12. See W. Lloyd Warner, Marcia Meeker, and Kenneth Eels, *Social Class in America* (Chicago: Science Research Associates, 1949) for a discussion of the six-fold

In 1952, they were more likely to be described by the townspeople as "honest, hard-working people, for the most part" and implicitly ascribed upper-lower or lower-middle class status. The latter generally referred to those who were skilled maintenance workers, loom fixers, fixers, or holding other responsible hourly-rated jobs and were qualified for the higher status in other respects. A small group of mill workers were still regarded as lower-lower class—"there's still an element among the mill people that don't amount to much"—but they were distinguished from the bulk of the work force, whereas thirty years previously they were considered by most townspeople as completely representative of it.

It is significant to note that under the present-day relationship the mill people, when they attempt to improve themselves, are no longer regarded as "aping their betters"; and mill employment does not in itself present any serious barrier to winning higher status in the social structure of the community. Also significant is that fact that during the course of numerous interviews, the writer heard the phrase "mill workers are as good as anybody" very infrequently, and then only from older workers who still remembered vividly the slights of the 1920's. Younger workers apparently felt no need to make the assertion. They took it for granted, and assumed that others did, that they were as good as anybody and that emphasis of the fact was unnecessary.

Perhaps the most telling example of the present relationship between town and village is offered by the actions, not the words, of one of the elements in the towns most sensitive to social differences, unmarried young women of middle-class families. From an average weekly wage of less than $20.00 before 1941, earnings in Georgian broad-woven fabric mills had jumped to an average of $46.95 per week by 1952. And this was an average figure; a clever young woman with supple fingers could count on earning at least $1.30 an hour as a weaver and might push the figure up as high as $1.70 an hour for a forty-hour week, with time and a half for overtime. The prospect of a weekly wage that was not likely to be under $50.00, and that with a bit of luck, effort, and overtime might be as high as $80.00 or better, proved a powerful inducement to young women to desert lower paying "respectable" occupations and take a job in the mill.

classification system, ranging from lower-lower class to upper-upper class, that is quite useful in analyzing the open-ended class structure typical of American society.

The writer has talked with many of them in weave rooms, spinning rooms, cloth rooms, and sewing rooms who had come from employment as receptionists in doctors' offices, clerical work, and school teaching, to their hourly-rated work in the mill. They did not believe they had lost class socially by their change of occupation. Most of them felt that actually their town friends who had remained at their lower-paying town jobs secretly envied them. The barrier was not completely gone, even yet; but by 1952 it appeared to be more psychological than social. That is, the young woman who in 1932 would have been insulted by the suggestion that she apply for a job in the mill and would have explained her response by stating with conviction, "No one who was *anyone* would think of working in a cotton mill!", would be more likely in 1952 to explain her antipathy to mill employment by saying, "I just don't think I'd like it in the mill."

The Community and Management People

The obligations of individual members of mill managements as citizens of the communities in which they live have become so intertwined with their obligations as executives of industrial enterprises that it is difficult for themselves, to say nothing of the observer, to tell where one role leaves off and the other begins. This close relationship between mill managements and their communities has led to numerous misunderstandings on the part of people who are familiar neither with the history of the mills nor the dimensions of life in the small town or small city under the folkways. They are accused of running the towns and of controlling the city councils, the boards of aldermen, the police departments, and the school boards. It is averred that all the church pastors are on their pay rolls and that local sheriffs are their right-hand men. Everyone in town, it is stated, eats out of their trough.

When one talks with people in management, one gets a different story. The more cynical of them are inclined to feel that they are being taken advantage of, that the community is overburdening them with responsibilities they cannot gracefully avoid but would be quite as happy to see performed by someone else. By the time they have finished attending to their civic responsibilities, in addition to their duties at the mill, they have very little time left for their families or themselves. They are expected to lead off every drive for funds for a community project with a contribution that will make everybody else give twice what they were expecting to out of mere shame. This is expected in addition to taking an active part in the direction of the drive.

Anyone familiar with small-town life would be perplexed if the situation were any different. The small town expects those who enjoy the advantages of position or wealth or even of a respectable earned income to carry a proportionately heavy load of the responsibility of community affairs. In more cases than not, the mill official, if he is not acting out of a sense of civic responsibility, agrees to serve on a civic board or committee, not so much for what it will get him if he does, as to avoid what his refusal is likely to earn him if he does not.

Actually, any appearance the mills may have of controlling the communities in which they are located comes about generally because as members of the communities themselves they are so closely in touch with them that they are not likely to make proposals that will not command substantial community support. They play a leading role on many occasions, but the leadership is of the type that is earned through being able to define a puzzling situation to the satisfaction of those who are involved in it. If they enjoy the respect of the community, it is because they meet the pattern of expectations that the community has with regard to them.

The Community and Industrial Relations

The implicit assumption of the communities that the mills operating within their borders or adjacent to them are "our" mills seems not to have diminished with the passage of time. It operates as powerfully today as it did before World War I, tying the mills irrevocably into the pattern of the folkways. We shall speak at greater length of this and of its consequences in the final chapter; for now we shall merely note that the origins of the major policies that shape the structure of the relationship between management and worker in the Piedmont cotton textile mill lie beyond the environs of the plant itself and even beyond the community. They strike deep, to the very heart of the region itself. But the community, as a major link in their transmission, plays a powerful and ultimately decisive role.

CHAPTER IX

The Solution of the Textile Piedmont

WE BEGAN THIS STUDY by outlining the basic problem of industrial relations. It arose, we discovered, out of the fact that certain characteristics fundamental to the industrial process challenged the industrial worker's ability to maintain the conditions necessary to a human way of life. Division of labor, low worker skills, high capital investments, and a managerial structure separated out of the production process—all inherent and inescapable features of an industrial operation since the advent of power-driven machinery—made it difficult for the industrial worker to maintain (1) the feeling of function, recognition, and status, and (2) the kind of concepts of his world, others, and himself that would enable him to maintain a satisfactory predictive relationship with the future. (For brevity and clarity in further discussion, we can think of the first group of necessary conditions as those leading to a feeling of security, the second as those leading to understanding.)

The unameliorated impact of the industrial process upon the human being was, we noted, potentially so traumatic in nature that it did not remain unameliorated for long. The whole history of industrial relations has been a history of various experiments and expedients looking toward its mitigation, a largely implicit but nevertheless continually probing search for some means by which the worker might live like a human being within the industrial *milieu*. Our present study is no more than an exploration of the dimensions of one solution that had been worked out, in a particular context and with particular resources, but still in answer to this general problem that was common to any industrial society.

The nature of the solution worked out by the cotton textile industry of the southeastern Appalachian Piedmont region has been implicitly stated as we have traced the development of the industry and of its industrial relationships. In this final chapter we should like to outline it somewhat more explicitly and concisely, but as a prelude to this it will be worth our while to consider at least briefly two other cases:

1. The general nature of the pattern that any specific solution must follow.

2. The particular pattern of the solution that has been devised for the industrial worker under the massways.

By contrast and comparison the salient features of the Piedmont textile solution will stand out more distinctly and perhaps somewhat more understandably.

THE GENERAL PATTERN OF SOLUTION

In this section we investigate the general pattern that the solution must follow simply by virtue of the fact that the problem is universally found within the context of human society.

The industrial worker, owning no tools and possessing no important or distinctive skills, has for this reason no inherent feeling of security in his job. He has no real sense of self-reliance. He is dependent rather than independent in the exercise of a function that is basic to his every other activity. Because of this dependence he is particularly conscious that he is able to exist only as an integral part of the social fabric. He, above all, feels as a living force the interdependence of humanity that arises out of and creates society.

As a human being in society and dependent upon that society, he must have the feeling of function, recognition, and status if he is to possess that stable foundation we call "security" from which he can make first approximations as to the shape of the future. This is, we recall, the basic living technique of all sensate organisms; man lives by predicting the future. Because these needs are so basic to his very existence, the industrial worker (as does everyone else) thinks of them as "rights" that are due him if one accepts the initial premise that he is a human being. He thinks of them as (1) "the right to work," his right to demonstrate his ability to perform a useful function; (2) "the right to be treated like a human being," the right to be recognized and accepted into the society on the basis of observed performance of his function; and (3) "the right to a fair day's pay," the right to the reward proper to the status earned by the performance of his particular function.

Yet within the context of the enterprise (and thinking of it as abstracted and isolated, for the moment, from the enveloping context of the total society) there is no asssurance that these rights can be enjoyed and that the initial needs basic to a human way of life be met. No management can guarantee him the right to work though it admits his moral right to the chance to earn a living. The first responsibility of management must necessarily be to the firm and not to him. The survival of the enterprise is paramount. It must of necessity take precedence over every other obligation that management may have, even though it involves denying the right of employment to those people who must be laid off during a period of retrenchment. The industrial worker realizes this. He is aware that the management that assumed its primary function to be the provision of employment for its workers might soon be in the position of not being able to provide employment for anyone. This admission of the necessity of management's action in laying him off, however, does nothing to increase his sense of security on the job, nor does it lessen appreciably his emotional set against management as he sees his children hungry and poorly clothed and wonders where next month's rent is coming from.

Management also agrees with the worker that he has a right to be treated like a human being while he is on the job. It ordinarily presumes that it is according such recognition to him. Yet because of an inadequate imagery of what human nature is like in general, because of well-meant policies that are either unrealistic or not put into practice, inadequate communication, and poor supervision, management's laudable intention to give the worker an adequate feeling of recognition and appreciation of the performance of his function may not be realized. In addition to challenging his feeling of security, this lack of recognition prevents even the first step from being taken toward the establishment of mutual understanding. The worker's sense of dignity and his self-respect may be violated, but there is little he can do about it, other than to quit his job.

Management is additionally in agreement with the worker that he is entitled to just compensation for his services. Its ideas, however, as to the definition of "just compensation" may vary considerably from his. The worker may feel that management ought to take into account such items as family responsibilities, length of service, and the cost of living, but management may consider that at any particular time his wage ought to depend only upon what he is doing at that time and nothing else. If there is a difference of opinion, the power of decision rests with management.

When we draw a circle about the enterprise and think of it as a kind of island, the worker is in a precarious position. He does not possess any feeling of security within the situation in which he finds himself, and he may in addition be denied understanding of it. Yet he can live in a human fashion only on the basis of his ability to make predictions about the future. If he is fortunate enough to possess understanding he is, it is true, able to make certain predictions even when he lacks the stable base of security from which to orient his glimpse of the future; but under such conditions his predictions are more likely to increase than diminish his anxiety. When he possesses neither security nor understanding, he gazes into a tomorrow that holds nothing but the hobgoblin shapes of uncertainty. He feels himself to be alone in a recalcitrant world, a world that is capricious and whimsical, senseless and arbitrary.

What can he do about it? Nothing, when we think of the firm as an isolate existing in physical proximity to, but in no way socially related to, its context. Nothing, except to look for another job, hoping that it will be better. But this is seldom a realistic answer to his difficulties. Theoretically the economist may think of labor as completely mobile. Practically, when the economist thinks of labor in terms of human being rather than of units of labor and of real industrial situations rather than industrial models, he admits that labor has very little mobility. A firm may be able to maintain a work force in the face of persisting inequities.[1]

In Chapter One and in this chapter we have been thinking of the firm as lifted out of the context of the society in which it actually exists. What happens when we put the firm back into its context, when we think of it as an integral part of human society, whether it be organized under the folkways or the massways? Do the added

1. See Lloyd Reynolds, *Labor Economics and Labor Relations* (1st ed., New York: Prentice-Hall, 1949), pp. 344-50.

resources of the total society provide possibilities for the solution of
the problem of the industrial worker that obviously do not appear
within the boundaries of the firm itself?

The answer is "Yes." The anomalous position in which the industrial worker finds himself when only the firm is taken into account,
which arises in large part because management is necessarily responsible to the firm rather than to him, is balanced out when we see the
firm as part of a total society. There is a circle of responsibility, now
completed, that reaches back to the industrial worker. Management is
responsible to the enterprise, but the enterprise is responsible to the
society; it must render a service or produce a good that the society
judges to be worth as much or more than the price asked for it. From
the point of view of the society, part of the price is the enigmatic
position of the industrial workers who are a part of it. The society,
in turn, is responsible to the individual people who make it up, including the industrial worker. The circle of control runs in the other
direction. The industrial worker as a part of society enjoys some
degree of control over it; society controls the firm; and the latter,
acting through its board of directors, controls management.

The industrial worker can appeal to the society of which he is a
member to exercise coercive control over the firm for which he works,
requiring it to grant to him those rights that it may have formerly
withheld. The firm cannot except under special circumstances be
forced to grant him the right to work; that is a responsibility which
the society itself must assume. The firm can, however, without jeopardizing its economic stability, be forced to grant him just compensation and the outward forms of humane treatment. It cannot be forced
to grant him understanding, for this can only be worked out mutually
between a management and its work force; but given a satisfactory
degree of indirect control over the firm through the society, the
worker theoretically can make fairly adequate predictions on that basis
alone.

We must note, however, that when the worker achieves security
through control but fails to achieve understanding, the solution is
essentially neurotic in nature. It is comparable to that fashion of dealing with the world adopted by an individual who for some reason
lacks adequate understanding of the people with whom he must live,
and relies upon his ability to exercise control over them to compensate

for his inability to predict their probable responses by taking their roles. Yet we must note also that understanding without some degree of actual or potential control, given the particular circumstances of the industrial *milieu*, is not sufficient to insure a satisfactory feeling of security. Nor can the complete solution be finally achieved completely within the firm even with the aid of coercive control from outside. The society must stand ready to afford the worker an opportunity to earn status outside the enterprise when for economic reasons no opportunity is available within it. From the standpoint of cold logic, this is not a matter of charity. The total society profits by employment of the industrial process; it ought therefore assume final responsibility for alleviation of such human problems as arise out of the employment.

The industrial worker, then, is dependent upon the larger society of which both he and the firm are a part to guarantee him those rights that the firm either cannot or will not grant him of its own accord. The important question is this: to what degree, under real circumstances, can he actually rely upon the society to implement this guarantee? How well, under actual conditions, do the twin circles of responsibility and control operate to give him a feeling of security as an industrial worker? Let us consider the case first under the mass society.

The Industrial Worker under the Massways

We can refresh our memory as to the dimensions of a mass society by reference to Chapter Two. Essentially, it is that type of social structuring that is necessary to achieve an effective degree of co-ordination under conditions where men are under the necessity of acting together, but where they are unable to fit their separate lines of activity together on the basis of their understanding of one another. They cannot depend upon being able to predict the nature of the actions of others, and thus plan their own in a manner that will reinforce rather than conflict with those of others, on the basis of their intuitive knowledge of the subjectively held intentions of others.

In the absence of adequate reciprocal understanding of this sort, the social bond in the mass society is conformity. Its organization is deliberate, arising out of man's logical realization of the necessity for co-ordinated action even though he neither knows nor shares the point of view of his neighbor. It deliberately adopts rules, regulations, laws, and ordinances. It deliberately sets up agencies to enforce the conformity with them that enables the society to operate—police, constabulary, militia—and empowers courts to decide the degree of nonconformity involved in an alleged transgression and its appropriate punishment within certain pre-established limits. The mass society prides itself on being a "government of law rather than of men," somehow overlooking the rather obvious fact that men make the laws.

The typical industrial enterprise is located in an urban area in which the prevailing tone is that of the massways. There is no necessity that the relationships between its work force and management must therefore also be of the mass variety. Its internal relationships can be and occasionally are of the folk even when it is surrounded by a sea of massways; but because of obvious difficulties that stand in the way of establishing the mutual understanding that must underly such a relationship—stereotyped images reciprocally held, poor communication, heterogeneous backgrounds, and differing points of view—such a case is the exception rather than the rule. Even more important to our immediate discussion is the fact that the enterprise is ordinarily integrated into the enveloping society through mass relationships. It operates under the constraint and guidance of ordinances, laws, and directives set up and deliberately enforced by formally created agencies. It is responsive only to the overtly coercive power of the massways.

When the industrial worker under such conditions turns to "society" for a guarantee of those rights that are necessary to him, he finds it difficult even to identify any tangible agency to which he can appeal. The enterprise in the mass society may, and often does, seem to its work force to be an isolate, existing outside any social context. For eight hours a day it *is* the society, as far as he is concerned. No one outside its gates appears to care what is going on within them. It may be crowded in among other buildings, circumscribed by streets and railways carrying thousands of people past it daily, yet it may appear to the worker to stand alone, to have no realizable tie-in with the life around it. The passer-by has much the same reaction. The industrial sections of large cities give one the impression of a merely physical crowding in of plant after plant, sandwiched in with slums like the sweepings that fall between the bricks in a walk. In chemical terms, there is a mixture but not a compound. The plant merely exists in physical proximity to other enterprises equally detached in a social sense. There is no community.

The society to which the industrial worker under the massways must turn for relief when he needs it is an intangible. It is not something the worker can realize, from which he can draw a real sense of belonging. It is a code of laws, a system of jurisprudence, a matter of rules and regulations. It is far away, impersonal, insensitive. The feeble cry of a single man protesting an injustice only serves to emphasize its aloofness. And if the combined cries of many men finally prod it into activity, its ponderous processes grind with maddening deliberation. The resulting law, or decision, or whatever may come out must be "general" in order to apply to the many; it may have little application to the situation of any one of the many, even if the decision is rendered with sufficient celerity to be of some practical good. The latter is unlikely to be true. The mass society operates to effectuate justice, but in the long run; and the industrial worker cannot wait out the long run.

Because of his need for short-run response to his appeals for assistance in setting up and maintaining conditions necessary for a human way of life, the industrial worker within the mass society is little better off, as an individual, than he would be if the society did not exist as a coercive agency to guarantee his rights within the enterprise. The assistance he needs individually and immediately is too likely to be finally applied for the impersonal benefit of the generation succeeding him. It is a fine thing that in the long run the society works to correct inequity and injustice, "but in the long run we are all dead." The worker cannot wait out the inexorable grinding of the massways. He wants his rights now, today, next week.

Because he is a human being, it is inevitable that he will do something to short-circuit the round-about processes of the mass society. As a human being, he is still capable of voluntary co-operation; and he is not alone in his need, his anxiety, and his frustration. Others in the enterprise share his plight. Almost as an emotional response, hardly realizing the logic of his action, he and the others go on strike. Economically the strike is a withholding from the market of the only product he has to sell, his labor, in order to bargain out better terms for its delivery; but emotionally it is a mass protest, a refusal to continue any longer in a relationship that denies essential human needs. The strike is not a phenomenon of the massways. It is used very effectively (though for an essentially different purpose) under the folk society. It is nothing new. Heroditus tells us of a general strike under the Pharaohs of Egypt. But in the industrial society under the massways, a new phenomenon appears. The *union* is developed as an institution that stands in a permanently coercive relationship over the enterprise. It is poised, ready for action, designed to bring management to an immediate accounting if the need arises.

The presence of the union demonstrates the conclusion of a work force that it dare not, in the future, place its faith either in management or in the society. It represents the judgment of the industrial worker that for practical purposes the plant is a closed social system, that there is no point in his looking elsewhere for relief or assistance. The rights which he regards as his he must guarantee himself, by means of the ever-present threat of his collective power as represented by his union. The union is his answer to a situation where he sees himself at the mercy of an impersonal management and forgotten by society.

Because the union without question interferes with the firm's social responsibility for production, it is at first looked on with disfavor by the society. It is branded as extra-legal, if not illegal, and the existing institutions of the society are used to discourage its growth. The major problems of the young industrial society are those of production; it is likely to be impatient with any hindrances to them, whether justified or not. As the society matures and its productive facilities become equal to the demands placed upon them, the society begins to take a somewhat more liberal attitude toward the union. First it is tolerated. Then finally, and this is perhaps as good an example of the impersonally logical and essentially economic basis of action in the mass society as any, when the industrial worker, collectively, becomes as important to the total society as a consumer of goods as his managements are in their production, the union is adopted by the mass society.

It becomes one of its recognized institutions. Its growth is regulated, its operations supervised, its rights and obligations spelled out in laws. Its conduct is administered by bureaus and adjudged by courts. After the course of a hundred years the mass society has acted to protect the interests of the industrial worker by deciding that organization of workers themselves into a coercive agency that can be used against management is not only equitable but necessary, a thing to be encouraged and protected for the sake of the society itself. This under due supervision, of course. If the Wagner Act was inevitable under the massways, so were the Taft-Hartley amendments.

The primary function of the union in the mass society is then to maintain coercive control over managements in order that the rights of workers to fair treatment and equitable compensation may be restored, in those cases where they have been denied, with sufficient speed to be of some practical help to those who have asked for it rather than to their sons and daughters. It cannot obtain guarantee of the right to work from individual managements; so in this respect it acts as an organized pressure group before the deliberative agencies of the mass society itself, demanding social security, federal and state creation of jobs when private industry is unable to supply them, and other measures designed to lessen the anxiety of the industrial worker whose skills are commonplace and who owns no tools. As a pressure group also, the union asks for restraints to be placed upon managements directly by statute law and administrative control, thus reinforcing its own coercive activities.

The general inability of work forces under the massways to predict the probable actions of their managements through understanding is compensated for by their collective power to force them to adhere to an objectively outlined and predictable pattern of action. The future seems less vague. Tensions are lessened and anxieties reduced. Formal communication at least is established with management where previously no effective communication of any kind existed. As a result of the increased morale and improved communication, long-run gains accrue to managements as well under the massways as a consequence of collective bargaining. But this is true only because, paradoxically enough, the union remains primarily an instrument of coercion, poised to exercise its power at a moment's notice in instances in which the rights of workers are disregarded, in which they are unable to set up and maintain conditions basic to a human way of life.

The union, as it actually exists, is not always sincerely representative of the rank and file. It is not always responsible to its membership. As is the case with all institutions, there is the constant danger that it may become more interested in its own perpetuation than in carrying out the function it was originally developed to perform. Even the most democratic union must become completely autocratic in times of stress; and its leadership, liking the taste of power, may find means to delay its surrender once more to the rank and file. Because its membership includes, according to Marxist theory, the most oppressed and potentially rebellious segment of the population, it is the constant prey of radical groups who wish, and are occasionally able, to use it to further their own ends. It may on occasion become the tool of racketeers. It occasionally becomes arrogant as it gains power and employs it arbitrarily.

But taking all this into account, it remains a necessary institution of the mass society, and its perfection proves to be an additional challenge to the citizens of that society. It is developed within the framework of production capitalism; and it is, in the mass industrial society, the bulwark of capitalism.[2] It has been developed in our nation within the American tradition, and it is a protection to the dignity that is the right of American labor but that cannot be maintained without the help of the union in an industrial society under the massways. "Besides exerting economic pressure, the union gives the workers a new sense of strength and becomes a powerful weapon to force management to recognize their worth as men. To compensate for their loss of status and for their anxieties in a changing industrial civilization, workers have been trying to find status and security in union organization."[3]

We must note that collective bargaining is only part of the solution to the problem of industrial relations under the massways. Actually it is three-fold in nature.[4] So far we have mentioned only two of its aspects; the union, which is the development of the worker, and labor

2. See Frank Tannenbaum, *Philosophy of Labor* (New York: Alfred A. Knopf, 1951), for a discussion of the union as a conservative force in our society.

3. W. Lloyd Warner and J. O. Low in "The Factory in the Community," *Industry and Society,* ed. W. F. Whyte (New York: McGraw-Hill Book Co., 1946), pp. 44-45.

4. See Glenn Gilman, "Industrial Relations in the Georgian Piedmont" (Doctoral dissertation, University of Chicago, 1955), Chapter I.

legislation, which is the contribution of the mass public toward the solution. Managements under the massways, themselves aware of the grave nature of the problem in its unameliorated form and not particularly happy with the solution as it has been developed by workers and the public, have been working since the days of Frederick Taylor toward the perfection of their own answer to the problem—scientific management. Their objective studies of the industrial worker have resulted in many and valuable contributions. On their own volition and largely as a result of their studies they have improved his working conditions, increased his pay, and reduced his hours. But they have missed complete success in their endeavor for two reasons. First, they must rely essentially upon manipulation of the industrial *milieu* to evoke the kind of responses they hope to get from the industrial worker, but they are embarrassed in this attempt in a mass society by their inability to predict with sufficient accuracy the manner in which the worker will interpret their manipulative activities. He is too complex an entity for scientific study. The nature of his interpretation of any configuration of circumstance and his ensuing response still defy satisfactory prediction on any basis except that of intuitive knowledge which lies outside the present realm of scientific investigation.

Second, even though they may under the massways eventually be able to substitute scientific information for subjective understanding in such a fashion as to be able to predict with the greatest accuracy the nature of his responses to any conceivable situation, they will discover their work to have been in vain if their objective has been to escape from the onerous burden of union and legal control. The one thing the industrial worker anywhere must have, if he is to possess that confidence in his ability to meet the future that is essential to the high state of morale his management seeks to engender, is the knowledge that he is able to control in some fashion any situation that threatens his security and thus his predictive relationship with the future. So long as management is responsible to the firm rather than to the work force, just so long can the industrial worker find ultimate security only in the presence of coercive authority that can be applied against management and in his favor.

The Industrial Worker under the Folkways

The basic plight of the industrial worker is no different in the folk society than in the mass society. Just as his opposite number does in the great industrial cities of the Northeast and the Midwest, the industrial worker in the Piedmont cotton textile industry lacks essential command over that portion of his daily life upon which all the rest hinges. He neither owns the tools with which he works nor is he, by and large, called upon to employ skills that make him irreplaceable in an economic sense. Within the context of the firm itself, he is potentially subject to all the anxieties and frustrations that plague the industrial worker anywhere.

The potentiality is theoretical, however. Practically, he is somewhat less subject to them even within the context of the firm itself. Unlike the typical work force under the massways, his is no mere physical aggregation of individuals ordered by the massways but with no real social bonding between its individual members except in the extreme case of common despair. The industrial worker in the folk regions of the United States seldom lacks organization whether he possesses a union or not. His organization is informal and implicit, but none the less powerful. It is that organization which proceeds out of possession of a common background of custom and tradition, mores and folkways; it is the kind of organization that is based on possession of mutual understanding, ability to foretell in advance the line of action of the other simply by putting one's self in his place; it is the kind of organization that is based upon possession of a common ground against which events are judged, a common point of view from which they are seen against that ground. It is above all the kind of organization that is shot through and through with sympathetic rapport, so that what happens to one happens to a degree to all.

Under such conditions, management *cannot* deal with the work force on an individual basis. It speaks of individual bargaining *versus* collective bargaining; but as a practical matter of fact, its every activity must be rehearsed as it will be viewed by the group rather than merely by the particular individual immediately involved. "You've got to watch your step with these folks," an overseer told the writer. "You forget yourself and get short-tempered with one of them, and you just haven't got him sore at you. There's his brothers, his sisters, perhaps his father and mother, his uncles and his aunts, his cousins, all his in-laws and his friends. You may have half the mill stirred up before you know it."

The informal organization not only facilitates communication, but it enforces it, in a manner of speaking. Because management is so well aware that group action is quite likely to follow upon what seems an action directed only at an individual, it is under the necessity of constantly revising and enriching its imagery of the work force. It cannot be content with mere factual information about the people who work for it; the nature of their feelings and attitudes must be ascertained in order that their roles may be effectively taken both individually and collectively. Management is immediately reminded of the unhappy consequences of neglecting any of the dimensions of human nature; it finds it unwise ever to settle back and relax in its certainty that it now knows all there is to know about the people. It finds it necessary constantly to pay attention to them. It is not permitted, even should it attempt to do so, to "take them for granted."

Concepts of what is right and wrong under the folkways make it difficult for a management to remain unaware of the attitudes of its people, even when it makes no deliberate attempt at communication. "It's your duty to tell the boss when you think he's wrong," a long-service employee told the writer. "Maybe he isn't doing the wrong thing on purpose—maybe his mind was on something else, or somebody told him the wrong thing, or something. If you tell him he's wrong, and he still goes on doing whatever it is the way he was doing it in the first place, why that's for him to decide. You figure maybe he's got a reason you don't know about. But it ain't right to stand by and let a man do something wrong, and not tell him about it."

We have previously noted that the spontaneous walkout has long been a weapon of southern work forces when they have felt themselves to be ignored. The strike, under such conditions, has a different aspect than in the mass society. Basically it is a communicative device, an emphatic demand for attention in a situation where the people feel themselves to be in possession of information that ought to be brought to the attention of management and that has obviously been overlooked in a managerial decision. It is this characteristic of the southern strike that explains its generally quick and satisfactory settlement as long as the union is not injected as an issue. Very often it has occurred in cases where for some reason the people are prevented from easy communication with top management. One plant experienced a series of such work stoppages during the early 1930's, often confined to single departments. A worker who had taken part in some of them explained the situation to the writer. "Mr. ———— (the president) and Mr. ———— (the general manager) were pretty decent people. You could get a square deal from them. The trouble was, you just couldn't ever get to them—there were a whole bunch of "little bosses" that blocked the way. We finally found out that the thing to do, when we had trouble, was just to walk out. Then we got to see the people we wanted to see, and things got straightened out. They finally caught on around the plant, and let us go up to see them in the first place when we wanted to, and there wasn't any more trouble."

Nor can policies be permitted to become rigid under circumstances of this sort. The work force under the folkways insists that every problem be settled in accordance with principles of what is right and wrong; and this can be accomplished only by policies that have sufficient flexibility to permit allowances to be made for differing circumstances. The relatively simple policy structure of the typical Piedmont cotton textile mill, in combination with its short and effective formal lines of communication and numerous personal contacts between top management and hourly-rated people, means that the latter are well aware of managerial attitudes and intentions and the probable nature of their modification under particular circumstances. There is high validity of prediction in both directions, a rather important requirement for effective co-operation. Much emphasis in present-day discussion of personnel relations is placed upon the necessity for a management to understand its work force; but it is equally or even more important than the work force understand management through knowledge of its policies as well as of its persons.

This high level of accuracy of prediction as to the probable intentions, objectives, attitudes, and value judgments of the other results in a variety of unconscious accomodation of interest behind every managerial decision involving the work force and every worker response to that decision. Any particular decision announced by management may appear to be completely unilateral in nature. Actually, a rehearsal of its probable consequences in terms of its assessment by the work force will either have consciously or unconsciously preceded its adoption. It will have been modified, revised, and reshapen in terms of the probable interpretation and response of the people. In its final form it represents a compromise between what management would like to do and what it feels the people would like to see done and there will have been a considerable amount of informal checking to assess the accuracy of this latter estimation. The decision, when it is announced, is likely to meet with general approval; the people who have ordinarily been aware of the circumstances that have called for the decision have themselves, in attempting to predict what it will be, been balancing what they would like against what they think the company will be able to do. The announced decision is not likely to be much different from the predicted decision because of the informal and almost intuitive accomodation of interests that enters into its formulation and its acceptance.

This high degree of informal organization of work forces under the folkways has actually worked to facilitate union organization in the Piedmont textile industry. In those cases in which a breach has been permitted to develop between management and the people and in which the informal leaders of the work force run into serious difficulties in their attempts to restore communication and rapport, the union can move in with amazing swiftness. It does not have to "organize" the plant. All it has to do is convince the leadership of an already informally organized group that it can be of some assistance. This characteristic has on occasion given the union a false impression of its persuasive powers. After some kind of a settlement has been worked out, the union is dismayed to find that it cannot hold its membership. It never had them; it was merely used on an *ad hoc* basis as a convenient way of getting a job done by an organization already in existence.

It was very unlikely, as a matter of fact, that the work force thought seriously one way or the other about a permanent and continuing alliance with the union. It just did not see it in those terms. The textile worker has not supported institutionalized collective bargaining simply because it has not fitted into the pattern of his day-to-day behavior. It has possessed only one feature of interest to him, its ability to run a strike in a professional manner. And even here, as we have noted, the purpose behind the strike is different.

Under more usual conditions, when the union is attempting to organize a plant where no labor dispute is in progress, it finds itself opposed by the informal organization. It discovers that before it can proceed with its own pattern of organization it must disorganize what is already in existence. It must attempt to create a breach between the work force and management to begin with; and then it must attempt to break up the informal organization itself, discredit its leadership and swing the people to the new leadership offered by the union. It is seldom successful in doing so. The folk group is too powerful. In case after case, the union is able to enroll in its ranks only those elements in the work force that are not in the folk organization to begin with. The remnants of the floating textile work force figure largely in this fringe group, as do local people whose behavior patterns are for some reason unacceptable to the solid core of the work force. The net result is that the union starts out in the plant without the support of the main body of the people, and draws its local officers from that group least likely to be able to win such support in the future.

A Southerner and firm supporter of the philosophy of organized labor, once a high official of the C. I. O. but critical of its organizational methods as employed in the Piedmont, gave the writer his version of a typical organizational meeting in the southern textile industry. "The only people they have there are the ones who haven't anything to lose. They're the fringe element, the ones the company wouldn't dare give a house in the mill village—drifters and misfits. Everybody gets up and cusses out management, and the one that damns it loudest and longest, they say 'That's our boy! We'll elect him president of the local!' The president of the company takes a look at who the union members have selected to represent them, and he says 'I know that character! He's dead drunk every Saturday night, he beats his wife all week long, and his children run the streets in rags. He's been arrested three times for vagrancy, and he was picked up once for theft but they couldn't prove it on him. If this is what I'm expected to bargain with—no, thank you! I'll fight the union 'till hell freezes over

before I'll bargain with him and his kind.' The respectable core of
the work force—the people the union should have tried to get on their
side in the first place—take a look at the slate of officers and tell
themselves, 'If this is what a union is like, we're not having any.' For
all practical purposes, the union is dead around that mill right then;
and it will be five years before the smell dies down and you can try it
again."

The response of the work force in general to the kind of organizational tactics that prove successful under the massways is either to become incensed or amused at the attempts of organizers to split the
hourly-rated group away from management. The latter response is
likely to be more frustrating from the union point of view. In either
case, the people are indicating their implicit resolve to retain the bond
of understanding that exists between themselves and management. It
is a necessary part of their lives in the industrial environment under
the folkways. Only the most dire emergency could bring them to
jeopardize it, and then they risk its loss only in a last desperate attempt
to re-establish it. Not only does it facilitate their ability to predict the
nature of the future, but it gives them a reasonable degree of assurance
that disputes and differences of opinion that are bound to arise can be
settled on a face-to-face basis, in terms of what is right and wrong,
against commonly held principles of what constitutes equitable treatment.

In addition, the flexibility of policy that is possible under the informal relationship that permits its revision whenever it would stand
in the way of what is agreed is the right thing to do means that disputes can be worked out with regard to the particular situation that is
involved. The relationship is problem-centered. Both management
and the work force, with equal determination that the "right" and
"reasonable" solution for each problem shall be found, regard policy
merely as an instrument that must be capable of variation from case
to case. Both sides are in agreement as to the simple principles of
equity that must be served. After an examination of the facts, both
sides are in general agreed as to what *should* be done. "Policy" is
not permitted to stand in the way, and what might under other circumstances have developed into a protracted and stubborn dispute over
matters of principle and policy is rapidly reduced to a question of de-

ciding the most practicable method of accomplishing what everybody is agreed must be accomplished. Emotionally based attitudes and hot tempers are rapidly short-circuited and drained off under a procedure of this sort; personalities and issues are kept out of the discussion. A standard rule of thumb for resolving differences, quoted time and time again to the writer by the overseers who are accustomed to finding themselves in the middle of a hot dispute between an hourly-rated worker and a second hand, is, "Let's stop worrying about *who*'s wrong and see if we can't find out *what*'s wrong!"

While the following incident does not involve a dispute, it illustrates not only the seemingly casual treatment accorded policy under the folkways, but also the frustrations inherent in attempting to organize a plant that blithely disregards their "sacred and inviolate" character as defined under the massways.

The owner-manager of a small country mill told the writer of an attempt to organize his work force shortly after World War II. "The union sent down this woman from New York. She was red-headed and full of energy. She got around to talk with everybody—visited them in their homes, talked with them out by the gate. The folks liked her—seemed to enjoy talking with her—but she just couldn't work up much interest in the union.

"Our machine shop was at the end of the mill nearest the village. If you stepped out the door of the shop and across the spur track, there it was. One of our machinists had his house right across the tracks, and he worked out a deal with the foreman of the machine shop so he could go home for his meal at noon or at night, depending on which shift he was on, and wouldn't have to carry a lunch bucket. There wasn't any harm in the arrangement; it would have been pretty small to have refused him his chance for a hot meal under the circumstances, actually.

"One afternoon when Ed was working the three o'clock shift, the organizer met him outside the mill just as he was going across the tracks for his supper. 'I thought you were working this shift, Ed,' she said to him. 'I am,' he told her. 'Is there something wrong at home?' she asked hm. 'Not a thing,' he told her. 'Then do you mind telling me,' she said, 'just why you're going home in the middle of the shift?' 'Don't mind a bit,' he said. 'I'm just going home for supper.' She threw up her hands in disgust. 'This is the last straw!' she said. 'I'm just wasting my time trying to organize a plant where the company hasn't got any more sense than to let the employees go home for meals on company time!' She was as good as her word, too. She packed up and left the next day. Nobody's been back since."

The need for control to enable the work force to see into a future it cannot understand is not present in industry under the folkways to the degree that it is where impersonal mass relationships impede the two-way communication process that leads to reciprocal understanding, where there is little common ground of agreement in terms of which differences can be worked out, and where inflexible policies hinder the settlement of problems in terms of their actual context. Yet we must never make the mistake of presuming that understanding is in itself a guarantee of labor peace. It may actually intensify conflict when one understands that the intentions of the other are not in line with one's own interest and that there is no intention to work out a suitable compromise. Managements in the Piedmont are like managements anywhere. They are made up of human beings and subject to all the faults that plague humanity everywhere. They can make mistakes. They can be stubborn. They can be callous, deliberately disregarding the rights of workers even when they are aware that those rights are being violated. They can be complacent or just plain stupid. They can be biased to the point that they are unable to take the roles of the people who work for them.

In addition to these possibilities, all of them operate in one of the few areas of intensive competition of the pure variety still remaining in the industrial world, with labor their major production cost. They are under constant temptation, even the best of them, to reduce unit prices by slashing wage rates. Though the corporation may be immortal, its management is not. The best of managements may be replaced by the worst. Granting all these possibilities and keeping in mind that the most sympathetic and understanding management is powerless in the face of the market, what guarantee does the textile worker have that a presently satisfactory in-plant relationship is going to continue?

Despite the generally high degree of rapport between workers and managements in this industry under the folkways, the industrial

worker in the Piedmont textile industry must still be able to depend
upon some outside coercive agency that will swing a recalcitrant management back into line if he is to enjoy a comforting degree of security.
There is always the strike, of course; but failing any other agency than
this to give him relief, why does he not institutionalize it by backing
it up with a permanent labor organization? The informal organization
in the mill does not answer to this purpose; it is a co-operative and
communicative device rather than essentially coercive. Is the textile
worker short-sighted indeed, as he has been accused of being, for not
adopting the institution of collective bargaining on a permanent basis
in order to wield a continuing coercive pressure upon his management?

As we did in the case of the worker under the massways, we must
seek the answer in the context of the total society of which the worker,
his enterprise, and his management are all a part. We note immediately factors that differ significantly from the contracting solution
discussed earlier. First and most important, the plant is part of a true
community in addition to its membership in the mass societies of
government and market. We have seen the Piedmont textile plant
brought into being to begin with as an agency of the community.
Migrating mills from the North were adopted by the community and
their northern managements "naturalized" into the folk society of the
Piedmont. This identity between the mill and the community has
remained something real, identifiable, and tangible. Its threatened
disappearance after World War I did not materialize; the folk society
was stimulated into a positive reaffirmation of it before its atrophy had
reached the danger point.

The society to which the southeastern textile worker turns for
protection is not, under the folkways, something vague, ephemeral,
and theoretical, an abstract concept of social justice, for instance. It
is as living and real as the people who walk the streets of the textile
town and collectively form it. Even during his time of trouble, this
society was a real entity to the textile worker. He continued to enjoy
the attention of a portion of it though, for a while, it was neither the
right kind of attention nor paid by the right group. As he made his
displeasure with the state of affairs that existed unmistakeably evident,
the entire community once more became interested in him and re-

mained so. It is made up of flesh and blood people whom the worker recognizes, people whose status he is aware of, the weight of whose judgments are grounded in the same ethical code as his own; when they are in possession of the same facts as he, they are likely to hold the same opinions as he as to what is right and wrong.

Except for brief periods in what was a minority of the mills, and these largely concentrated in the decade between 1925 and 1935, the implicitly enforced set of community expectations with regard to the conduct of industrial relations in the Piedmont textile plants has been the worker's protection against the possibility of an arbitrary and unsympathetic management, and has done much to protect him from the impersonal vagaries of the market.

The worker has depended upon the power of community opinion to bring into line, in the subtle fashion of the folk, those managements that would deviate from the "right" pattern of conduct.[5] Community opinion as to what constitutes "right" treatment may deviate from the opinion of the outsider; but what is important is that it will in more cases than not seem reasonable to the textile worker. He has in general been reasoning from the same premises, is in possession of the same facts, and comes to the same conclusions. It is because the "policies" that order his industrial life are, in their most essential aspects, folkways that have their roots in the community and strike back into the very region itself that the textile worker has faith in their eventual ability to make things right. A single management may evade them for a while, but not for long. Eventually they will swing him into line with a power that makes federal and state legislation and formal collective bargaining appear infantile by comparison.

The power of these folkways over management lies in the fact that they are for the most part unrealized as compulsive forces. Piedmont managements are themselves of the folk. They are members of their communities as well as managers of mills. They have internalized community expectations and attitudes and made them a part of their selves, a powerful censoring device that enters into their every decision. Without consciously realizing why they do it, they follow

5. See Liston Pope *Millhands and Preachers* (New Haven: Yale University Press, 1942) for an account of the attitude of the Gastonia community and its manifestations during the early days of the Gastonia strike before it was complicated by the issue of communism.

practices that have been developed under the folkways as the most effective and efficient means of meeting fundamental human needs under given conditions. Yet these guides for action do not become static and rigid, despite their compulsive nature at any one time. Because they have never been formalized, they are constantly under a process of revision. One does not call a meeting of the Board of Aldermen to revise the folkways. The folk do it themselves.

W. Lloyd Warner, discussing the industrial history of "Yankee City" while it was still of the folk, remarks, "The essential point to remember for these leaders of industry and finance is that they were subject to local control (1) because they were dominated by local sentiments which motivated them 'to take care of their own people,' and (2) they were under the powerful influence of the numerous organizations to which they belonged and of their personal contacts with local citizens, which directly related them to influences from every part of the city."[6] Without changing a word, he could have been speaking of the present-day textile Piedmont.

The president of a large selling house with its offices on Worth Street was talking with the writer of the personnel policies of the mills whose accounts his firm handles. "These people are wasting half their profits trying to run their mills the way their communities think they ought to be run. It doesn't make sense. What they should do is call in the unions, get the mills organized, and run their labor relations on a rational, business-like basis!" The intimation of the speaker was that the mill managements were irrational in the area of personnel relations. The social psychologist might perhaps define their actions as super-rational, displaying intuitive awareness of a higher logic not capable of objective definition.

The exact pattern of these folkways varies from plant to plant and from community to community, depending upon what seems right in view of local circumstances. But in general, they operate in such a fashion as to afford protection to the industrial worker in those areas where he cannot protect himself. Certainly they operate in the interest of other elements in the community as well. They are not grounded completely or even immediately in high principles of hu-

---

6. Warner and Low, *op. cit.*, p. 38. This paper shows an industrial relationship to have existed in "Yankee City" before its folk society degenerated that was very similiar to the present-day relationship in the Piedmont.

manitarianism, in objective recognition of the aesthetic desirability
of ethical conduct. They are practical ways of solving practical problems, in a given context, that arise because men must live and work
together if they are to survive. Whatever their immediate origin may
be, they cannot gain the status of folkways unless they promise in the
long run to effect the greatest good for the greatest number. They
will invoke community disfavor and attack if they appear to be
inimical from the standpoint of community welfare.

The community expects the mill to operate as long as it can borrow
money to meet its pay rolls, despite the state of the market, and this
dampens the cycle of the market before it involves the worker; he is
neither as prosperous during good periods nor as desperate during
bad because of it. The community expects, when layoffs become necessary, that the "loyalty" of long-service workers will not only be taken
into account but that the senior breadwinner of each family unit will
remain on the pay roll as long as possible. The worker can predict
the pattern of the layoff, if it comes, quite as accurately as if he were
operating under a union-administered seniority system, but he can expect also that "reasonable" deviations will be possible in individual
cases. The community expects management to treat the worker
"right"; the worker benefits through an informal but effective policing
of labor relations in the plant that stands ready and willing to apply
coercive measures if "right" pattterns of conduct are not maintained.

The community expects mill officials to contribute generously of
their time to community affairs, as all small towns do, no matter what
the role of their leading citizens may be. The net effect is to knit
the mill still more closely into community affairs, to make the mill
officials more cognizant of community problems and more susceptible
to community attitudes. The community expects the mill company
to contribute generously of its money to the local school system, over
and above whatever taxes it and its people may pay. The result has
been that in Georgia, at least, until recently the only adequate school
systems outside metropolitan areas have been those in which community funds have been supplemented by grants from textile mills.
Community ministers expect the mill not only to contribute generously
to community churches, but to employ a class of workers that will
support churches with their presence. The result is to increase the

homogeneity of the work force and the proportion of its members who are likely to hold most stubbornly to implicit ideas of what is right and wrong.

The community expects the mill to sell electricity and gas to the mill village residents at cost, to charge extremely low rents for the houses, and to remit rental utility charges in case of layoffs lasting more than two weeks. It expects community pastures and garden spots to be made available to those workers who desire them. It expects that advances will be made against future earnings to reliable workers in the case of protracted layoffs. It expects the mill to "make a job" for a worker crippled by an industrial accident. It expects the mill to provide some measure of security for a family stricken by serious illness.

We could go on down the line with regard to these community expectations. The advantages of each of them to the community as well as to the worker is obvious. A steadier income for the worker means a steadier flow of cash into merchants' tills. The more the mill can hold down expenses for the worker in housing and utilities, the more of his pay check is left to spend up town. Employment spread among family units keeps down relief rolls and taxes, as does mill-assumed responsibility for worker security along other lines. Mill interest in community affairs means a flow of mill money into community projects. Yet, though we can point out aspects of each expectation that are economically advantageous to some group in the community other than the mill worker, and though in cases certain special groups may be particularly benefited, none of the expectations are detrimental to any group. All contribute in some degree to the benefit of all, and the mill worker is at the head of the list.

This is what we meant when we said in Chapter Three that the folkways constitute a design for living. *They represent an intuitive accomodation of individual interests in a social situation in such a fashion that the ultimate interests of all are most effectively served.* The concept of Adam Smith that the greatest good results to all from each seeking earnestly to serve his own self-interest is regarded nowadays as rather naïve. Those who scoff at it, however, fail to realize two important facts. Adam Smith was the product of a folk society in which he saw such a condition actually in operation. Second, they are generally unaware of Smith's excellent insight into human nature, as demonstrated in his *Theory of Moral Sentiments*. He was well aware of the operation of sympathetic response; he could not conceive of a "self" that did not, to some degree, respond to the plight of every member of the community. Under such conditions, "self-interest" takes on a new meaning.

Yet there is always the possibility that a particular management may not be subject to the control of the folkways merely by having made them a part of its own thinking. We noted how various pressures during the 1920's served to isolate some managements from their work forces; and there was a corresponding tendency during the same period and for the same reason for managements to lose touch with their communities. The manager of a particular mill may rebel against the folkways. He may be under pressure from an absentee management that regards compliance with them as poor business and unnecessary. In these and like cases where the folkways are disregarded or violated, the response of the community is swift and generally effective. It does not rely upon the formal methods of obtaining compliance that would have to be resorted to in the mass society. It depends upon the informal controls of intimate human societies, flattery, cajolery, persuasion; or if these are not effective, adverse opinion, gossip, ridicule, withdrawal of communion, non-cooperation. The positive methods of coercion first listed have a high degree of success in the folk society. Though they are objectively applied, they are unlikely to be recognized as coercion at all. In a way, they are not. One appeals to a man's "better nature"; and if the attempt to bring it into the picture is successful, it takes over. One has merely triggered a process of self-coercion.

The next step, if positive but indirect methods fail, may be to work through an intimate friend of the deviant individual. There is no general voicing of disapproval of his conduct to his face; but various people concerned over the turn affairs are taking may approach someone whom they know to be in his trust and confidence. "You know, you'd ought perhaps speak to Joe," they are likely to say. "Being as close to it as he is, he probably hasn't realized it, but he's heading for trouble at the mill if something isn't done about things out there pretty soon." The friend may already have "spoken" and Joe has scoffed at his fears. In that case, there is nothing more that can be done in a positive fashion. There is no conscious and deliberate agreement that negative methods are now to be employed, but they come into the picture.

All of us are familiar with the power of these negative patterns of coercion that are at the disposal of the folk society with its close human contacts. There is nothing blatant about them, nothing studied. Far from being able to meet them head on and defeat them, one cannot even prove that they are being used. One senses an adverse opinion mainly through the non-symbolic elements of communication. The pastor's handshake is not quite so firm as he greets one at church on Sunday morning. The local banker is too formally polite. The members of one's golf foursome, usually mercilessly critical of one's activities, studiously avoid mention of the variant policy. An adverse opinion need not be voiced "in the little world where people come together" to be felt. One feels estranged, separated, cut off from communion with what is going on by a wall of polite behavior, and one wonders "what people are saying."

If the deviant is so stubbornly persistent as finally to cut himself off completely from communication with the folk group, then he has set up a mass relationship; and the folk can use the coercive devices of the massways with telling effect if necessary though not always for the purpose for which they were designed. There may be harassing ordinances; interminable delays; red tape, once casually brushed aside, now scrupulously insisted upon; permits not renewed or not granted; strict enforcement of obsolete regulations suddenly discovered to be still on the books. And there is always the power to tax. The writer visited one mill just as its management had finally relaxed after a week of considerable anxiety. A second hand, a few weeks previously, had discharged an elderly worker in a burst of anger and without just cause. The superintendent offered the old man his job back; but his pride was hurt, and he announced his intention to retire permanently to his farm miles out in the country. The next week the superintendent had some business in the county court house. He happened to glance into the room where the county Board of Tax Equalization was in session, and there sat the old man—senior member of the board! It appeared that in addition to his farming and his mill work, he was a political figure of some importance in his community. "We discovered the old fellow carried enough weight with that board to have talked it into doubling our assessment, if he'd wanted to. Fortunately he'd had time enough to cool down, and nothing happened; but there were a few worried people around the mill until the board adjourned!"

If the controls of the local community fail, there is a community still more powerful, that of the industry itself. Here again the controls are informal and largely those of opinion. We have noted the manner of their operation during the 1930's, and they are even more effective at the present time. The industry is no more inclined to look with favor upon union penetration today than it was twenty years ago; and it is more convinced than ever that violation of the rights of employees by any particular management is an open invitation to union organization. There is little question in the minds of any management as to what the opinion of the balance of the industry will be if it persists in a course of action that is contrary to regional standards of equity and justice in personnel relations. If its mill should be organized, other managements would commiserate with it in its misfortune, but it would get scant solace out of the sympathy. Whether justified or not and whether true or not, it would imagine behind every spoken phrase the unspoken thought, "If you'd treated your people right, you wouldn't *have* a union in your plant!"

The communities in which the mills are located, including the mills, their managements, and their work forces as constituent elements, stand in a powerful coercive relationship to management. The weight of their corrective influence is buttressed by the folkways of the region itself, which seek to realize the stern and implacable ideals of a Calvinistically oriented Christian ethical code under real conditions and in real situations. Further coercive power is potentially available through the weight of opinion of the industry which is not in sympathy with any management that will permit a fundamental breach to develop between its people and itself. The result is an effective and efficient structuring, outside the context of any particular mill, that operates swiftly for the proection of a work force that is being subjected to denial of those basic conditions necessary for the maintenance of a human way of life.

The industrial worker under the folkways is actually less in need of this social control than is his opposite number under the massways, because a much greater rapport exists between himself and his management. This higher degree of understanding permits him to make valid predictions as to the future and under ordinary circumstances to feel secure within the industrial context despite his own lack of control over it. His feeling of security is further increased, however, by his implicit reliance upon the forces of the folk society of the Piedmont to bring a management that would violate his rights into swift and satisfactory compliance with what he, the worker, regards as "right" treatment. He feels that the society itself, through its natural processes, provides him with an effective guarantee as to those rights that he cannot, as an individual in industry, depend upon obtaining through his own efforts if they are withheld from him.

When there is added to this the fact that he already feels himself to be (though he does not perhaps consciously realize it) a member of a highly integrated and effective informal organization within the plant, we begin to see why he is not interested in the union. It is, actually, a make-shift and pathetic affair compared with what he already possesses. It is a substitute for the kind of relationship that he enjoys in the original state.

It is not within the province of this study to predict how long he will continue to hold this opinion, but this much seems rather clear. Any decision he may reach in the future will be based, as have those in the past, upon the degree to which he can feel that he is living like a whole man in the industrial *milieu*. For as long as he can feel himself to be an accepted member of his community with the responsibilities and privileges due him as an individual, and for as long as he can regard himself with respect as a voluntarily participating member in a co-operative association, he will continue to look with favor upon a folk structuring of the reciprocal relationships between himself, his management, and his community.

The past success of the Piedmont textile industry along the line of industrial relations has been the result of its ability to translate the folkways into an industrial environment, to realize abstract concepts of human dignity and brotherhood in the concrete situation of the workaday industrial world. As long as this remains its essential philosophy for labor relations, and as long as the region continues to generate true communities to exist and police these intuitive guides for men living and working together in a human fashion, the Piedmont cotton textile industry will continue to be what it has been since the opening days of the Cotton Mill Campaign—a tremendous and challenging experiment in industry under the folkways.

MODERN MILL COMMUNITIES

One of the Earliest Textile Mill Plants *Circa* 1887

Modern Textile Plants

Loom-Weaving Operation

High Speed Warper

Warper Tender at Warper Creel

The Lunch Hour Break

Mill Cafeteria for Employees

Employees Leaving Mill at Shift Change

The Mill Community

Ed Beazley

Mill Housing Around the Plant

Mill Houses

Textile Mill Employee Homes

School Buildings

Employee and Community Recreational Facilities

Employee Vocational School Class

Community Center for Employees

A Mill Baseball Diamond

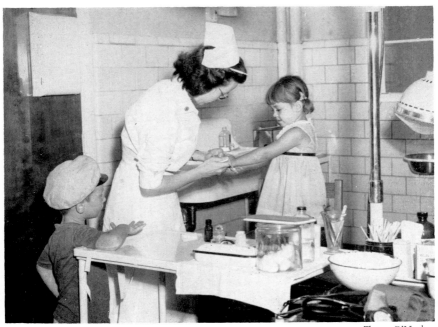

Textile Clinic for Employees and Their Families

Hospital in Mill Community

Modern Textile Engineering School

INDEX

Index

Abbot, Grace, 162
Absenteeism, 214-15
Absentee management, 183-86, 219-22
Accessions to Georgia mills, 1947-1952, 254-56
American Federation of Labor, 171, 187, 237
Appalachian Mountains, 29
Appalachian Plateaus, 29
Appalachian Valley, 29
Artisans, in early Piedmont, 43
Ashby, Irene, 161, 163
Atkinson, Edward, 76
Atlanta Constitution, 75

Bachman, Jules, 93n
Bacon, Nathaniel, 48
Baltimore Journal of Commerce and Manufacturing, 76
Bassett, John Spencer, 33n
Becker, Howard, 55n, 58n
Berglund, Abraham, 177n, 214n
Berkeley, Governor, 48
Black, Robert C., 35n
Blue Grass Basin, 29
Blue Ridge, 30, 33
Blumer, Herbert, 5n, 54n, 78
Boll weevil, 130
Bowman, Isiah, 28
Bureau of the Census, 66n, 209n, 251n, 256n

Capital investment and modern industry, 17; and the industrial worker, 19; in southern mill building, 83; in the northern industry, 114
Cash, W. J., 50n, 78, 82n, 111n, 140, 145, 149, 151, 165, 174, 175, 191n, 193, 194n
Charleston Courier, 74

Child labor in the mills, 159-63; and the folkways, 159; management attitudes toward, 160; economics of, 161; Piedmont opposition to, 162
Christian ethic, 10, 37, 63, 262
Civil War, 45
Civilization, as product of mass society, 55
Clark, Victor S., 19n, 65n, 68n, 76, 90
Coastal Plain, 30, 33, 34
Collective bargaining, 296. *See also* Labor unions *and* Union-management relations
Commission houses, 84, 100
"Commodity" theory of labor, 190-92, 222-26
Communication, as basis of personnel relations, 239, 241
Communist Party, 172, 185
Communities and industrial relations, 88-89, 192-96, 287, 308-15; nature of community expectations, 88, 211, 310-12; period of apathy, 195-96; re-awakening of interest, 231
Communities and managements, 82, 88-89, 157, 177, 286-87; nature of controls over management, 313-15
Communities and mills, basic relationship, 103-4; in the North, 116
Communities and workforces, 163-67, 190-96, 226-32, 284-86, 308-15
Company store, 152-53, 280-81
Competition in textile industry (general), 95; inter-regional, 109-20
Concepts, in human behavior, 13
Cooley, Charles Horton, 5n, 6n, 9n, 54n
Co-operation, as basic industrial relationship, 133
Copeland, M. T., 76
Cotton aristocracy, 35, 70, 86
Cotton culture, 34; in ante-bellum Piedmont, 44; under Reconstruction, 45, 70

Cotton gin, 34
Cotton Mill Campaign, 64, 74-79; as a social movement, 76; results, 89; termination, 103; the "new" campaign, 190
Cotton textile industry, general, 91-102; technology, effect on industrial relations, 91-93; managerial structure, 93; labor costs, 94; competition, 95; profits, 99; economic factors, effect on industrial relations, 101; competition between North and South, 109-20
Cotton textile industry, Northern, 109-20; wages, 109; static nature of, 112; industrial relations, 115; community relations, 116, taxation of, 117; summary of factors leading to decline, 119
Cotton textile industry, Piedmont, 46-48, 64-124; war and Reconstruction, 46, 67-68; ante-bellum mills, 65-67; industrial recovery after Civil War, 68-69; investment in, 83; location of, 85-88; community support of, 88; integration, 89, 121; as an institution, 104, 203; competition with North, 107-20; modernization of present industry, 121; concentration of ownership, 122; northern ownership, extent of, 122; statistical picture of Georgian industry (1952), 251-52. See also Workforce, Piedmont
Cox, Reavis, 98n
Cultural activities, mill support of, 283-85
Cultural heritage, Piedmont region, 36-43
Culture, as product of folk society, 55

Danville strike, 170
Davidson, Elizabeth H., 159 n, 163 n
Davison's Textile Blue Book, 105, 251n
De Bow's Review, 65
Decentralization of industry, 47, 48, 49, 317
Decline of the Northern industry, summary, 119
Democracy, in pioneer culture, 41; in Piedmont politics, 48-50
Depression of 1929, effect on textile industry, 179
De Vyver, Frank T., 177n, 214n
Dewey John, 5n
Dewey, Richard, 5n
Discrimination against mill workers, 164-67, 193-96, 227-32
Dividend rates, early mills, 84

Division of labor and modern industry, 16; and the industrial worker, 18, and cotton textiles, 91
Drucker, Peter, 12n, 17n
Durkheim, Emile, 10n, 54n

Eastman, Charles, 44
Eels, Kenneth, 284n
Educational level of mill workers, 195, 196, 253, 255
Efficiency experts, 180-83, 217-19
Elizabethton strike, 170, 183
Empathy, as uniquely human possession, 7
"Employer-employee" relations, 139
Ethnic origins of Piedmont people, 32-33

Fall line, 30
Faulkner, Harold Underwood, 34n, 51n
"Flight of the spindles South," 107
"Floaters," 136
"Flying Squadrons," 171
Folk-mass check list, 58-61
Folk society, 53-63; social bond within, 54; and the individual, 62-63; in building of mills, 79-84; and "social security," 212; and labor unions, 236, 303-7
Folkways, 58-61; envelopment of the mills, 89; as "personnel policy" in early mills, 149; and the industrial worker, 300-17; and management, 309-15
Frontier, as influence on Piedmont culture, 36, 49-52
Function as requirement for human way of life, 12; and the industrial worker, 18; and the textile worker, 92; in Piedmont mills, 138

Gainsbrugh, M. R., 93n
Gastonia strike, 170, 172, 184
Geddes, Patrick, vii
Georgia Department of Labor, 251n, 252n
Gettys, W. E., 77n
Gilman, Glenn, 298n
Golden Rule, as basic personnel principle, 262
Grady, Henry, 75
Gregg, William, 74
Grievances, 276

Hammond, J. H., 65
Hayes-Tilden campaign, 73

Herring, Harriet, 44n, 65n, 66n, 131, 151, 152, 153n, 154n, 157n, 158n, 166n, 213n, 229n, 280
Hinrichs, A. F., 92n, 96
Home ownership, by textile workers, 254
Horney, Karen, 5n
Hughes, Everett Cherrington, 104n, 203
Human nature, 5-16; predictive basis of, 5; and sympathy (empathy), 6; and the self, 8; and the industrial process, 17-23, 288
Human way (of predictive behavior), 11; and security, 11; and understanding, 13; and novelty, 15; and the industrial worker, 15
Humber, W. J., 5n
Hume, David, 6n

Idealism, as pioneer characteristic, 39
Industrial process, 16; and human nature, 17-23, 288
Industrial relations, definition, 3; and the folkways, 89; and economics of textile industry, 101; in the Northern industry, 115
Industrial relations, problem of, 4, 17; the general solution, 289-93; the mass solution, 293-99; the folk solution, 300-17
Industrial Workers of the World, 172
International Union of Textile Workers, 186

Johnson, Gerald, W., 81

Kennedy, Stephen, 96
Kier, Malcolm, 179n, 214
Knights of Labor, 186

Labor costs, in textiles, 94-95
Labor force. See Workforce
Labor mobility. See Mobility
Labor unions, organizing activity in Piedmont, 186-97, and the folk society, 236-37, 303-07; as social institutions, 296-98
Labor unrest in the Piedmont, 170-76; contemporary analysis of, 172-75; national contributing factors, 176-90; regional contributing factors, 190-97; local contributing factors, 197-205
Lahne, Herbert J., 113, 114, 115, 130, 149, 150, 151n, 152, 154, 159n, 161n, 162n, 170n, 186, 187, 188n, 209n, 210n, 211n
Lay-offs, pattern of, 210
Lemert, Ben F., 103n, 119n, 130, 209

Linton, Ralph, 12n
Low, J. O., 17n, 298n, 310n

Machinery manufacturers, role in mill building, 84
McIver, R. M., 54n
McKelvay, the Reverend Alexander J., 161, 163
Maine, Sir Henry, 54n
Management officials, statistical data concerning, 259-62
Managerial attitudes, in early mills, 135, 138, 145, 146-47, 149; change during 1920's, 201-5; re-orientation of, 238-40
Managerial structure of modern industry, 17; and the industrial worker, 21; in the textile industry (general), 93; in the present Piedmont mills, 258-59
Mannheim, Karl, 40n
Marion strike, 170
Marketing of cotton textiles, 100-1
Mass society, 54-61; social bond within, 54; as source of civilization, 55; and the individual, 62; and the Piedmont mills, 90; and the industrial worker, 293-99; and collective bargaining, 296-99
Massways, 58-61
Mayo, Elton, 17n
Mead, George Herbert, 5n, 6n, 9n, 13n
Meeker, Marcia, 284n
Michl, H. E., 113
Middle class, role in building of Piedmont mills, 46, 69, 77, 86; value system and mill workers, 194, 195-97; and mill hands, 194-96, 227-32
Migration of cotton textile industry, 107-9; statistical analysis of, 108
Mill village, 149-54; origin, 149; extent of housing, 150; appearance, 151; improvement of, 151, 208, 225; and labor mobility, 153; and welfare work, 154-59; present status, 278; trend toward sale, 279
Mill workers. See Workforce
Mississippi Valley, 29
Mitchell, Broadus, 46n, 75n, 76, 78, 79n, 80, 83n, 101, 127, 128, 129, 133n, 135, 139, 170, 171n, 172, 173, 183
Mitchell, George, 170n, 171n, 183, 188
Mobility of mill workers, 136; and the mill village, 153
Mountaineers, 129, 139
Mumford, Lewis, 16n
Murchison, Claudius, 98n, 101n

Murphy, the Reverend Edgar Gardner, 161, 163

Nashville Basin, 29
National Industrial Conference Board, 96
National Planning Association, 120
Northrup automatic loom, 106
Novelty, as requirement for human way of life, 15
NRA Cotton Textile Code, 211

Odum, Howard, 27n, 49n, 60n, 52, 53, 54n, 56n, 63, 69, 77
Olmstead, Frederick Law, 35n
"Open-door" policy, 247
"Operator-operative" dichotomy, 138-39
Organizing, in Piedmont, 186-90
Otey, Elizabeth, 159n

Park, Robert E., 5n, 54n, 55n, 58n, 62
Parker, Lewis W., 80
Parsons, Talcott, 13n
Personnel function, in early mills, 167; shift of responsibility for (mid-twenties), 198, 204; re-assumption of (mid-thirties), 238-48; basis of, 240; and the supervisor, 244-47
Personnel management, present Georgia mills, 262-84
Personnel office, 269
Personnel policies, nature of, 264-68; under the folkways, 302-3, 305-7
Personnel practices, nature of, 269-84
Personnel principles, nature of, 262-64
Phillips, Ulrich B., 32n
Piedmont Organizing Council, 187
Piedmont Region, 28-63; physiography of, 28-32; immigration into, 32-36; ethnic background, 33-36; cultural background, 36-43; economic background, 44-49; political background, 48-49; frontier heritage, 49-52; social structure, 49-63; social typology, 52-63
Pioneer characteristics, 36-43
Pope, Liston, 83n, 172n, 184, 309n
Power, water, 30, 31, 46, 85; electric, 47, 119
Prediction, as basic life technic, 5; human pattern of 6; social, 8
Profits in cotton textiles, 99-100

Quigley, Thomas, 201n, 224n

Railroads, 47, 48

Raleigh News and Observer, 74
Recognition as requirement for human way of life, 12; and the industrial worker, 19; and the textile worker, 93
Reconstruction, 45, 70, 72
Records, employee, 234, 273
Recreational facilities, present mills, 280
Recruitment, 271
Redfield, Robert, 54n, 55n, 56n, 58n
Regionalism, 27
Reynolds, Lloyd, 144, 233, 234n, 291n
Rhyne, J. J., 136, 155n, 162n, 164n, 229n
Riegel, Robert, 42n
Rieve, Emil, 112n
Riezler, Kurt, 5n, 9n, 13n
Ring spindles, 106
Robertson, Ben, 32n, 133n
Role-taking, 7
Roper, R. W., 65

Sapir, Edward, 5n, 55n, 58n, 63
Sauer, Carl O., 28n
Scientific management, 215, 217-19
Sea Islands, 34
Security, as requirement for human way of life, 11; and the industrial worker, 18-23; and the textile worker, 92-93
Selection, 271
Self-realization, 8
Semple, Ellen, 32n, 47
Senate Document No. 126, 106, 114
Senate Document No. 645, 159n, 160n, 161n
Senate Report No. 325, 77
Settlement of Piedmont, 32-36
Shenandoah River, 29
Shibutani, Tomatsu, 5n
Simpson, W. H., 109
Skill, requirements of modern industry, 17; and the industrial worker, 20; increasing demand for in Piedmont textiles, 178; training for, 213
Skills and craft in early Piedmont, 42, 44
Skinner, Constance Lindsey, 41n, 49n
Smith, Adam, 6n
Spindleage, cotton system, in 1860, 66; in 1870, 72; in 1880, 72; in 1890, 89; 1890-1923, 104-7; 1923-1952, 108-9
Starnes, George T., 177n, 214n
Statistical Abstract, 66n
Status as requirement for human way of life, 12; and the industrial worker, 19;

in Piedmont mills, 92; and the textile worker, 134

Strikes, at Danville, 170, 187; at Elizabethton, 170; at Gastonia, 170, 172, 187; at Marion, 170; at Greenville, 172; spontaneous, 187, 189, 216; General Strike of 1934, 188; as social phenomena, 295; as communicative devices, 310

Sullivan, Harry Stack, 5n, 7n, 9n, 10n

Sumner, William Graham, 54n, 166n

Supervision, in early mills, 141-49; relation with management, 144-49, 244-46; informal training of early supervision, 148; and labor trouble, 199; statistical data, 257-58; present training, 274-76

Sympathy (empathy) as basis of human nature, 6

Tannenbaum, Frank, 17n, 298n

Tenantry, in Coastal Plain, 70; in Piedmont, 71

Tennessee River, 29

Thomas, W. I., 5n

Thompson, Holland, 68n, 69n, 83n, 161

Tonnies, Ferdinand, 54n, 58n

Training, employee, 248, 273-74; supervisory, 248, 274-76

Transportation, 31, 35

Turner, Frederick Jackson, 38n, 41n, 42n, 49n, 50n

Turnover, in Georgia mills, 254

Understanding, as requirement for human way of life, 13; and the industrial worker, 18-23; and the textile worker, 92-93

Unemployment, 177, 209

Union-management relations, 233-38, 296-98

Unions. *See* Labor unions

United Textile Workers of America, 171, 186, 187, 237, 240

Vance, Rupert, 28n, 32n, 47n, 48n, 50

Wage differential, 109-12

Wage levels, 109-12, 177, 207-8

Warner, W. Lloyd, 17n, 284n, 298n, 310n

Weber, Max, 13n, 39

Welfare work, 154-59

Wertenbacker, Thomas J., 32n

"White collar" and "mill hand," 194-96, 227-32

White collar group in Piedmont mills, 255

Whitehead, Alfred North, ix, 37, 63

Wilcox, Clair, 99

Wirth, Louis, 55n, 58n

Wolfbein, Samuel Levin, 113, 115, 117, 118, 120

Woodmason, the Reverend Charles, 37, 57n

Workforce, northern industry, 115; source, 127-32; adjustment to manufacturing, 133-35; casualties of the transition into industry, 136-37; mobility, 136-37, 153-54; temperament of, 137; relations with management, 138-39; initial relation with communities, 163-67; on the auction block, 190-92; estrangement from communities, 192-96; rising educational level, 196-97; re-integration with communities, 226-32; statistical analysis of (Georgia, 1952), 252-57

Work loads, 178, 214